Leadership
Coaching
for Educators

*This book is dedicated to my late father Harold and mother Dobbie,
to my beloved children Michael and Emily,
who have inspired me to always continue learning and growing to be an
ever-better parent and citizen.*

Leadership
Coaching
for Educators

BRINGING OUT THE BEST IN
SCHOOL ADMINISTRATORS

KARLA REISS

CORWIN PRESS
A SAGE Publications Company
Thousand Oaks, CA 91320

For information:

Corwin Press
A Sage Publications Company
2455 Teller Road
Thousand Oaks, California 91320
www.corwinpress.com

Sage Publications Ltd
1 Oliver's Yard
55 City Road
London EC1Y 1SP
United Kingdom

Sage Publications India Pvt. Ltd.
B-42, Panchsheel Enclave
Post Box 4109
New Delhi 110 017 India

Printed in the United States of America

Library of Congress Cataloging-in-Publication Data

Reiss, Karla.
Leadership coaching for educators: Bringing out the best
in school administrators / Karla Reiss.
    p. cm.
Includes bibliographical references and index.
ISBN 1-4129-3739-6 (cloth)
ISBN 1-4129-3740-X (pbk.)
   1. School administrators. 2. Educational leadership.
3. School improvement programs. I. Title.
LB2831.6.R44 2007
371.2'011—dc22

This book is printed on acid-free paper.

06   07   08   09   10   9   8   7   6   5   4   3   2   1

Acquisitions Editor:	Elizabeth Brenkus
Editorial Assistant:	Desirée Enayati
Typesetter:	C&M Digitals (P) Ltd.
Indexer:	Juniee Oneida
Cover Designer:	Michael Dubowe

Contents

List of Figures

Preface

"Oh Yes You Can!"

—Bolder Boulder race motto

In 2003 I picked myself up and relocated to Boulder, Colorado, after spending a lifetime in New York. I left behind family, friends, and everything I had known so I would be able to live where I could be inspired by the awesome beauty of this part of the country. I was seeking a way to satisfy my spirit of adventure, love of nature, and desire for a lifestyle change. I'd also become crystal clear—thanks solely to the coaching process—about my life's work and personal mission to bring the benefits and power of executive and leadership coaching to school systems.

The first week I arrived in Boulder, I discovered a training program to prepare for a gigantic 10K race held annually on Memorial Day. The Bolder Boulder attracts 50,000 people to this stunning town. *"Oh Yes You Can!"* is the motto for the race and the training program. I had never run a race in my life. In fact, I never ran as far as a block. I was struck by the motto as I contemplated jumping into the training. Me . . . run? I felt it would be my initiation to life in Boulder, so I took the leap and signed myself up.

"Oh Yes You Can!" is a great example of the mindset and message our inner voices need to adopt to create the changes we want in our schools and in our professional and personal lives. It's the heart of coaching process—making the internal shift from "no way" to "yes!" Every week during the 10 weeks of training, a van carrying supplies was parked nearby with *"Oh Yes You Can!"* imprinted on the side. Just when I thought I would quit, especially after a long training run, when it seemed too difficult, I'd look up and be reminded . . . I can!

I've run the 10k twice now. I could *never* have accomplished it without the constant support, encouragement, and inspiration of our coaches and the supportive system of learning, training, and community that enabled me, and thousands of others, to accomplish what would have been difficult, challenging, or impossible alone. Much of what I learned and experienced can be applied to professional school leadership coaching and can be useful in understanding and making organizational change in complex school systems.

PURPOSE

This book is intended to raise awareness about coaching to a higher level and provide a rationale for considering coaching as a strategy for peak performance leadership. Thus far in the field of education, coaching has been known as an effective practice that supports classroom teachers. However, school system leaders can greatly benefit from coaching, just as their peers in business have done for many years. It can strengthen their capacities and abilities to lead challenging change in schools when they have access to executive and leadership coaching *and* learn effective coaching skills and techniques to interact with staff, students and the education community.

The objective of this book is to provide school system leaders, and those responsible for designing and developing school improvement programs, with a basis for (1) deeply understanding what coaching is and what coaching isn't, (2) defining and clarifying the role of a coach, and (3) establishing an awareness of a common set of core competencies adopted by the rapidly growing coaching profession. It provides a depth of knowledge about coaching and tips for understanding and developing a good coaching relationship in the hopes of preventing and avoiding coaching as yet another new thing that comes and goes. Coaching, done well, holds enormous potential for creating lasting change—something school systems have struggled with for so long. In addition to clearly defining coaching and essential coaching competencies recommended for skilled coaching, readers will find

- A comparison of sports psychology and professional coaching
- How to get started as a coach
- How to create a coaching mindset
- Insights into dealing with resistance
- An easy-to-use POWERful Coaching Framework™ for conducting coaching sessions
- Discussions of issues for implementing coaching in school systems
- Tools and templates

This book is about coaching—not mentoring, not a combination of roles—but intentionally, purely, coaching. While there are numerous helping roles, for coaching to be successful, it requires a thorough understanding of what it is and how it differs from mentoring, consulting, and other combined roles. Coaching is a process and a relationship that empowers individuals to explore their innermost thoughts, strengths, beliefs, and goals to create outer results. It holds enormous potential for creating inside-out change in individuals and school systems.

Leadership Coaching for Educators provides a common core of knowledge and understanding about coaching to help educators design and develop effective coaching programs. The book can help educators create uniform coaching programs across buildings, districts and states. It can help educators know that obtaining external results for their organizations is often about changing the internal thoughts and beliefs people hold that have prevented change from happening.

The knowledge base that comprises the information provided is based on recommendations from the International Coach Federation, my intensive professional coaching training and my years of experience as a professional coach. To become effective, educator coaches need an abundance of training with guided feedback. They need to learn and practice numerous skills, processes, know-how, and techniques. Successful, effective coaching is a whole lot more than asking some reflective questions. It goes much deeper and creates a relationship unlike most others.

This book is best used as a learning and planning guide, a discussion and resource tool. It is not intended as a training manual, nor should it be used as one. It provides a knowledge base, awareness of necessary skills and a handful of helpful tools that coaches use, as well as tips for implementing coaching. Ideally, educator coaches should be no less trained and skilled than professional coaches are. Becoming so requires a depth of understanding of the coaching skills and processes that lead to personal change, and in turn, organizational change. Acquiring coaching expertise requires many months of skill development and guided practice supported by experienced, credentialed coaches.

HOW I CAME TO COACHING

I don't remember much about my grandfather, who died when I was a teenager. What I do recall is a saying I often heard him repeat: "Every day, and in every way, I'm getting better and better." I've since learned it was originated by Émile Coué, a French pharmacist. As a veteran staff developer, I've often thought about that saying and how it related to my professional work, to the ongoing challenges and common goals educators face for helping students achieve their full potential. *Everyone* involved in the continuous improvement of school systems needs to be constantly improving—not only students but also every staff member, every leader needs to be engaged in ongoing learning about themselves and how they can contribute to improvement of their schools, systems, and communities. Coaching has tremendous potential as a school improvement strategy for achieving greater results for students, improving and strengthening leadership, and creating the lasting change that has eluded school systems.

I came to coaching via a unique path. As coordinator of staff development for a regional educational service center, I with my colleague, Jane Lombardo, launched a large, regional professional development project that included peer coaching as a process preferable to delivering staff development in workshop mode. I quickly became a believer in its potential. I was also somewhat perplexed. I wondered how this useful process could be utilized in a more effective manner, how it could be expanded so that principals, superintendents, teacher leaders and others in leadership roles could benefit.

I saw its value and sensed that it was exactly what was missing from the multitudes of school improvement efforts I had witnessed for more than 20 years. I'd worked with and facilitated numerous school improvement efforts, developed planning processes, and set up and conducted hundreds of workshops and conferences with more than 50 districts. Yet I still felt there was a void, especially in the area of leadership development. I saw what I'll call a broken system—new demands to meet higher learning standards, new accountability systems placing enormous pressure on school leaders, fewer and less qualified administrative candidates taking the leap from the classroom with the lack of meaningful support to deal with everyday challenges they faced, all leading to a growing crisis in recruiting and retaining strong, effective school leaders. I saw a huge need for leaders to have access to executive coaching, just as leaders of business and nonprofit organizations have. I set out to develop this work and fill in the missing piece.

Sounds ordinary so far, doesn't it? At just the right time, opportunity knocked. As I sought more information about coaching, I applied for and was selected to participate in a television documentary with well-known life coach and author, Cheryl Richardson. Suddenly, I had a chance of a lifetime—to learn first-hand about, and receive coaching from, one of the nation's most well-known coaches. For six months, six other participants and I worked with Cheryl to create "The Life Makeover Project," a five-week television series for Oxygen TV. I was hungry to learn more about coaching and interested in finding ways to bring coaching to school leaders. On the personal side, I'd just become an empty-nester, a change I found to be more challenging than I expected. I was puzzled about how to create a life without the role of mom and the demands of parenthood.

The experience was completely transformational. I became convinced that coaching has a much larger place in schools. I made the decision to obtain a professional coaching credential and dedicate myself to bringing coaching to educators and school systems. I attended and graduated from the Institute for Professional Empowerment Coaching in Manasquan, New Jersey, and received additional training at the College of Executive Coaching. I developed a model for leadership coaching and currently provide executive coaching for leaders and conduct training programs for educator-coaches.

ABOUT THE CONTENTS

I invite readers to either start or continue their journeys into coaching with this book, to use it to review or revise their current programs. I invite you to join me as you explore and consider coaching as a methodology for improving schools, improving who we are as adult learners, becoming more of who we are, sharing our best selves with others, and creating deep, lasting change.

It's best to think of this book as a "Coaching 101" resource and guidebook, like a travel guide with lots of overview information about the place called *coaching*. It will be especially useful for the following audiences:

- Superintendents
- Assistant superintendents for instruction
- Assistant superintendents for human resources
- Directors of professional development
- Principals
- Aspiring leaders
- Professors of education and leadership
- Developers and facilitators of leadership development programs
- Regional education service center personnel
- State Departments of Education staff

There are three main parts: Part I focuses on background information and a rationale for coaching as a school system improvement strategy. Part II defines coaching skills and knowledge, and Part III contains practical implementation techniques, processes, and concerns. I have developed a unique coaching model, the POWERful Coaching Framework™ that offers guidance for new and experienced coaches to address key factors during coaching sessions. Part III is truly the meat of the book. Readers may benefit from reading it first.

Chapter 1 describes coaching and provides information about studies of the effects of coaching in business and nonprofit sectors, the rapidly emerging coaching profession, and its growing presence in school systems. It presents a rationale for considering executive and leadership coaching as a strategy for improving the performance and confidence of school system leaders. It describes the connections between emotional intelligence and coaching, and it compares sports psychology strategies for achieving peak performance with coaching.

Chapter 2 delves into considerations for developing a philosophy and mindset about coaching and people being coached, the coachees. It describes attributes of a great coach and what potential coaches can anticipate when working with reluctant and resistant coachees versus those who are eager and enthused. People come to coaching for a variety of reasons, from wanting to obtain new skills to developing themselves professionally, for solving life problems or addressing issues pertaining to an entire organization. This chapter presents coaching as a process for working with the inner self, the whole person, and aligning what people value most with their outer work.

Chapters 3 through 5 are entirely focused on the International Coach Federation's Professional Coaching Core Competencies. These competencies were developed to provide continuity and a common set of skills and methodologies for creating change in individuals. They form the basis of the majority of professional coach training programs, and can provide a common core of learning for educator-coaches. They assist coaches in helping coachees when they are stuck. They provide strategies for overcoming resistance people are likely to face in their coaching roles. Within these chapters, readers will find information about starting the coaching relationship, ethical considerations, communication and focus on learning, action and results. They identify the skills coaches need in order to be effective and successful, and they should be part of any coaching training initiative.

Chapter 6 addresses resistance—the greatest challenge faced by school leaders. It identifies several concepts, models, and strategies for overcoming it. This is where training is crucial. Often we are stumped with what to do when people we are charged to work with will not budge. When properly trained, coaches work with people from the inside out. They get inside the heads of coachees to create shifts in thinking or belief systems and help them create new outlooks and thus new actions for improved results.

Chapter 7 contains a practical, easy-to-use model for conducting a coaching session. The POWERful Coaching Framework™ helps coaches address important elements of the coaching process that result in continual action steps toward mutually defined goals. The chapter describes phases of the coaching relationship a coach can expect and includes thoughts and strategies about developing a professional coaching plan. It also discusses the use of assessments to pinpoint areas of development.

Chapter 8 addresses considerations for implementing a successful coaching program: confidentiality, communication, selecting and training coaches, and the use of external versus internal coaches. It proposes coaching as a whole-school improvement model and discusses the future of coaching.

The group of resources at the end of the book contains a number of tools and templates useful in the coaching process.

We have a long way to go until schools fully integrate coaching well and results are known. I invite you to share your stories, your challenges, and your successes. You are welcome to contact me or visit my Web site for ways of connecting with fellow educators around the world who are as passionate as I am about coaching, who are learning and growing in their role as coaches and who are excited and enthused about the results they are creating.

AUTHOR'S NOTES

1. Throughout the book, readers will find success stories and examples of coaching scenarios. All are based on my work and experiences with actual coachees in school systems. Due to the confidential nature of the coaching relationship, their names and districts have been changed and their identity is kept private.

2. Persons receiving coaching are identified, in this book, as *coachees*. They can also be referred to as coaching coachees, as is common in the coaching profession. Here, coachees can be any recipient of coaching: superintendents, principals, teachers, students—anyone.

3. I would like to thank and acknowledge the Institute for Professional Empowerment Coaching for the interpretation of portions of their copyrighted material used in their professional coach training programs. The Institute for Professional Empowerment Coaching can be contacted at www.ipeccoaching.com

Acknowledgments

"It's always worthwhile to make others aware of their worth."

—Malcolm Forbes (as quoted in
Management Tid Bytes, 2004)

Nothing "big" ever happens in isolation. It absolutely takes a team, a community of people who contribute to your success in numerous ways. I have many people to thank. Without them, this book and this work would be on the back burner—a thought, a wish, a dream. With them, this book and this work can contribute to the world of continuous school improvement, and I thank them all for their unique insight, feedback, enthusiastic support and encouragement.

I am beyond grateful to Bruce Schneider, PhD, president and founder of the Institute for Professional Empowerment Coaching. Your program is unequalled. I'm convinced you have graduated the best-trained coaches in the country. Thank you for the quality and integrity of your program and for requiring and demanding so much from us busy adult students. It is no wonder your program has expanded from one location in Manasquan, New Jersey, to several across the country. The world is a better place because of the difference the coaches you've graduated are making in the lives of thousands of people and organizations.

To Cheryl Richardson—my first coach—thank you for the opportunity to work with you on Oxygen TV's "Life Makeover Project" and to learn firsthand what it truly takes to make personal change in one's life. You inspired and encouraged me to start writing; I never imagined I'd be writing this book only three years later. I'll never forget my Quantum Leap—and the many leaps I've taken in my personal and professional life since then. How could I have known that climbing atop a telephone pole, wobbly and terrified, could be so transformational? I fear nothing now, thanks to you and the incredible program you designed. I'm grateful to have been chosen from thousands to participate in our six-month journey through change. I learned firsthand the power and potential of coaching and the precious gift of having an ally who totally believes in you.

Dennis Sparks, Executive Director of the National Staff Development Council—thank you for bringing attention to educators about the promise and potential of coaching. In 2001, your life coaching pilot program helped dozens of superintendents and principals learn how coaching can help them in their daily work. You started a movement.

Three years ago, I approached the directors of the newly funded Long Island School Leadership Center with the hope of finding a few school leaders to join my pilot Leadership Coaching for School Change program. To Dr. Gerald Dempsey and Michael Keany, thanks for listening to my idea and being open to the concept of executive coaching for school leaders. You have been so supportive and wide open to exploring this work. I am so grateful to both of you for helping turn my vision into reality.

My thanks and appreciation go to Briggs McAndrews, Superintendent in Residence for the New York State Council of School Superintendents, and George Meyer, Associate Professor of Leadership, Quincy University, Quincy, Illinois, other early adopters of leadership coaching. You saw, as I did, the need for leadership coaching, for this kind of support that could truly help school leaders deal with their daily challenges with renewed confidence and inner strength. Together, you sponsored and supported my first coaching skills teleclass, which enabled educators to learn to coach across the country. Thanks to Dr. David H. Larsen, Executive Director, Connecticut Association of Public School Superintendents, for inviting me into your process for training superintendents to provide coaching support to new superintendents.

Thanks to Len Lubinsky, consultant and coach, for your willingness to co-present our leadership coaching workshop, "Get Out of Your Comfort Zone," at the American Association of School Administrators' (AASA) national conference in 2003. Although we were total strangers with only our shared belief in coaching in common, you graciously accepted my phone call one day and were open to collaborating with me on this new, emerging work. It was a pleasure working with you.

Eight o'clock on a Sunday morning, I thought no one would attend my coaching workshop. Thank you to Jay P. Goldman, editor of the AASA's *Administrator* journal, for waking up and showing up. Your presence in the session led to my first published article. Your issue on executive coaching in November 2003 provided valuable information about coaching as an emerging professional growth process of importance for strengthening school leadership.

Putting a new idea out there for the world to judge is risky. I am forever grateful to Jane Lombardo, Director, Suffolk's Edge Teacher Center, Long Island, New York, and Mary Ann Luciano, Director, Catskill Regional Teacher Center, Oneonta, New York. Together, we launched the first leadership coaching project for teacher center directors in New York. Thank you for believing in me and my vision for this work. It was fun being snowed in at our first retreat and sharing my work around the state. Eternal thanks for your support. I'm glad to know the work has continued.

I've learned volumes about people, change and organizational systems from consultant Robert Ebers. You have perfectly blended the roles of coach, mentor and consultant. Thank you for guiding my learning and growth.

To colleague and consultant Ann Delehant, as a participant in the National Staff Development Council life coaching pilot, your openness and willingness to share your insights were helpful in confirming my gut instinct—that leadership coaching has a major place in our school systems. It was fun to learn and grow together in this work.

There is nothing like being surrounded by coaches. Never before had I experienced such enormous energy and positive vibes. Thank you to my fellow peer coaching students at the Institute for Professional Empowerment Coaching and the patient and skilled instructors. Special thanks go to Nancy Massar for many hours of deep thinking and learning together about the importance of language in the change process. To my friends and colleagues with whom I've shared my learning, new skills and new profession, thank you for your patience, feedback and support.

My family, especially my children Michael and Emily and their spouses Bridget and Matthew, has witnessed so much change in me and watched my life completely transform. You have been there and supported me in every way. Watch out—I may not be finished!

I have high hopes for coaching in education. To the readers of this book, thank you for your interest in this growing body of work. Creating lasting change in schools is possible. I am certain we can reach lofty and challenging goals.

Corwin Press gratefully acknowledges the contributions of the following individuals:

Shelby Cosner, Assistant Professor
University of Illinois at Chicago
Chicago, IL

Charles Elbot, Director
Office of Character and School Culture
Denver Public Schools
Denver, CO

James Halley, Superintendent
North Kingstown Public Schools
Kingstown, RI

Kim Hendon, Curriculum Specialist
Talladega County Central High School
Alpine, AL

Matthew Jennings, Assistant Superintendent
Berkeley Heights Public Schools
Berkeley Heights, NJ

Michael Keany, Director
Long Island School Leadership Center
Huntington, NY

Joellen Killion, Director of Special Projects
National Staff Development Council
Arvada, CO

Lorna Lewis, Assistant Superintendent for Educational Services
Three Village Central School District
East Setauket, NY

Jim Ritchie, Retired Professor
Department of Educational Administration
San Jose University
San Jose, CA

Jan Robertson, Associate Professor
University of Waikato
Hamilton, New Zealand

Glen Sewell, Principal/Superintendent
Wheatland Union High School District
Wheatland, CA

Karen Tichy, Associate Superintendent for Instruction
Catholic Education Office
St. Louis, MO

Linda Vogel, Assistant Professor
Department of Educational Leadership
University of Northern Colorado
Greeley, CO

Paul Young, Executive Director
West After School Center, Inc.
Lancaster, OH

About the Author

**Karla Reiss** founded The Change Place, a coaching and consulting firm dedicated to the continuous improvement of individuals, teams and organizations after 20 years in education. She and her team of certified coaches provide executive and leadership coaching for school leaders and coaching training and consulting services for school systems.

As a school administrator, Reiss worked with more than 50 school districts in a variety of school improvement roles: coordinator of professional development at Western Suffolk (NY) Board of Cooperative Educational Services and director of planning at Southern Westchester (NY) Board of Cooperative Educational Services. She has conducted and implemented professional development and school improvement planning opportunities for K–12 staff and district leaders. She is trained and experienced in strategic planning and organizational development. She served on the New York State Education Department's statewide steering committees for Comprehensive District Education Planning and Practical Uses of Data for Teaching and Learning projects. She was president of New York State Staff Development Council and served on the Executive Board of the Long Island Association for Curriculum and Staff Development.

Karla Reiss graduated from the Institute of Professional Empowerment Coaching in 2002 and is a Certified Professional Empowerment Coach. She received additional coach training at the College of Executive Coaching. She holds a bachelor of science degree, a master's in special education, and a professional diploma in school district administration. She is the author of two articles: "Why Coaching Matters," published in the American Association of School Administrators' *Administrator,* November, 2003, and "Coaching for Leadership," published in the Association of California School Administrators' *Leadership,* January 2004.

She has two grown children and lives adventurously in Boulder, Colorado. Reiss can be reached at www.thechangeplace.com or changemaven@thechangeplace.com.

Let the Change Begin

We cannot change the world we see
Till change begins in you and me
We change the world around us when
The change begins within

Let the change begin
Let the change begin
Let the change begin within

The lesson from the willow tree
Is strength in flexibility
When nothing seems to go my way
It's time to learn to sway

So, let the change begin
Let the change begin
Let the change begin within

Patiently
Courageously
Be the change you wish to see

Let the change begin
Let the change begin
Let the change begin within

Words and music by Jana Stanfield and Megon McDonough. Eagle Woman Music ASCAP, www.megonmcdonough.com. Used with permission. Let the Change Begin (Jana Stanfield, Meson McDonough): © Jana Stan Tunes (ASCAP).

PART I

Making a Case for Leadership Coaching

Introduction

Impossible is a word to be found only in the dictionary of fools.

—Napoleon Bonaparte

The first time I offered complimentary executive coaching sessions at a conference for school administrators, I was stunned to discover that by 8:00 a.m., my schedule was fully booked for the day. I was the last person to leave the conference. Every person entered the session with a challenge he or she was facing on the job and left 30 minutes later with actions to take the next day. Everyone thought, initially, I would tell them what to do to remedy their problem. Every administrator quickly learned that coaching is a collaborative discovery process. Each one left the session feeling positive, more confident, and empowered to solve his or her problem.

Welcome to the powerful world of coaching! If you are reading this book, it is likely you have begun the quest—the journey—to know more about coaching, to determine if and how to bring coaching into your school, district or university. This book will provide you with what you need to know to get started, to plan and implement a successful program. I believe that coaching, done well by skilled coaches, holds enormous promise for creating ongoing, continuous improvement of all aspects of the education system—for creating lasting change . . . at last.

It can be very tempting to jump on the bandwagon and start a coaching program in your school or district. It's well worth doing. Coaching is a hot, new field and a buzz word that is used more and more often to describe a role that is *not* coaching. As you take the trip down the coaching road, my advice is to "walk, don't run," to "proceed with caution." Take time to learn about the role, the process and the coaching relationship. Take time to discuss and reach mutual understanding with your colleagues about how coaching differs from other helping roles. Before you implement yet another new thing, learn about the role of coaches and the skills, techniques and processes they use. Learn about coaching's potential

> [Coaching is] the heart of management, not at the edges. Coaching is everything you do to produce extraordinary results amid change, complexity, and competition. Coaching is everything you do to improve your strategic thinking about the future you want to create. Coaching is everything you do to ignite personal and team learning in solving organizational problems while building the capability you need to succeed. Coaching is everything you do to give you and your entire organization an edge and advantage. You don't need coaching for ordinary results.
>
> —Robert Hargrove (2000)

> Executive coaches are not for the meek. They're for people who value unambiguous feedback. All coaches have one thing in common: it's that they are ruthlessly results oriented.
>
> —Anonymous

for changing thoughts, beliefs and minds and touching the essence of who we are as human beings. I believe coaching is the missing ingredient from our school improvement efforts, and when a well-designed coaching program is successfully implemented, school systems, staff and students will soar.

There are many compelling reasons for the coaching process to find its way into the boardroom, the principal's office and elsewhere throughout a school system, as well as in the classroom. Coaching as a strategy to reform schools is in its infancy. We have yet to fully appreciate its potential for strengthening schools and boosting the performance of school leaders responsible for high levels of achievement in others in a demanding, complex environment. We have a long way to go, and my hope is that this book will provide the basic knowledge educators need about coaching to design and develop successful programs.

I see a future for coaching as a continuous improvement process that will penetrate the system. Imagine a district where . . .

- Every educator has personal and professional goals that continually evolve
- Every educator is taking daily actions to achieve them
- Every school and central office has well-trained coaches available to coach all staff
- School leaders are incorporating a coaching approach for more effective communication with colleagues, board members and staff
- Teachers are skilled in coaching students to empower their learning

All school leaders deserve access to a coaching relationship and benefit from learning coaching skills and techniques to enhance interpersonal communication throughout their school systems. I have great hopes for coaching and its yet untapped potential for creating successful school change and hope that throughout the course of the book, you, the reader, will discover some of the potential coaching has for effective and lasting school change.

Why Coaching?
Why Now?

Every moment of one's existence, one is growing into more or retreating into less. One is always living a little more or dying a little bit.

—Norman Mailer

IN THIS CHAPTER

Rationale for leadership coaching

The growing coaching profession

The link between coaching and emotional intelligence

How coaching enhances results in business and nonprofit organizations

Achieving peak performance through coaching

Coaches are everywhere these days. It's "cool" to have a coach, yet it is often a misinterpreted and misunderstood role. Look around your community and you are likely to see a growing number of professional coaches. There are parent coaches, life coaches, executive coaches, abundance coaches, business coaches, and school-based instructional coaches.

The term *coach* isn't new and is known by just about everyone. Surely anyone who's participated in a sport has had a coach and an inkling of what a coach may do. However, the coaching role in a professional setting is different and needs to be defined, understood, and distinguished from other helpful roles.

> Executives and HR managers know coaching is the most potent tool for inducing positive personal change, ensuring better-than-average odds of success and making the change stick for the long term.
>
> —John H. Eggers and Doug Clark (2000)

Executive and leadership coaching is finally beginning to emerge in schools, providing confidential, individualized professional growth in a convenient, ongoing format that is focused on the leader's specific challenges. It is a common strategy available to leaders of business to enhance their performance and strengthen their organizations. School leaders need the same service and benefits to successfully lead their schools and districts to high levels of achievement.

The role of instructional coach is becoming common in schools. The function of instructional coaches is broad and multifaceted and includes many roles merged into one. Instructional coaches are described by Killion and Harrison (2005) as

- Catalysts for change
- Classroom supporters
- Curriculum specialists
- Data coaches
- Instructional specialists
- Learning facilitators
- Mentors
- Resource providers
- School leaders

School-based coaches have a challenging and complex role offering individualized support to the classroom teacher. They are usually expert in specific content areas, typically literacy or mathematics—necessary specialties. However, when they are faced with challenges and staff members that don't *want* to change, they often hit a wall. School-based coaches need more preparation in dealing with the people aspect of change. How do they handle the teachers who don't think they need to change? Or resists change? Or resists the presence of a coach? What do school-based coaches do when teachers don't trust them or the process or when personal issues may impact their professional performance? What strategies do school-based coaches have when coachees believe they are already doing their absolute best or don't believe in the new methods? My experience working with school-based coaches tells me they are frequently stuck, stumped and frustrated when confronted with these very common situations. Although the focus and intent of this book is to develop quality school leadership coaching programs, the information, models, tools, and techniques can be used successfully by school-based coaches.

School systems need to provide programs to prepare coaches that have sufficient *coaching skills, techniques,* and *appropriate practice* to be highly effective in their roles to help teachers create change.

> *Trying to implant a goal that is incongruent with the self-image is like trying to plant grain by dropping seeds on rock-hard, bone-dry ground. No one can consistently outperform his or her self-image. No one can overcome it with willpower. No one can sneak past it and perform in an incongruent manner. The bottom line is that you cannot "do" things without "being" the kind of person who does those things. You must "be" to "do."*
>
> —Dr. Maxwell Maltz
> (as quoted in Agno, 2003)

Chapters 3 through 5 provide a core of common learning that both instructional and executive coaches need to support others through the change process. With more coaching skills and techniques, school-based coaches will be equipped to deal more effectively with changing behavior by working with coachees to change perceptions and limiting thought and belief systems. School-based coaches need a vast repertoire of techniques that go beyond mentoring and facilitation skills, looking at data, or any external strategies. School-based coaches need strategies for working with the inner life of coachees.

It is time for coaching to expand beyond the classroom and become *the* school improvement strategy to boost performance of everyone who touches the lives of children. As school systems across the country and around the world struggle to create higher-achieving organizations and improve student learning results, effective coaching can boost effectiveness for all educators—leaders, teachers and students—and help districts achieve the high levels of performance they seek. I imagine a future system where school leaders incorporate a coaching approach when communicating with their staff, where principals coach teachers and teachers use coaching techniques with students. I anticipate that the culture of such a system will change dramatically, and results will skyrocket.

WHAT'S THE PAYOFF?

How likely is it that your district would be willing to invest precious staff development resources in something that only has a 5% to 15% chance of

Figure 1.1   Impact of Training Components on Teacher Learning and Application

Training Components	Impact of Training Components on Teacher Learning and Application		
	Concept Understanding	Skill Attainment (mechanical use)	Application
Presentation of theory	85%	15%	5%–10%
Modeling by trainer	85%	18%	5%–10%
Practices and low-risk feedback in training setting	85%	80%	10%–15%
Coaching	90%	90%	80%–90%

Source: Adapted from Joyce and Showers (1995) and Collins (1997).

success? Not likely, yet many are doing just that. As demands on districts to improve student achievement continue, districts are wise to consider how they spend their school improvement and staff development resources.

The research on effective staff development has shown little impact of traditional training programs on creating change in the classroom (Collins, 1997; Joyce & Showers, 1995). It recommends models that provide ongoing support and are job embedded, and it specifically recommends coaching. This is not news to experienced staff developers. Looking at Figure 1.1, you can see that without coaching built into the improvement process, only between 5% and 15% of learning is transferred.

Implementing new learning doesn't occur by learning new skills or information but by providing support through coaching to embed them. Put another way, if your staff development budget is $100,000 and is focused on a workshop model, although learning is taking place, you are getting a benefit of only $5,000–$15,000 worth of learning that transfers to the classroom. With coaching, your investment would yield a whopping $80,000–$90,000.

Another survey supports these same findings: "In a 1988 study of 3,300 managers and human resource professionals, it was concluded that, of $48 billion spent on training and change programs, only 12%–15% was considered money well spent" (Lebow, 1990).

Let's take a closer look. Figure 1.2 shows what should happen when a new skill is learned. It's usual to go through an awkward stage where the skill isn't natural or bringing results (Rackham, 1979). With coaching and persistence, learners eventually succeed in seeing results from the new behavior. Figure 1.3 demonstrates actual results *without* coaching. Notice the dip and flat profile.

Figure 1.2   What Should Happen With a New Skill, With Coaching

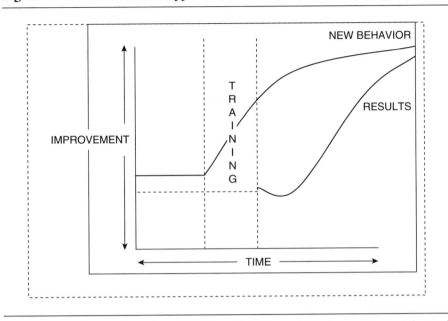

Source: Copyright © November 1979 from *Training and Development Journal* by Neil Rackham. Reprinted with permission of American Society for Training & Development.

Suppose you want to learn to be a better public speaker. You've just gotten your first job as a principal and find that although you have dreaded public speaking, you now have to do it and do it well. You've set a new goal to improve, and off you go. You read a few books and observe people making good speeches. But—you can read all you like about techniques of making and delivering a good speech. You can know how to write one. You can know a lot. However, it is only when the new learning is implemented over time that change and growth happen. It's likely you'll feel tense, nervous, and anxious in the beginning; it's a normal response. You're likely to slip back into your old ways or avoid it altogether. When practicing the new skills, it won't feel good, or comfortable. You're in a new zone, what I call the *discomfort zone*, and it most likely does not feel good.

It is in that discomfort zone that it's tempting to retreat. It is in that discomfort zone where a person benefits from coaching. Little by little, practice session by practice session, with feedback, it begins to feel better.

> Asked for a conservative estimate of the monetary payoff from the coaching they got, these managers described an average return of more than $100,000, or about six times what the coaching had cost their companies.
>
> —"Executive Coaching" (2001, p. 19)

In time, it will feel normal. The new skills will be embedded, and the feelings of discomfort will lessen. Feeling skilled and confident will be the new norm.

Figure 1.3   What Actually Happens to a New Skill, Without Coaching

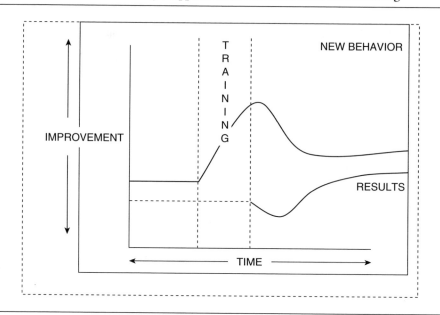

Source: Copyright © November 1979 from *Training and Development Journal* by Neil Rackham. Reprinted with permission of American Society for Training & Development.

Additional evidence of the benefits of executive coaching for business leaders was identified in a 2001 study of the impact of coaching (Manchester, 2001). One hundred executives from Fortune 100 companies received executive coaching that was both change oriented—aimed at changing certain behaviors or skills—and growth oriented—aimed at sharpening performance. Organizational benefits included

- Increased organizational strength
- Increased executive retention
- Increased productivity
- Increased quality
- Reduced complaints
- Improved working relationships with staff
- Improved teamwork
- Improved job satisfaction
- Conflict reduction
- Increased organizational commitment

The results of the executive coaching program delivered an overall, estimated return of 5.7 times the initial investment. The figure is even higher (788%) when employee retention was considered (Manchester, 2001).

Given the evidence that coaching is effective and cost-effective, schools should be considering how to begin, extend and expand their current coaching programs from the classroom to the boardroom. Clearly, extending coaching beyond the classroom to include executive and leadership coaching would be beneficial for the entire system.

COACHING DEFINED

The term *coach* comes from a French word meaning, "to transport important people from one place to another." *The Cambridge Dictionary* (2006) defines it as "used to take groups of people on journeys." A coach was known as a vehicle, a thing. Now the term is used to describe a person, a process, a role, and a profession. A modern interpretation would refer to a person being moved to a higher level of competence, confidence, performance, or insight. It is imperative that, in establishing a successful coaching program in schools, district leaders have a common understanding of the definition, role, skills and process of coaching. Coaching is all about change. It's about supporting people and organizations through change, helping them get from one place to another in their professional and personal lives.

The coaching profession has emerged from a number of fields and combines elements of what has been learned about human performance and achievement. It has roots in psychotherapy, particularly solution-focused and cognitive behavioral therapy. "Carl Jung, Alfred Adler, Carl Rogers and Abraham Maslow are antecedents to today's therapy practice—and modern day coaching. Coaching was born as a result of great advances in psychotherapy and counseling, and then blended with consulting practices and organizational and personal development training trends. Coaching takes the best each of these areas has to offer and provides a now standardized and proven method for partnering with people for success" (Williams, 2004). In Chapter 3, coaching is further defined and distinguished from mentoring and other helping roles.

Today, individuals work with coaches to achieve challenging goals, to create the life of their dreams, to achieve high levels of performance or enable their businesses or organizations to prosper. Executives collaborate with coaches to think through challenges, develop strategies and be more effective with greater confidence.

> *Professional coaching is an ongoing partnership that helps coachees produce fulfilling results in their personal and professional lives. coachees deepen their learning, improve their performance and enhance the quality of their life.*
>
> —International Coach Federation (n.d.)

The International Coach Federation (ICF) is one of the leading professional organizations that support the rapidly growing coaching profession. It has developed competencies for coaches (see Chapters 3–5) and credentials for coach training organizations. It defines coaching as follows:

> Coaching is an ongoing relationship which focuses on coachees taking action toward the realization of their visions, goals or desires. Coaching uses a process of inquiry and personal discovery to build the coachee's level of awareness and responsibility and provides the coachee with structure, support and feedback. The coaching process helps coachees both define and achieve professional and personal goals faster and with more ease than would be possible otherwise. (ICF, n.d.)

A skilled coach helps individuals create change—in what they think, in what they believe, and ultimately, in what they do. A coach is a highly skilled professional who works with people to unlock their hidden potential to bring about extraordinary results. Coaches inspire people to get out of their comfort zones to reach their full promise. Coaches provide ongoing support through challenging change efforts to help individuals and organizations create lasting change.

Coaching is about aligning one's inner values, gifts, passions, personal mission, and strengths with the coachee's outer world. It's about making desired change to achieve an external or internal goal. Coaching is a process, a powerful, confidential relationship, a strategy and dozens of skills and techniques that support an individual or an organization through a change process. Coaches are change agents. They are experts in creating change in people and organizations.

Coaches help people think beyond their daily issues and see a bigger picture. They help daydreams become reality by helping coachees focus on their most important priorities and take action toward them. They help find time, manage challenges, and deeply connect with one's most precious dreams and desires. Coaching is an action-oriented, results-focused, and positive process. It helps busy people feel they're in action toward their highest priorities versus being in constant motion and feeling unaccomplished. Coaching focuses on the inner self, on gaining clarity about what excites us and how we may need to grow and change, to achieve the outer results wanted in professional or personal lives.

Coaching is an alliance between two people: the coachee, who wants or can benefit from coaching, and the coach who is skilled and experienced in listening deeply to what the coachee wants and what's in the way of achieving it. Together, they create a pathway to change. The coach offers support throughout the change process.

I like to compare what a coach does with a chiropractor. A chiropractor helps you feel better by putting your body back into alignment. When one part of your body is out of whack, other parts of you feel the affects. Your physical health suffers. When your spine is properly aligned, you feel great. Your systems are aligned; you feel good and healthy again. Life works!

Think of a coach as performing the same function—however, they're aligning your thoughts, beliefs, goals and actions to achieve desired, extraordinary results. Coachees feel more alive. They are energized, empowered, focused and optimistic.

The coaching profession is built around certain philosophies about people and insights into why they behave as they do. Coaches are taught to "see" the highest potential in everyone they work with. Coaches believe each person is an expert in their own life, and each is creative, resourceful and whole and therefore capable of creating their own solutions. Coaches are your allies, your cheerleaders and inspiration. They hold the coachee accountable for accomplishing agreed-on tasks.

It is *not necessary* for a coach to have content knowledge or expertise in the field of the person he or she is coaching. This comment may be surprising and controversial. When you are trained and skilled in coaching techniques, you have the ability and skill to coach anyone, in any field. Many educator-coaches are functioning in a blended model of coaching, combining coaching and mentoring. When I'm training new coaches, they find that this is a difficult concept to grasp initially. It can be challenging to stay in a coaching role, particularly when you want to share your personal experiences. Coaching and mentoring are different roles and different processes, each requiring different skills and experiences. Coaching is an inquiry, a discovery and learning process, whereas mentoring is about sharing experiences and what's worked for another. In Chapter 3, the difference between coaching and mentoring is further clarified.

Coaches can either be 100% in a coaching role when working with individuals or they can incorporate coaching behaviors into their daily interactions with staff or any others, depending on their levels of training. Leaders, instructional coaches, and teachers can consider using

> Having specific knowledge of a coachee's situation may actually be a hindrance to the coaching process, as it is only natural for the coach to compare the coachee's situation to what he or she knows. In nearly every case, more helpful is a fresh and objective perspective that allows the possibility for new solutions to old challenges, which is exactly what the coachee wants.
>
> —Bruce Schneider, President, Institute for Professional Empowerment Coaching (personal communication, October, 2005)

a coaching approach as a communication style and create a results-focused, goal-oriented, and action-oriented class, building, or district.

Coaching is about the future—intentionally creating a desired future. It's a confidential, collaborative partnership in which the coach is totally focused on the success of the coachee, the organization and the results that person desires.

COACHING: A BOOMING PROFESSION

Once upon a time, the only type of coaching most of us were familiar with was sports coaching. Now, coaching is "in." There are thousands of coaches with as many specialties. As of this writing, anyone can call himself or herself a coach. You can simply wear the title, with little or no formal training. However, calling oneself a coach may not assure anyone that there's consistency of training or sufficient know-how to help people and organizations create lasting change. There are credentials for becoming a professional coach.

> Executive coaching is growing by about 40% a year.
>
> —"Executive Couching" (2002, p.51)

Thomas Leonard is considered to be the founder of the modern coaching profession. He founded the International Coach Federation in 1995, as well as several coach training schools, including CoachU, CoachVille, and the Graduate School of Coaching.

He died suddenly in 2003, leaving behind a rapidly growing new profession.

> Business coaching is a major growth industry. At least 10,000 coaches work for businesses today, up from 2,000 in 1996. And that figure is expected to exceed 50,000 in the next five years.
>
> — Steven Berglas (2002, p. 86)

In 2005, the ICF reported over 8,500 coach-members and 132 chapters in 34 countries—double the number of members two years before that and an exponential increase since the Federation's formation. Coaching is flourishing as results are becoming known. For organizations, it has become an effective, beneficial strategy for managing change, developing and retaining leaders, and changing the culture of organizations. For individuals, it has awakened or rekindled purpose, mission and passion, enabling people to connect what matters most to them in their daily lives.

THE NEED FOR LEADERSHIP COACHING

Susan was a second-year leader of a professional development organization. She had been a teacher for many years but was not yet comfortable with being so visible in her new role. She was quiet by nature and struggling to feel more confident. She was frequently nervous and unsure of herself when we began coaching, excited about her position but filled with self-doubt.

Her external goal was to implement a new program in a number of schools. She voiced some limiting beliefs and fear that others would view her as not knowing enough. Her inner voice held her back. Her external goal was inhibited by her inner mind. Although our goal for coaching was an externally focused one, the strategies and steps to accomplish them were *internal.* Without coaching, Susan had no one and no process for dealing with the root cause of her anxiety. Two years later, Susan was an accomplished, confident leader in her district.

Hand in hand with the enormous demands placed on school systems to raise standards for students has come increased pressure on school leaders at every level. The decline in the number of applicants and increase in retirement of current leaders has caused great concern for communities across the country. A number of studies and reports have provided recent data that confirm these issues:

- *School Leadership for the 21st Century: A Statement of New York State's Blue Ribbon Panel on School Leadership* (New York State, 2000) reported that retention rates for urban superintendents average between two and a half and three years.
- *Leadership for Learning: Reinventing the Principalship*, a national report issued by the Task Force on the Principalship (2000), stated that 50% of superintendents report a shortage of qualified candidates nationally to fill principal positions.
- *The View From Inside: A Candid Look at Today's School Superintendent*, a study conducted by Colorado Association of School Executives ([CASE], 2003), looked at four areas of the superintendency: superintendent effectiveness, recruitment and retention, school board relations, and professional development. Former Executive Director Bob Tschirki said the 2003 study reveals increasing concerns about the demands on school district leaders:
  – A shortage of fiscal resources
  – Conflicting state and federal school reform mandates
  – Strained relationships with school boards impacting their effectiveness

These concerns contribute to high turnover and a perceived shortage of qualified candidates seeking the position. Superintendents reported that graduate programs didn't prepare them for the day-to-day work of being a superintendent. When asked what training would be useful now, superintendents called for one-on-one mentoring and coaching.

- The New York State Council of School Superintendents ([NYSOCSS], 2004) conducted its fifth study of the superintendency in New York State; *Snapshot V. NYSCOSS* predicted that by 2008, nearly two-thirds of their members will be in the first five years of their first superintendency. "The superintendency has become less attractive as a career in recent years, both due to the increasing demands of the position and the perception of a deteriorating working climate" (p. 7).

This alarming data confirms that something else is needed. Busy school leaders need a different system. They need just-in-time opportunities for ongoing, confidential dialogue with a thinking partner to dialogue, brainstorm and develop strategies that benefit the system.

> *Superintendents need mentoring and coaching to be more effective in their jobs, especially with regard to school reform initiatives and building relationships with stakeholders.*
>
> —Bob Tschirki (CASE, 2003)

There has been growth in the number of focused professional development programs for new and aspiring principals and superintendents. More is needed. Executive coaching for principals and superintendents and leaders using a coaching approach with others will enable them to manage the numerous challenges today's leaders are facing with improved confidence and competence. Because of the action-oriented nature of the coaching process, leaders will walk away from *every* coaching session with a set of actions to take that are directly related to their current issues or challenges. Leader and coach consider obstacles and strategize together to overcome them. Because coaching has a built-in accountability system, there is constant movement toward the organization and coachee's goals.

> *The leader of the past knew how to tell. The leader of the future will know how to ask.*
>
> —Peter Drucker
> (as quoted in Hesselbein, Goldsmith, & Beckhard, 1997)

School board members need knowledge of executive coaching and its potential impact. They need to know that most people who benefit from coaching are already successful professionals who strive to make a greater impact and become ever better at what they do in order to strengthen their schools or districts. Coaching is not solely for people who are perceived as needing help; it is highly effective for ensuring that all leaders are achieving at their peak potential. Coaching is a perk, not a punishment.

Traditional approaches to professional development are local, regional, state or national workshops and conferences, which are often insufficient for those in leadership positions. *Snapshot* (NYSCOSS, 2004) reported that "72.7% thought they did not have enough time to spend on personal professional development" (p. 14). Busy school leaders have little ability to drop what they're doing to attend training programs, although they would like to. A well-structured coaching program enables ongoing, customized professional growth by the coach coming to the district or being available via telephone. Coaching provides convenience and is 100% focused on the leader's issues and concerns for achieving specific, measurable results.

EXECUTIVE COACHING FOR SCHOOL LEADERS EMERGES

In 2000, Dennis Sparks (2002), Executive Director of the National Staff Development Council, launched a life coaching pilot initiative. Fifty principals and superintendents received weekly life coaching for one year. It was the first known project that brought life coaching to school leadership. The results were positive, and participants reported feeling more focused, purposeful and confident. "I would like to see school leaders (who are already great just as they are) become more purposeful, more clear, more confident, more balanced, and happier in their professional and personal lives. It follows that schools led by such leaders will become better places for students and staff" (p. 22), Sparks said.

> [Coaching] helped me to see situations with a different pair of eyes. The coach "nudged" me to create possible solutions I might not have seriously considered on my own. The coach provided the gentle support that kept me focused on attaining personal and professional goals.
>
> —KC, School Leader, NY (personal communication, July 2002)

In 2002, I launched two leadership executive coaching pilot programs in New York, one for aspiring leaders and another for leaders of professional development centers. The Long Island (NY) School Leadership Center offered their enthusiastic interest and assistance in helping me to launch a four-month leadership coaching pilot program. Both veteran and aspiring leaders were invited to participate, and they received a combination of group and individual coaching sessions. After four months, a first-year principal felt far more competent in her role, one participant landed the job of her dreams, and other participants reported increased comfort dealing with interpersonal communication and greater confidence to pursue their first administrative positions.

In another project, I worked with experienced leaders of professional development agencies over a six-month period. Their goals ranged from interpersonal relationships, managing and making time for organizational priorities, and boosting their confidence and effectiveness in their roles. In this project, I used a leadership assessment that pinpointed their strengths and confirmed the leadership areas where they needed further development. Goals emerged from the assessment that became the targets of our coaching sessions. Among the reported gains were improved interpersonal relationships with staff, increased confidence, courage to step out of their comfort zones and try new strategies and skills and take on new leadership roles. One participant produced a product to bring to market; another made great strides in completing her doctoral dissertation and achieving long-desired, increased fitness levels.

Both projects convinced me that school leaders need, appreciate, and benefit from coaching, that the coaching partnership works, and that results are often beyond those that the coachee begins with. In my experiences coaching school leaders, I've found that leaders seek coaching for a variety of reasons. Typically, they are

- Transitioning and integrating into new, higher-level positions
- Deciding whether to stay in their current positions or move on to others
- Strengthening their leadership competencies and confidence
- Strategizing to prepare for and obtain their next positions
- Struggling with staff
- Having conflicts with school board members
- Seeking their first superintendency
- Seeking feedback
- Interested in learning about their strengths and areas for personal development
- Interested in managing and balancing their personal and professional lives

Other leaders sought coaching when they had lost a position or were about to. Often they were unaware of the cause and sought support and assistance in determining their next positions or strengthening their skills and confidence to move on. For the most part, they had received little specific honest feedback and came to coaching to seek insights about themselves.

The future success and strength of our school systems lie in the leadership ability of its administrators. Executive, or leadership, coaching can have a strategic impact on the performance of an organization's leaders. Most districts need to greatly improve student achievement results. Results don't happen when people are only focused on test scores or accountability issues. School systems must support leaders to help their staff with the intangible elements of human interaction—the soft people skills. To achieve extraordinary, external results, we must focus on *developing and sustaining individual, team and organizational behaviors* through improving personal relationships. *Executive and leadership coaching* builds the organizational capability to achieve those results by strengthening those skills, one leader at a time.

THE COST OF NOT COACHING

In a recent conversation, a leader of a medium-sized suburban district claimed that the prior six leaders the district had hired didn't work out. Each one, he claimed, shone during the interview phase. However, when they started their new job, they didn't have what it took. Six in a row! It seemed evident to me was there was a systemic problem: a lack of support for these newly hired leaders. There was no support system, and each of the six was let go in a short time. Think of the time spent and cost of advertising that then had to be repeated.

I've heard it said that the skills that helped you succeed in one job will not be the same ones that help you succeed in a higher position. As leaders move up into higher levels, the skills needed to be successful change from technical to managerial to personal (see Figure 1.4). The softer skills—emotional intelligence and people skills—become far more important and crucial to success. In my coaching practice, I find that the majority of coachees are dealing with interpersonal conflict, time management, and self-control issues.

A derailed executive is described as "having reached the general manager level; is fired, demoted or reaches a career plateau. The derailed leader had been originally seen as having high potential, an impressive track record and holding a solidly established leadership position—until derailed" (Chappelow & Leslie, 2000, p. 7). Five key characteristics describe these executives:

1. Problems with interpersonal relationships

2. Failure to hire, build, and lead a team

3. Failure to meet the organizations objectives

4. Inability or unwillingness to change or adapt

5. A lack of a broad functional orientation

Figure 1.4 Changing Requirements for Success

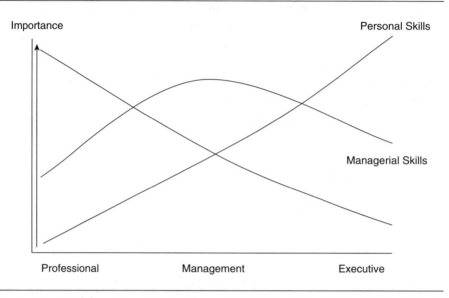

Source: *Reprinted from Preventing Derailment: What to Do Before it's Too Late* by Michael M. Lombardo and Robert Eichinger, Copyright © 18989 Center for Creative Leadership.

I cannot help but wonder how often school leaders are dismissed instead of supported. Let's look at an example of a derailed school leader. Robert was a 30-year veteran teacher and content area administrator in a small district. He came to me for coaching after he'd moved to a larger district and was soon without a job. He didn't know what had happened. He'd had no feedback. Although he was successful and confident in one district, as soon as he moved on to a much larger one, he began to sense it wasn't a good match. He'd hoped to work until retirement but found himself out of work one year later. It was too late to save his position, and it was too bad for everyone involved. Coaching helped Robert prepare for his next move with renewed self-esteem and confidence. Had coaching been available to him, perhaps the situation would have been remedied. The district would have saved the time and dollars invested in hiring him, and Robert would have been supported rather than dismissed.

The costs are great to a school system when there is frequent turnover among leadership. Imagine if there was a process for improving relationships rather than continuing frustration with interpersonal conflicts. Imagine the dollars that would be saved by dealing directly with conflict and improving the day-to-day struggles and stresses that leaders and school board members face. Imagine increased stability and longevity, highly possible when leaders receive the benefits of a coaching relationship.

Given that the cost of superintendent searches ranges from $5,000 to $100,000, it makes smart sense for districts to protect their investments by providing strategies that lead to leader retention and that will support them in transitioning to a new position or a new district. It would be a mistake to view coaching as only for leaders who "need it." It's not a weakness to rely on another for support. It's smart practice. Ongoing professional growth and continuous learning is everyone's role. Considering that in the area of professional development, only 29% of superintendents felt they were "somewhat prepared" for the role (CASE, 2003), there is clearly a need for providing leaders with appropriate support to do their very best.

COACHING IN THE BUSINESS WORLD

Leading an effective, high-performing school system is surely as challenging as leading a Fortune 500 Company, a large hospital, or any complex organization. There are many parallels to the business world. In corporations, managers have multiple departments to lead, budget and personnel issues and personalities to deal with, boards to respond to, and lofty goals to accomplish. In the business world, the goals may be product branding, profits, and market share. Technological advances and a more global society have created enormous pressure for companies to outperform the competition, creating high-stress workplaces and low morale. In the educators' world, the goals are student

> To create a high performance team, we must replace typical management activities like supervising, monitoring, checking, and controlling with new behaviors like coaching and communicating.
>
> —Ray Smith, CEO, Bell Atlantic
> (as quoted in Edge First, 2000)

achievement and helping all students reach their full potentials. Although the goals are vastly different, the daily challenges of leading a complex organization are strikingly similar. In many ways, districts around the country are looking to, and learning from, their business counterparts.

Executives of major corporations have used executive coaches for years to deal with the complexities of running large companies. Many companies have internal, professionally trained coaches on their staff whose purpose is to improve the performance of individuals and teams and boost results for the business. Coaching has become *the* strategy for management and leadership development programs versus traditional kinds of training. Department managers and upper management leaders are often left to deal with complex people issues, and many of them are unskilled and untrained in this arena. Many business owners and managers are uncomfortable dealing with difficult people or difficult situations. Leaders may be wonderful visionaries and poor at people skills, or terrific at people skills and poor at managing change, decision making or solving problems. Coaching has become increasingly utilized and popular because the relationship between coach and coahee deals with those uncomfortable situations in a private, confidential manner. It provides support, feedback, a place to vent frustrations, and a safe space to brainstorm possible solutions.

> The scarcest resource in the world today is leadership talent capable of continuously transforming organizations to win in tomorrow's world.
>
> —Noel Tichy (Tichy & Cohen, 1997)

Approximately 59% of organizations offered coaching or other developmental counseling to their managers and executives in 1999, according to a nationwide survey of more than 300 companies by Manchester, Inc. (2001), a human capital consulting firm. Another 20% said they planned to offer such coaching within the next year. In the survey, the primary reasons corporations hired coaches were as follows:

- To sharpen leadership skills of high-potential individuals
- To correct management behavior problems: poor communication, failure to develop subordinates, indecisiveness
- To ensure success—or decrease the failure rate—of newly promoted managers
- To correct employee relations problems: poor interpersonal skills, disorganization, demeaning or arrogant behavior
- To provide management and leadership skills to technically oriented employees

In 1999, the International Coach Federation and Linkage, Inc. (2000) conducted a survey on the use of corporate coaching in over 4,000 companies. A summary of the findings showed the following results:

- Companies that use external coaches use them for executive ranks.
- There was improved performance for individuals.
- The use of coaching was seen as an ongoing tool for leadership development and managing organizational change.
- A need for standardization was felt—a clear definition of coaching, a list of competencies for coaches, a way to measure the effectiveness of corporate coaches, and a formal process to certify coaches.
- A desire was expressed for objective, documented evidence of coaching success.

- The primary benefits of coaching were seen (in this order) as (1) improved individual performance; (2) increased bottom-line results, including profit, coachee service and competitiveness; and (3) and development of people for the next level: raising confidence, skills and self empowerment, goal achievement, relationship improvements, and retention.

Scores of corporations use executive coaching as their primary improvement process for leaders, individuals and entire teams, including Time, Inc., Colgate Palmolive, Goldman Sachs, and Intel. In 2005, NASA implemented an agencywide, three-stage program providing coaching for middle and upper level leaders.

Coaching is used in business in a multitude of formats. CEOs use one-on-one executive coaching. Frequently, coaching is also available for middle managers. Some companies have full-time, in-house coaches who work with anyone who wants or needs support. These people may coach individuals, executives or teams. They may shadow, observe team meetings and provide feedback. They often administer assessments to determine specific areas for coaching. Middle to upper level managers often apply a coaching approach versus a top-down management style. Although they may not be credentialed coaches, they have learned to use coaching skills as an effective communication style. School systems have much to learn about the benefits of coaching from business.

COACHING IN THE NONPROFIT WORLD

Nonprofit organizations are exploring the coaching movement, too. Like school districts, each nonprofit organization has a clear, purposeful mission, a board of directors, and a leader—an executive director. They operate much like school districts, sharing fiscal concerns, attempting to make positive change in the world and make a difference for people. They share similar political issues with school districts: finding sufficient funding sources to fulfill their missions, board politics and media concerns.

A study of the effects of executive coaching on executive directors of nonprofits (CompassPoint, 2003) reported numerous positive findings. The Executive Coaching Project studied the impact of executive coaching to develop and sustain effective leadership. Twenty-four executive directors received a year of weekly coaching. Like superintendents, executive directors are called on to be strong managers, strategic thinkers, reflective philosophers, successful fundraisers, public speakers and inspirational leaders. Participants received 40 hours of one-of-one coaching. Overall, executive directors agreed that their coaching outcomes met and often exceeded their expectations. They reported a high degree of satisfaction, with a mean rating of 4.6 on a scale of 1 to 5. Key findings from the study include

- Increased confidence in exercising leadership
- Improved ability to connect with the organization's vision
- Increased confidence in leading toward fulfilling the vision
- Increased task completion and productivity
- Improved personnel management skills
- Better relationships with staffs and boards of directors
- Improved decision making
- Improved communication and teamwork
- Increase in balancing personal and professional lives
- Increased confidence, which resulted in increased happiness at their jobs and better developed interpersonal skills
- Reduced stress and burnout
- Overall increased job satisfaction
- Increased financial stability
- Improved internal communication
- Improved ability to fulfill the mission and vision of the organization

The report concluded that, overall, coaching had a profound impact on executive directors and the organizations they led. Coaching, according to the study, is a relatively inexpensive, high impact way to develop the leadership of executive directors. As one participant stated, "Coaching more than exceeded my expectations because I really doubt I'd still be here without coaching. In the face of really difficult changes, I got regular, reliable feedback of how I was doing during this period of change. It made me feel that I was on the right track. I doubted myself and was hard on myself. Now I feel successful" (CompassPoint, 2003, p. 11).

COACHING: A STRATEGY FOR ACHIEVING PEAK PERFORMANCE

No serious athlete would consider training for an Olympic event, or other challenging sports competition, without the assistance of an inspiring, skilled coach. Most people are familiar with athletic coaches—they work with athletes to move them from one place of competence to another. These focused, dedicated, goal-oriented people seek out coaches to help them gain and strengthen their physical skills and, more important, help them find the mental focus and thinking needed to be successful at a high level. It makes good sense for educators to learn from professional athletic coaches the techniques they use to help ordinary people achieve extraordinary results.

Although sports coaching and "professional" coaching differ in some aspects, there

> *Most successful pros have mentors, coaches, and gurus who motivate, activate, and inspire them to great performances.*
>
> —Bobby McGee (2001),
> *Olympic running coach*

are similarities. In both, coachees strive to reach a challenging goal and rely on a skilled, supportive coach with whom they are accountable. Results are achieved by following a thoughtful plan that includes specific, daily action toward the targeted goal. Both supply objective, encouraging feedback to help the coachees continue toward their goals. A sports coach, as well as an executive or personal coach, deals directly with achieving peak performance through a close collaborative relationship that focuses on the mind to achieve greater results. According to Olympic running coach Bobby McGee (2001), 80% of training for a challenging race or competition is mental versus physical. He uses a five-point strategy with his athletes: affirmations, focus, routine for dealing with anxiety, visualization, and dealing with discomfort. I have applied this strategy to coaching school leaders to reach their maximum potential (see Chapter 6). In fact, *all* the "professional" coaches I know use these techniques when coaching executives, leaders, individuals and teams to create and achieve change and overcome personal and professional challenges.

Achieving peak performance in the boardroom or the classroom can be no less challenging than on a race course or high diving board. Sports coaches help athletes visualize success by focusing on what they *want* to achieve rather than on what they *don't* want. These are common techniques to achieving superhuman performance. They help athletes eliminate negative thoughts that might interfere with achieving their goals. They help manage their lives to make appropriate time for training, nutrition and rest. They help athletes create conditions for success. Professional and executive coaches perform similar functions.

Improving thinking skills, improving imagery skills, and taking purposeful action are key ingredients to achieving challenging goals. It takes discipline, just as athletes work toward their goals on a daily basis, for coachees working on any personal or organizational goals to practice positive thinking and helpful mental habits.

Our thoughts create our reality. When negative thoughts are more prevalent than positive thoughts, negative results will occur. We can choose thoughts that will move us toward a goal, or away from one. How would it be to think . . . ?

New Thoughts	versus	Old Thoughts
I won't give up.		I'm a quitter.
I can do that.		I'm not good at that.
I have what it takes to succeed.		I don't have what it takes.
Anything is possible.		That will never work.
I make time for what's important.		There's not enough time.

By practicing affirming thoughts on a daily basis, a new mindset evolves, and new actions are the result. Everything is energy; our thoughts are energy, too. An abundance of positive thoughts sends positive energy flowing through the coachees into their environments. Aligning vision with thoughts and beliefs allows people to experience success mentally before experiencing it physically. This is the essence of sports coaching *and* the essence of professional coaching. With executive and leadership coaching available to all school leaders, they will have the opportunity to reach their peak levels of performance and lead their staffs, students and systems to success.

COACHING: IT'S ALL ABOUT CHANGE

Change is so challenging that 90% of people who underwent bypass surgery did not change their lifestyles, even when faced with possible death (Deutschman, 2005). At a Global Medical Forum summit, health care leaders convened to discuss the concern that 80% of the health care budget was consumed by five health care issues: smoking, drinking, eating, stress, and insufficient exercise. Dr. Edward Miller (2005), dean of Johns Hopkins Medical School, noted that 600,000 patients a year with severe heart disease undergo bypass surgery, a traumatic and expensive procedure that can cost more than $100,000—a total cost of $30 billion (p. 54). He noted that many patients who *could* avoid repeat surgery rarely do. Health care issues are caused by the choice of lifestyle versus disease. "The central issue is never strategy, structure, culture, or systems. The core of the matter is always about changing the behavior of people" (p. 55), said John Kotter in the same article (p. 55). "Behavior change happens mostly by speaking to people's feelings. In highly successful change efforts, people find ways to help others see the problems or solutions in ways that influence emotions, not just thought" (p. 55). A study of bypass surgery patients showed that those who were told what to do (regarding living a healthier life) did not make lasting changes. Only when they were provided with support (a team of professionals) to implement lifestyle changes did they succeed.

A few years ago, I heard a radio reporter comment that nearly 80% of people who got a new hairstyle reverted back to their original style within a few months. I don't know if it's true, but it's no secret that people resist change, and there's probably no greater frustration among leaders of organizational change efforts.

So how do we obtain lasting change? How do we start? How do we overcome resistance? How do we get change right? In my workshops, I find that school leaders can easily and rapidly rattle off dozens of projects and programs that have come and gone. Their level of frustration is high, and often leaders and their staffs are reluctant to implement one more new thing. School system resources are precious dollars that no district can waste on another failed change effort. Supporting change efforts with a coaching approach that addresses the soft, people issues and deals with coachees' feelings can help sustain those efforts and add lasting value to school improvement investments.

EMOTIONAL INTELLIGENCE AND COACHING

Emotional intelligence is known to be a greater predictor of success in a leadership role than technical or cognitive skills. The higher the position, the more important it is. "Emotional competence made the crucial difference between mediocre leaders and the best. On average, close to 90% of success in leadership was attributed to emotional intelligence" (Goleman, 1998, p. 33). And Cherniss (2000) says,

> There now is a considerable body of research suggesting that a person's ability to perceive, identify, and manage emotion provides the basis for the kinds of social and emotional competencies that are important for success in almost any job. Furthermore, as the pace of change increases and the world of work makes ever greater demands on a person's cognitive, emotional, and physical resources, this particular set of abilities will become increasingly important. (p. 10)

Typically, managers and supervisors don't deal effectively with their staff to assess or manage emotional competencies. They are either uncomfortable doing so or unskilled. Who then can address those delicate personal issues? Skilled, trained coaches and organizational psychologists are two professional groups equipped to deal directly with emotional intelligence to improve leadership effectiveness, productivity and overall well-being. School systems must embrace executive and leadership coaching as a common practice, as it directly deals with the hearts and souls of the coachees. In the confidential space of the coach-coachee relationship, coachees are safe to reveal themselves and their inner, personal issues. They reflect on, and work on, the areas of emotional competency that are holding them back from high levels of success.

Let's look more closely at suggested guidelines for dealing with emotional intelligence, developed for the Consortium for Research on Emotional Intelligence in Organizations in light of the coaching process (Goleman & Cherniss, 1998). The guidelines represent current knowledge about how to promote emotional intelligence in the workplace. They apply to most management and executive development efforts as well as training in supervisory skills, diversity, teamwork, leadership, conflict management, stress management, and so on. The guidelines are based on an extensive review of the research literature in training and development, counseling and psychotherapy, and behavior change. Each item describes precisely what coaches do on a regular basis.

Best Practices to Enhance Emotional Intelligence in the Workplace

1. Assess the organization's needs.

2. Assess the individual.

3. Deliver assessments with care.

4. Maximize learner choice.

5. Encourage people to participate.

6. Link learning goals to personal values.

7. Adjust expectations.

8. Gauge readiness.

9. Foster a positive relationship between trainers and learners.

10. Make change self-directed.

11. Set clear goals.

12. Break goals into manageable steps.

13. Provide opportunities to practice and give performance feedback.

14. Rely on experiential methods.

15. Build in support.

16. Use models to demonstrate competency.

17. Enhance insight.

18. Prevent relapse.

19. Encourage use of skills on the job.

20. Develop an organizational culture that supports learning.

There's a high correlation between these interventions and support that executive and leadership coaches offer and the development of emotional competencies necessary to success on the job. Most often, even when coachees begin a coaching relationship with specific, external organizational goals, the coaching conversation quickly shifts to their internal, personal resources and capacity for carrying them out. In that respect, executive coaching is personal coaching, just as leadership development can be equated with personal development. It is common for professional coaches to incorporate the use of assessments to identify areas of strengths and developmental opportunities with coachees (see Chapter 7, Using Assessments).

SUMMARY

Creating systemic change has been a challenge for school leaders for decades. Increased pressure on school systems has caused an alarming decline in the number of qualified candidates interested in leading our schools. Clearly, additional models of supporting school leaders on the job can attract them into these challenging positions and provide the confidential support to retain them while improving performance.

Numerous studies have long supported coaching as a beneficial process for creating collaboration and professional growth among teachers. The role of school-based coaching continues to grow and expand, and it is important that classroom coaches increase their coaching skills and knowledge.

We are making great progress. Yet we have a very long way to go before we realize the full potential and value of coaching in school systems. Coaching techniques and strategies are useful throughout the school system. Why limit coaching to some classrooms? Why not make coaching available to every educator who faces the enormous challenge of successfully educating every child? I believe that when coaching is available to principals, department chairpersons, and central office administrators, we will see enormous shifts in culture, communication, attitude, and outlook—factors crucial to making lasting change.

Let us borrow the knowledge from classroom coaching models, the success of business and leadership coaching, and the rapidly growing coaching profession to create a new level of support for leaders and school systems. School system leaders can deal more effectively with their daily challenges and achieve a level of peak performance just as CEOs of businesses and top athletic competitors have. We can incorporate the same peak performance strategies for our leaders and ensure that school-based coaches have adequate preparation as coaches. We can support and encourage them by acknowledging the challenge of the job and providing what is needed: ongoing support and opportunity for professional growth, confidence and increased competence available with professional coaching.

Reflective Questions

- How does your current perception of coaching differ from ICF's definition?
- How can your school's leader or leadership team benefit from working with a coach?
- What steps can you take to create increased awareness of the benefits of coaching?

PART II

Coaching Mindsets and Skill Sets

Getting Started as a Coach

The best coaches set in motion a continuing learning process that helps people develop a tolerance for their own struggles and accelerates the unfolding of skill and contributions that would not have been possible without the magic attention of a dedicated coach.

—Nancy Austen and Tom Peters (1985, p. 445)

IN THIS CHAPTER

Coaching mindset and attributes

Why people come to coaching

Coaching the whole person: values, outer and inner goals

Introduction to professional coaching organizations and competencies

Olympic running coach Bobby McGee (2001) states, "Athletes tend to assume that training and talent precede performance, and that a strong mental approach is something you either have or don't have. The truth is, the harder you train mentally, the better you perform physically and your improvements will go as far as your mind will take you" (n.p.). The same is true of professional coaching: By helping teachers and leaders shift their thoughts and beliefs to create new actions and results, leadership coaches can be successful in helping them achieve greater results and reach their lofty goals. Educators make ideal coaches; they have already chosen a helping profession and are passionate about helping students learn, grow and improve themselves.

This chapter can help you form a philosophy about the coaching process and develop a knowledge base necessary for successful coaching. If you are just beginning your role as a coach, this chapter can provide coaching basics to ensure that your coaching relationships are successful and get off to a good start. If you are already in a coaching role, the skills and processes within this chapter can help you deal with the struggles and challenges you may encounter. Note that the content and recommendations are derived from the world of professional coaching. There is no intent to compare different coaching models or imply that one is preferable over another, but there are likely to be similarities and differences. With the concepts in this chapter, you can coach anyone, in any area of education, or outside of education. Use them with students, teachers and staff, or your friends, children, or spouse. Use them to shift your leadership style from leader-as-manager to leader-as-coach or to change your general communication style.

Most educators would agree that it's important for students to be lifelong learners. Coaching is an ongoing learning process, a discovery process in which the coachees learn about themselves and how they experience and interact with the world around them. It's in perceptions, interpretations, assumptions and beliefs that people think something can either be accomplished—or not. Educator-coaches who have developed a coaching philosophy and have sufficient basic coaching skills, strategies, techniques, and processes can be more successful in supporting their coachees through transitions and creating lasting change for their school or district.

DEVELOPING A COACHING MINDSET

It's important for long-term success that coaches develop an attitude—a philosophy—about people in a continuous learning mode. The relationship coaches develop with their coachees depends on how they see them. If they see them as broken and needing fixing, they are likely to create relationships that cause them to feel and act defensively. If coaches see coachees as learners and in a positive light, they'll create a different dynamic, one that is healthier and has the potential to create positive interactions, trust, and ultimately positive change. It can be helpful for coaches to adopt what I call a *coaching mindset*. With it, coaches can be far more successful in their coaching role, and they can develop the sense of trust and collaboration that leads to a constructive, long-term relationship. And as an added bonus, it is nearly impossible for coaches to learn to coach others without learning and growing themselves!

Developing a coaching mindset is a process of adopting some particular ways of thinking. They're not specific skills but are attributes or characteristics that can help coaches grow in their role and become more masterful and successful. These ways of thinking can be especially helpful when a coach feels stuck with a coachee. The Coaching Mindset Self-Assessment (see Resource A) is a continuous-learning tool. It is for coaches to use as an ongoing assessment of their professional growth. Just as with the people they coach, coaches may have inner thoughts and beliefs that get in the way of their success.

COACHING MINDSET ATTRIBUTES

Active Listener

The coaching process and relationship focus on the coachee, not on the coach. When you are engaged in a coaching conversation, you want to be totally focused on the coachee. Become acutely aware of how you listen:

- Are you tuned in to your coachee or thinking about other things?
- How closely are you listening to what is being said without filtering it through your own thoughts and beliefs?

Nonjudgmental

As a coach, you want to suspend your own personal thoughts or judgments about the coachee's personality, performance, thoughts, or beliefs. When you approach your coachees without judgment, you open the door for trusting, unguarded relationships and ultimately for change to occur. You can be more able to see things from their perspective, and help them identify how they can move forward. You are neutral. You have no opinion, only the goal of helping them move forward.

- What do you need to let go of in your attitude about others to approach your coachee without judgment?

- How might your reaction or approach with a coachee be different if you were to suspend all judgment?

Possibility Thinker

As stated in Chapter 1, coaching is about change. Often coachees have not made desired changes because they simply haven't seen any other way. As a coach, you believe all things are possible. There are no limits, and anything can be accomplished. Obstacles and problems are nothing but opportunities. Every problem has a solution. In fact, there are usually multiple solutions. As a coach, you are to help the coachees think beyond their current thoughts (see Chapter 6).

- To what extent do you think out of the box?
- How willing are you to step into the unknown?
- Do you help your coachees think of multiple possibilities and new options?

Compassionate

Great coaches truly care about their coachees. They express appropriate concern for them when it's fitting.

- How do you express your feelings of empathy?
- How do you show others that you care?

Inspirational

Helping people change is almost always about dealing with their inner thoughts and self-doubts. Providing inspiration works wonders, especially when it is specific and concrete. Convey to your coachees that you can see them as successful in what they are trying to accomplish and why. Inspirational comments must be truthful and sincere, or your coachees will see them as fake and phony. Become their cheerleader and personal champion for their success.

- How often do you tell others they *can* reach their goals?
- Do you believe they can?

Personable

Coachees can relate to coaches in a positive manner when coaches are perceived as pleasant and friendly. Coachees will feel connected with you when you are approachable, pleasant and open.

- How comfortable are your colleagues in sharing their professional and personal concerns with you?
- When you have a bad day, how do you let go of your own struggles so you can coach from a pleasant, positive mindset?

Intuitive

When coaches deeply listen to their coachees, they will hear the coachees' self-doubts and their limiting thoughts and beliefs revealed, and they develop the ability to trust their gut. They are seeing the bigger picture, getting a meta view of the coachees and the issues that are keeping them stuck. Because coaching is not about telling the coachees what to do, you will develop your intuition to guide them to things they will agree to do to move forward.

- How intuitive are you?
- How can you communicate your intuitive thoughts to coachees?

Sincere

A successful coach will demonstrate a high level of caring and concern for the coachees. When you coach from a place of truth and honesty, that is conveyed to them and improves your relationships with them.

- Do you approach your coachees with sincerity?
- How would your coachees know if you're being sincere?

Trustworthy

The ideal coaching relationship is a confidential one. This is a crucial element of a successful coaching relationship. Whether you are an instructional coach making classroom visits, or a leadership coach, you want to establish trust. Without trust, the relationship is likely to suffer. Keep your word, show up on time, and follow through with any promises or commitments you make.

- What additional steps can you take to create trust with a coachee?
- How can you communicate the importance of trust with the coachee?

Risk Taker

If you are timid or avoid taking risks yourself, how can you support and encourage coachees to try something new? Successful coaches are courageous and willing to take risks, to experiment. The more courageous the coach, the more likely the coachees will be willing to take action into the unknown. Stepping out of one's comfort zone is a crucial element of changing behavior, actions, and results. It's the key to change. The coach must be willing to abandon the tried and true and support coachees to take risks. Being out of one's comfort zone is the place where learning and lasting change happens.

- How willing are you to try something new—a new activity, a new thought process, or new way of doing something?
- Do you resist or get excited by something new?
- What risks have you taken lately in your own life or work?
- How courageous are you?

> It isn't so much we're afraid of change or in love with the old ways. It's just that place in between, like being in between trapezes. It's Linus when his blanket is in the dryer. There's nothing to hold on to.
>
> —Marilyn Ferguson
> (www.thinkexist.com)

Action Oriented

Coaching is only effective when a person does something—takes an action toward an agreed-on goal. A skilled coach knows how and when to move the person forward. Your coaching sessions will result in action steps that your coachee will take between sessions. A great coach will not end a session without a commitment to two to four action steps the coachee has agreed to take. Remember, being in motion is different from being in action!

- Do you have a bias toward action?
- Do you think too much and act too little?
- Do you make sure your coachee has actions to work on between coaching sessions?

Focused on Results

Successful coaching happens when coachees accomplish something they (or the organizations) want yet haven't done on their own. Always keep the coachees' or organization's goals in mind and be sure the action steps are pointing toward them.

- Have you established clear and specific goals with your coachees?
- What would success look like if it were accomplished?
- How able are you, as a coach, to help coachees visualize results?

Knows Core Coaching Competencies

Resistance to change is one of the greatest challenges and frustrations for leaders of complex organizations. A skilled coach is competent in various coaching techniques and processes that help people explore resistance and change their behavior and actions. A great coach knows that change is possible and happens by aligning the inner self with outer results. With training and practice, coaches get to the root cause of resistance and work with individuals to create shifts in thoughts and beliefs that lead to different actions. Change is easier when the coachee seeks it. When the impetus for change is external or the coachee resists it, change is more challenging. Good coaches understand that different people need different levels of support through a change process and they use their effective coaching skills to move them through the process.

- How can you practice and integrate the core coaching competencies (see Chapters 3–5)?
- What additional resources can you identify to boost your coaching skills and techniques?

Curious

Because coaches want to help coachees get to the core of any issues, they want to help them understand why they think or believe as they do. Asking lots of questions demonstrates your curiosity and helps coachees think out loud. It helps them gain clarity. Being inquisitive helps coaches explore and go beneath the surface to uncover patterns of negative, limiting thoughts.

- Do you ask more questions or tend to give more answers?
- How comfortable are you asking versus telling?

When wearing a coaching hat, always view the coachees through the coaching mindset. Accept them for where they are in their personal or professional lives. View them as people on a journey from one place to another. The coach is the vehicle or guide for helping them move along their own journeys. The coach is their sounding board, their inspiration and their partner in success.

COACHING TIPS:

- ❖ Make multiple copies of the Coaching Mindset Self-Assessment (see Resource A). Use it in the beginning of your coaching work and every three months thereafter.

❖ Work with another trusted coach; share your results. Identify three areas you will focus on during the next three months. Talk about ways you can improve in these areas. Commit to them.

❖ Meet again in three months to review your progress and identify three more areas for your professional growth.

CONSIDER THE COACHEE

Although everyone can benefit from coaching at one point or another in their lives or work, there is a wide range of individuals who may become your coaches, ranging from those who seem eager and enthused to those who are reluctant and resistant. When coachees are eager and enthused about their goals, they will be a pleasure to work with. They make coaching seem a breeze. When people are reluctant and resistant, they may challenge you every step of the way. This distinction is not to label or judge but to recognize that a coach may find some coachees wide open and ready for change, some who are fixed in their thoughts and outlooks, and some who are somewhere in between. It is important for coaches to also recognize that a coachee may be open to coaching on certain issues and not others.

For Example

Joe was one of the most eager, enthusiastic coachees I've ever worked with. He was gung-ho about his performance goals and surged ahead every week. He also identified one personal goal in addition to his professional ones—to improve his relationship with his daughter. Yet although it was an important goal for him, he resisted taking action toward it beyond what he'd already tried. He avoided talking about it. He was full of fear that the relationship would worsen. In this instance, Joe was only willing to take very small, safe steps. We spent a great deal of time in our coaching sessions talking about what he feared and brainstorming about other actions he could take. In time, Joe and his daughter were reunited and enjoying a good relationship again.

As previously mentioned, coaches need to know numerous skills and processes for helping people through resistance (see Chapter 6). Remember to maintain a neutral, nonjudgmental perspective, even when coachees are resistant.

And to reiterate, it would be a mistake to think of coaching only for those staff members who someone else thinks need it. Coaching is a positive process whereby anyone, including already successful people, can benefit. In organizations, coaching is often "given" to someone who is perceived as needing assistance in improving performance. The coach, therefore, needs to develop an understanding of each person he or she is working with. The coach needs to take time to know the coachees and learn why they may be resistant and what thoughts and beliefs they need to overcome in order to help them tiptoe into the land of change.

The important thing to recognize is that coaching is a continuous learning process. Like snowflakes, no two people are alike. All will have their own starting points.

The Eager and Enthused

These are the dream coachees. The eager and enthused will be excited to work with a coach. They want to grow in their professional roles. They're open to new ideas and are ready to take steps or risks. They see a preferred future for themselves or their organizations or both. They're positive people who want to become even more capable than they already are. They're willing to think beyond their own mindsets and able to reach decisions through collaboration. They are likely to be successful already and seeking more. Perhaps they want to learn something new or to make a bigger difference in their organizations or have a larger impact on the world. They have many ideas and goals and are ready to move forward. They may need a coach to help them focus and take steps toward reaching their goals. They may need some inspiration or someone to rein them in, as they are likely to have so many ideas that they need help concentrating on or prioritizing them.

They are likely to accomplish their weekly action steps with ease and enthusiastically report them to you, often before your next coaching session. Most often, eager and enthused coachees will ask for, seek out, or request a coach. They are highly "coachable," and delightful to work with. You are likely to feel an enormous sense of satisfaction when coaching the eager and enthused.

> To exist is to change, to change is to mature, to mature is to go on creating oneself endlessly.
>
> —Henri Bergson
> (www.creatingminds.org)

The Reluctant and Resistant

These are the coachees that are likely to challenge you on a regular basis. They're likely to be the ones that are "given" coaching rather than seeking it for themselves. They may resent or resist the coach or the process and act defensively. They are why it is essential for anyone in a coaching role to have sufficient skills and training under their belts and numerous strategies in their bags of tricks. They may use passive-aggressive tactics to avoid making changes in their lives or on the job. They are not typically open to new ideas or to reflecting on their thoughts and beliefs. They will make excuses for not completing their action steps. They will question and challenge you. They will be less likely to see past obstacles. In fact, they will use obstacles as the reason they didn't do something. They're more likely to be negative thinkers and have closed minds. They are less "coachable" and may seem difficult to work with. Coaches may feel a great sense of frustration when working with them. However, successful coaching of someone who's reluctant and resistant is possible. Don't give up!

COACHING TIPS: Turning Reluctance and Resistance Into Eagerness and Enthusiasm

It is helpful for coaches to consider who they are coaching, from the beginning of the coaching relationship. Did they seek you out or were they assigned to work with you? Do they have a choice of working with a coach or not? Do they have a choice of coaches? If you find yourself in a position of coaching someone who doesn't wish to be coached, here are some tips:

- ❖ Take it slow.
- ❖ Set small, achievable goals initially.
- ❖ Thoroughly explain the coach's role in the beginning.
- ❖ Focus on building trust.
- ❖ Be okay with small, tiny actions.
- ❖ Use the coaching mindset to determine what changes *you* may need to make.
- ❖ Set realistic expectations.
- ❖ Let them choose their own goals for coaching, especially in the beginning.
- ❖ Ask permission to coach on specific or sensitive topics.
- ❖ Celebrate their success with sincerity.

When you are successful in helping reluctant and resistant coachees become eager and enthusiastic, they are likely to become great advocates for coaching. (See Resource B: Coachee Readiness Checklist.)

DIFFERENT REASONS TO COACH

People seek out or enter into coaching relationships for various reasons. Regardless of why someone needs or wants coaching, the process and skills you choose to use are likely to be strikingly similar, no matter what the goals are. Thinking about different reasons for coaching is simply a way of examining motivations that people may have when you begin working with them. It is also helpful in determining schedules and length of time needed for different coachees.

Coaching to Increase or Gain Skills

Coaching is an appropriate strategy when someone wants to acquire a new skill. As mentioned earlier, you don't have to have the skill yourself in order to successfully coach someone. You help coachees explore the various ways they can obtain the skills they are seeking. Skills such as managing classroom behavior, analyzing student data, or managing budgets are examples of new skills educators may need. Coaching to gain skills is typically a short-term process, often six months or less.

For Example

Gloria, a first-year principal, was anxious about making her first graduation speech. She was young, concerned about being perceived as childlike, and had never given a speech before. Our coaching began by identifying the goal: to make a well-received, inspiring speech by "x" date. We had a few weeks to prepare and brainstormed various things she could do to feel better prepared. The following are some of the actions she took:

1. Looking for a Toastmaster chapter in her area

2. Attending a Toastmasters meeting and listening to others making successful speeches

3. Joining Toastmasters

4. Writing and delivering a speech, with feedback from the Toastmasters group

5. Searching the internet for graduation speeches written by others

6. Videotaping herself giving a speech

   By taking weekly actions toward her goal, Gloria was able to acquire the skills she needed, boost her self-assurance, and deliver a successful speech with confidence. It's important to note that I, the coach, didn't tell her what to do, but together we identified things that could be done, and she made choices about which ones to do.

(Continued)

(Continued)

> Ultimately, the core of the issue was that Gloria wanted to feel more confident. Her goal was connected to a *feeling*. She wanted to *feel* secure and self-assured. Some actions were about obtaining the skill, and by taking weekly steps toward them, she became more sure of herself and achieved the goal.

Coaching Tip: Focus on the *feeling* the coachee wants to achieve. That will be the inner motivator and help the coachee stay in action toward the goal.

Success Story

I never thought of myself as a writer. As a student, I hovered over my papers so no one would see what I wrote. I dreaded the process and cringed at the thought of reading any original writing aloud. Before I became a coach, I had one—to help me negotiate a major life transition. I'd gotten the empty nest and was feeling overwhelmed by how huge a change it was for me. My coach encouraged me to write about it, because one of my goals was to explore my creative side. I simply began to write, to get things off my chest. Step by step, action by action, one page led to two, then four. My coach gave me wonderful feedback—it was good, she thought. She thought other people would want to hear my story, knowing many people experience the empty nest and are upset by it. As the coaching process evolved, lo and behold, a new goal emerged. I agreed to write a complete article and submit it for publication. I confess I was terrified, believing my experience was nothing unique. As I felt more confident, the goal changed. It became bigger and for a broader purpose. This was huge and way out of my own comfort zone! I learned to write a query letter and to identify appropriate magazines. Eventually, I completed an article and submitted it to a large women's magazine. I had already begun to shift from thinking, "I can't write" to "I can!" Although the article wasn't published, shortly afterwards, I did have two articles on coaching published in two education journals. And . . . in my wildest dreams, I would never have anticipated I would be writing this book!

As a coach, you guide coachees to achieve beyond what they believe is possible. Be aware that goals can and will change as coachees adapt to their new mindsets.

Coaching to Improve Professional Performance

Coaching to improve performance is about improving in specific areas, boosting results or specific performance objectives. When coachees are not delivering the results the organization needs, when they're in a brand-new leadership role or needing help in a particular area, coaches coach to improve their performance. As I've mentioned before, it is often about the internal self. A coach might help coachees reflect on what they are doing that may be contributing to a situation or what they can do to improve it. They'll help coachees think about the ideas and beliefs that get in their way. The coach may be acting like a sports coach, helping coachees gain the strategies for peak performance. Good coaches help them discover their internal dialogue and identify thoughts that influence their performance. Frank Shorter, 1972 Olympic marathon gold medalist, told nay-sayers in his past that he ran marathons "to find out how good I could get" (F. Shorter, personal communication, Bolder Boulder training club lecture, April, 2005). He created a habit of "backing up and reviewing" his performance as he sought greater goals. Just like athletes, educators may find nay-sayers who believe that the lofty goals set for students are out of reach. When faced with challenge, and often doubts, coaches help boost their coachees' courage muscles to achieve their goals.

> *I absolutely believe that people, unless coached, never reach their maximum capabilities.*
>
> —Bob Nardelli, CEO, Home Depot
> ("Home Depot," 2002)

Coaches often integrate appropriate assessments to identify coachees' strengths and areas for growth. There are numerous assessments published by valid, reliable sources that are effective tools to use with coachees (see Chapter 7).

For Example

A middle management coachee once came to me and reported that everything had been going well for him . . . until a new supervisor came on board. Bill was suddenly insecure and confused. A leadership assessment helped him look at his strengths as a leader and identified areas for improvement. Bill hadn't had any specific feedback from his new supervisor, just a vague sense that she wanted him out. Self-doubt and a bit of paranoia took over. The assessment helped him see himself as a leader in a new way and pinpointed where he could work on himself. He later moved on, with confidence and his newly acquired leadership skills, to another district in a broader role.

A typical time frame for performance coaching on specific goals is three to six months. It is certainly possible for multiple goals to be addressed over a longer period of time or for coaching to be ongoing. I suggest you use these time frames simply as a reference, not a hard-and-fast guideline.

Coaching for Enhanced Professional Growth and Development

Coaching is an ongoing learning process. It's about coachees learning about themselves and how they are progressing in their world, about their growth for future roles or goals. In what ways do the coachees wish to grow? What new learning will help them reach their goals? What does a coachee need to achieve a higher level of success? It may be that a coachee wishes to move up the organizational ladder or make the transition from teaching to administration, from department chairperson to principal, or from principal to central office. What new insights or personal attributes will help the coachee be successful? The attributes someone possesses to obtain a new position at a higher level may not be the attributes that will keep him or her in that role. When coaching someone who perceives others as the problem, remember, you coach the *coachee* to think and act differently, to yield a different result. In an organizational setting, the person you are coaching is part of a larger system; however, in your confidential sessions, coaching them to react differently or to choose different responses, thoughts or actions will help them develop the personal attributes they'll need to more successfully deal with the external situations. Coaching for this purpose may take nine to twelve months.

For Example

Karen was a guidance director with her heart set on becoming an assistant superintendent. Although she felt confident in her ability to do the job successfully, she realized the path to that position was not typically from the guidance office, and she thought that would be an obstacle. She wanted to overcome her feelings of doubt and uncertainty. She was so sure they would prevent her from reaching her goal that she'd been "apprehensive" to apply for the position. My intention as her coach was to help her negotiate the obstacles and reach her goal. We set out to create a plan. Through the coaching process and her willingness to take action, she ultimately achieved her goal in the specific district she'd hoped to serve. The following are some of the actions she took:

- Creating a crystal-clear description of her ideal work in her ideal district
- Creating a personal mission statement that demonstrated her purpose beyond herself

- Interviewing several assistant superintendents to get a more accurate picture of the position and determine if it aligned with her personal mission
- Contacting the superintendent in the district she hoped to work in for an informal conversation
- Interviewing for the position and determining that it wasn't a match with her purpose (The interview team was so impressed with her ability to clearly articulate what she wanted to do for the district, and why, that they eventually revised the position, making it more of a fit with what she wanted to do.)
- Interviewing again and accepting the revised position

Karen learned what would be acceptable and what was not. She became comfortable saying no to the position because it originally didn't fit her ideal job description. Eventually, the position shifted into one more aligned with her passions and goals. The result was a happy marriage between Karen and her new district—a wonderful success story, for Karen and the district.

COACHING TIPS:

❖ Role-playing is useful to help ease a coachee through difficult conversations.
❖ Practicing a new skill with the coach first will boost the coachee's confidence.

Too often, I find myself coaching administrators in positions that aren't working for them or for the district. They either don't like the situation or aren't seeing eye-to-eye with the school board or other staff members. Because of the confidential nature of coaching, I often learned that the motivation to change positions or leave one district for another had been factors such as increasing their salaries or planning for a more financially secure retirement rather than wishing to use their experiences to reach more students and serve their communities. A mismatch between a new leader and a district can be extremely costly, both in financial terms and in lost energy, vision and direction.

Coaching for Organizational Improvement

I predict that this will be the coaching model for school systems in the future. Organizational coaching refers to coaching many people toward agreed-upon goals that benefit the organization. The coach keeps the organization's goals in mind, coaching individuals, teams, and committees to achieve them. Many large corporations have internal coaches on staff who work with anyone who can benefit from the process. In the ideal system, the organization is "open"—goals are known and public. Everyone is working on an identified goal, and the culture is open enough that people are comfortable sharing their goals and progress toward them with each other (see Chapter 8).

Coaching will have the greatest impact when it permeates the system. When every staff member has access to well-trained, skilled coaches, a culture of continuous improvement will exist throughout a district.

Life Coaching

A life coach helps a coachee live a more meaningful, fulfilling life. There is little difference in the coaching process, although goals will be more personal. A coach may help people uncover squashed dreams or desires, find balance in their lives, reduce stress, or rediscover their passions and joys. Organizational coaches, however, would be wise to include personal goals *when the coachee wishes.* They are likely to be more energized, motivated and confident on the job when they are happier in their personal lives.

For Example

Carol was working in a position she no longer liked and was considering a change. As a single mom, she was concerned about giving up security and benefits she thought she needed. Through our coaching work, she identified a huge missing piece of herself—her creativity. She began to remember when she was most joyous; it was when she was creating things with her hands. Long ago, she had made some jewelry and remembered loving the process of making something sparkly and beautiful. Her job wasn't a very creative one. We began to bring back to life the part of her that had been dormant. At first, we suspended the idea of her leaving her job and simply focused on her joy. She started to make jewelry again in her spare time. But making beaded earrings wasn't enough. She really wanted to bring her sparkling goodies to the world to help people who needed beauty in their lives. She began to donate them to breast cancer patients. Her work became noticed. She received donations and funding to create more and was featured on a local television news program for the contribution she was making. Once she brought more joy to her life and to others, she surprised herself by discovering . . . she was much happier at work. Her job was the same. It was *she* who changed.

COACHING THE WHOLE PERSON

Let me emphasize this: Whether you are coaching a teacher or a school leader, do not be surprised to discover that you may be coaching areas outside of external, work-related goals. Professional development, through coaching, will almost always lead to coaching the inner person. Coaches should be aware of this and develop a comfort level with dealing with personal issues. Remember, coaching is about learning. As a personalized, customized, personal and professional development process, anything can come up.

> *We don't see things as they are, we see them as we are.*
>
> —*Anais Nin (www.brainyquote.com)*

Success Story

Melissa was a leader of a large professional development organization. With scant budgets, a small staff, and lofty goals, she felt overwhelmed and overworked. In addition, there were internal staff challenges, a trying teenager at home, and the desires to complete her doctoral dissertation and to lose some weight. Although she loved her job, she felt pulled in many directions. It seemed impossible to do everything she wanted.

We created a list of three goals: improve her ability to manage multiple tasks at work, make progress on her doctorate, and lose weight. One by one, we began to deal with the daily and weekly challenges. We identified ways she could carve out special time each week to focus solely on her dissertation. Sometimes she arrived early at the office and learned to say no to distractions. Other times, she took a 30-minute lunch break in her car. It was the only place she could focus her thoughts. She focused on her health goal and found that by doing so, she had more energy and felt less drained at work. She learned and practiced new communication strategies to deal with her office assistant and also used them for dealing with her family to garner support for everything she was trying to accomplish.

By having a clear set of prioritized goals, we were able to design weekly action steps that led to a greater sense of accomplishment, both at the office and at home. Also, by focusing on personal goals as well as professional ones, she was able to improve many areas of her life.

Coaching the whole person yields results in many areas. It creates a can-do attitude that impacts everything. And you *are* coaching the whole person, even when you are working with someone in a work setting, focused on work-related goals. You may learn about things happening in his or her personal life that may be an energy drain. Perhaps a child or family illness is causing distraction at work. As a coach, you may be able to help your coachees manage all the parts of their lives.

For Example

Chris came to me during her job-seeking process. Her goal, at first, was to obtain her first position as a superintendent. She had had several leadership positions that provided her with enough experience and confidence that she would be successful and provide strong leadership for a district. Through our coaching sessions, she identified a few other goals: spending meaningful time with her husband and her recently widowed father as well as spending time doing personal activities she loved and hadn't had time to pursue. Because she ranked these other goals as highly important to her, she eventually decided not to pursue the superintendency, as it would prevent her from living the life she pictured for herself.

She ultimately chose a leadership position in a nonprofit organization which had an education mission. She recognized she could use her leadership skills and experiences in an organization whose mission she believed in while being better able to integrate her other priorities. Although I have no doubt that Chris would have been a successful superintendent, she would have quickly felt drained and depleted by the demands of the position.

It's easy to forget that we have choices—every day, in everything we do. We can choose what to say, act, or think. We can choose positive thoughts or negative ones. The choices we make or attitudes we adopt will either move us closer to a goal, farther away, or in another direction or keep us stuck. We can change our thoughts at any time by simply choosing other ones. As coaches, you'll want to help coachees recognize that they have choices and that making new choices will yield a different result.

The choices people make are a result of their attitudes, which determine their actions, which influence their accomplishments. Where we are today is a result of the choices we've made and the attitudes we've accepted. Negative attitudes will inhibit us from making certain choices. Sometimes, individuals who were raised in households where negativity was common have adopted similar mindsets, or they've learned to blame others for circumstances rather than own the outcome.

I remember one of my coaching student colleagues. He was a very young attorney who had built a large, successful law firm by the age of 30. We were amazed and asked him how he accomplished so much at such a young age. He talked about his upbringing. He had lived in a household where he was always told he could do anything, that he had what it takes, and he

> To create a new, happier life, all you need is an open mind and wisdom to challenge the belief system that currently creates your reality.
>
> —Bruce Schneider (2001), Founder, Institute for Professional Empowerment Coaching

grew up believing it. Not everyone is so fortunate. During the coaching process, the coach and coachee will create new mental tapes to replace the ones that aren't working. They will learn how to create new attitudes, new choices and new outcomes.

For Example

Marie, was especially stressed about a staff member who wasn't performing well, especially in the area of budgets. She depended on Ann for producing reports in a timely manner and noticed they were always late and full of errors. Marie viewed Ann as hostile and doing it on purpose. Through our coaching, she recognized that Ann was not a numbers person, and producing budget reports was simply outside of her natural ability and skill set. Once Marie recognized that Ann simply didn't have the know-how, she was able to approach her from a supportive, helping perspective rather than one of anger and frustration. She chose a new attitude. She chose a new way of seeing the issue, which in turn, led to a more productive outcome. She found ways to help Ann learn more about budgeting. Ann felt supported, and both their relationship and the work improved.

Helping coachees reframe how they view particular situations will help them make different choices. When coachees see new possibilities, hence new choices, they can begin to take different actions.

CONNECTING OUTER GOALS WITH THE INNER SELF

Professional coaches spend a majority of their training learning to help their coachees identify their personal and unique gifts, their desires, passions and joys. They help their coachees think about what a meaningful, satisfying life would look like for them and then identify ways of bringing all of who they are into the world, either through their professions or in other areas of their lives. Focusing on the inner self is one of the major differences between coaching and mentoring. When everything is aligned within people—their talents, their passions, their purpose and missions in life—with how they spend most of their time, it all works. It's when there's a disconnect between who people truly are and what they are doing that there's a breakdown, and they become unhappy or numb and just go through the motions at work or at home. They become less effective or ineffective.

> *Nothing changes without personal transformation.*
>
> —W. Edwards Deming
> (As quoted in
> Baker & Baker, 2001)

People want to live fulfilling, meaningful lives. And each person has a personal definition of success. It's when the definitions or pictures of success are in conflict with the reality of their lives that people become dissatisfied. There's a disconnect between what is and what they'd like to see happen. Often, that future vision is vague or not yet discovered, but there's a subtle, dull sense of a meaningless life.

Most of us haven't been trained or encouraged to live our lives by design. It's so easy to become bogged down with responsibilities at work and home and fall into a habit of thinking there's no time for things we love to do. We make time for things we have to do and put things we want to do at the bottom of our lists. No wonder we're struggling and trying to find balance and more happiness at home and work. Coaching provides a process for creating a purposeful life—for discovering or rediscovering who we are and bringing it into the world. Coaching helps us integrate our gifts, dreams, talents and skills into our daily lives. It helps coachees create their lives on purpose, by connecting the inner self with the outer world. It is a great strategy for reducing burnout.

You might be wondering what all this has to do with improving schools. How could focusing on one's spirit, essence, or core self enhance school results? "Issues of the human soul are not just "touchy-feely" issues dealing with the soft side of life. They are issues that go to the heart of how well our organizations are functioning, and core concerns of performance, productivity and competitive success" (Seiler, 2003). Yet often, school systems focus on external strategies that are perceived to change results and rarely focus on the deep changes that individuals must make to achieve them. I come again to this theme: The coaching process often addresses the inner self and engages participants in ongoing learning about themselves. It's about discovery, taking a look at one's beliefs, thoughts, and results. With a shift in perspective and a new view of the world, new actions are taken, and different

> *You must give birth to your images.*
> *They are the future waiting to be born.*
> —Rainer Marie Rilke

results are the outcome. It's the attitudes or mindsets of individuals that make or break an organizational change effort. Frequently, leaders of change efforts avoid dealing directly with the softer human issues. The hard issues are easy to see, easy to measure, and more comfortable to confront than the human issues. When an effort is made to truly address the attitudes and mindsets of individuals within organizations, giant leaps will be made in change efforts. "Our general mental and emotional well-being, self-image, self-esteem, values, beliefs, and feelings about the world and our place in it, all affect our state of mind. An individuals' performance is directly related to his/her state of mind" (Oakley & Krug, 1991).

For Example

When I began coaching educators, I had a small group of aspiring administrators that I was coaching individually and as an ongoing, confidential group. During our first group meeting, I'd asked them to think about their future: where did they want to be, what did they want to do over the next 5, then 10, then 20 . . . up to 100 years. I encouraged them to think about the impact they wanted to have on the lives of others and how would they want to be remembered. There was a kind of stunned silence and strange looks. Initial responses were things like, "be a good parent" and "help kids learn." I'd asked them to think *really* big—beyond what they'd been thinking for themselves, their work and their families. It truly was the first time they'd thought about themselves having the power to influence many people and make a big difference in their lives. Over time, each one developed a personal mission statement that began to shape the way in which they created their lives "on purpose." They began the process of identifying their inner selves and connecting them with their outer work.

VALUES MATTER

Walt Disney (as quoted in Gratton, 2006, p.1) once said, "When your values are clear, your decision-making is easy." It's one of my favorite quotes and one I often use when coachees are conflicted between their options. We all have choices to make in our professional and our personal lives. Often people stress over their decisions. Living a life designed around what you value most equates to a meaningful life. Values represent what's most important to us, our core essence. Becoming clear about

> *Work is love made visible.*
> —*Kahlil Gibran (1923/1995, n.p.)*

what we value helps us to better understand ourselves. It helps create a fit between personal and organizational values. When personal values can be matched with an organization's values, there is a greater chance of hiring the right leader or retaining those already in place.

Coaches help their coachees become crystal clear about what they value most. Once a coachee identifies his or her core values, the coach and coachee can begin to see how they are expressed in work and life. How do they show up? When an individual makes one decision over another, that person is *honoring a value*. It is easier and less stressful to make difficult decisions when you know which values matter and which ones you choose to honor. I have found that this is a huge "Aha!," and decisions are made effortlessly.

Let's say you hope to stick with your workout plan and hit the gym four times a week. You've chosen a goal of living a healthy life, and going to the gym is an action that will help you reach your goal. You've made a promise to yourself, and perhaps your coach, that you will spend 60-90 minutes, four times a week, working out. Three weeks later, an important meeting, your child's spring concert, and dinner with a friend come up. There goes the plan, you think. You feel pulled in too many directions and want to do all of them. Remembering your top values— in this instance, family and health—you say no to the dinner and yes to everything else. You've made the decision with reduced stress, greater clarity, and no guilt.

When you are coaching, you probe your coachees to identify those things they value most. For one person, it may be adventure, love, creativity, and family; for another, it may be humor, calm, integrity, and service or art, learning, commmunity, and loyalty. You want to help them bring those values to their lives and to their work. If you value openness and trust, seeking a position in a district that tends to be a closed system is likely to be a costly mismatch. It is not a coach's intention to change a person's values but to acknowledge them as the coachee's core essence and help manifest them.

People become disenchanted or depressed by agreeing to things that other people want them to do versus those things that reflect who they are and what brings them joy and happiness. Having a clear set of personal values helps people know when to say yes or no to something. When the time, resources and energy that coachees spend are aligned with their values, there will be increased happiness, less stress, more energy, and an increased sense of accomplishment in all aspects of their lives.

> *Expressing your values in the workplace is an investment in the long-term future of your company.*
>
> —Ira Jackson (as quoted in Albion, 2000, p. 109)

For Example

A newly appointed assistant superintendent was experiencing some regret about his new position. He was conflicted over whether or not he had made the right decision to leave the principalship. Although he felt completely confident in achieving success in his new role, he ached for the people he had left behind and for the faces of the children he no longer saw. "My soul hurts," is the way he expressed it. He was seriously frustrated, especially because his former principal position was vacant, and he had the opportunity to return. He was distracted and mentally absent, wishing he were back in his old district with all those great people he had worked with for many years. He acknowledged how much he missed them and seeing kids every day. Through our coaching process, he remembered the time he'd yearned for the new position. He'd been ready to move on, to "make a bigger difference." He'd forgotten *why* he chose the new position. His conflict was between being with the staff and children he cherished and his burning desire to make a bigger difference and affect even more staff and many more children. When he focused on the values he wished to honor, he became more comfortable and at peace with his decision and without regret. He recognized that he could visit his former staff and remain connected with them. He could develop similar relationships in his new district. He could spend more time with children. What he valued most was connection, community, and leadership, and he could live those values in his new district. He decided to remain, and with renewed clarity, he was more committed and happier than he had been.

School planning team members often seek to identify their shared core values—a worthy process. However, the leadership coaching process can help leaders first identify their personal core values and bring them to life in their daily work.

> No matter what your profession, your job, or your industry, it is up to you to bring your values to work.
>
> —Mark Albion (2000, p. 109)

EMPOWERING OTHERS FOR SUCCESS

Generally, professional coaches refrain from giving suggestions to coachees when in a pure coaching role. This may be surprising news to coaches and coachees. It is in the coachee's best interest for the coach to ask questions that help the coachees observe their thoughts and beliefs versus having the coach telling the coachees what to do. This might be a major shift in communication style and is frequently a challenge for new coaches. It's easy to fall into a helper, problem-solver role. However, when you lead or guide coachees to discover their own solutions, options or actions, they will be far more meaningful to them, and it's much more likely they'll agree to them.

This is not to say that coaches don't offer advice at times. Coachees will often directly ask for ideas, suggestions and advice. Remember that the purpose of coaching is to help the coachee move from one place to another. There may be many pathways to a goal. A wise coach responds according to what is best for the coachee.

PROFESSIONAL ORGANIZATIONS

As stated in Chapter 1, coaching is a series of skills, a process, a relationship, and a booming profession. The International Coach Federation (ICF) is a nonprofit, professional association that has more than 8,000 members worldwide. As mentioned earlier, it has developed a set of ethics and standards for the coaching profession, known as Professional Coaching Core Competencies (see Chapters 3–5). The ICF sponsors an annual conference, publishes a professional journal, and serves as a leader and source of information about coaching and for certifying credentialed, professional coach training schools. Professional coaching programs must design their training offerings around the 11 Professional Coaching Core Competencies in order to offer graduates a Professional Coach credential. The competencies provide continuity and commonality and ensure that graduates of ICF-credentialed programs are skilled in essential coaching proficiencies.

For ICF credentialing, a professional coach school must provide a minimum requirement of 125 hours of training and practice in coaching skills and techniques; many schools having more than 300 hours. Some schools offer on-site training, while others offer convenient teleclass training where participants join a group telephone session with a professional coach-trainer and other students. Note that there is *nothing* embedded within the coaching competencies that refers to specific content knowledge. The competencies form the heart and the essence of coaching. Each of the next three chapters delves into the competencies in more detail.

The International Association of Coaches (IAC) is another professional organization devoted to the coaching profession, with a focus on supporting the coaching coachee. Founded in 2003, the IAC has also developed ethical guidelines and a credentialing process based on its identified coaching competencies.

CORE COMPETENCIES: IMPLICATIONS FOR EDUCATORS

Whether or not education organizations, districts, or universities utilize professional coaches, it is helpful to approach coaching with a common understanding and knowledge about coaching and the skills coaches need. The ICF Professional Coaching Core Competencies described in Chapters 3–5 identify the necessary skills. Keep in mind that these competencies are the ones necessary for professionally trained coaches to have to become certified. The more K–12 districts, universities, and organizations can incorporate these competencies into their coaching training programs, the more successful they are likely to be. If you have already implemented a coaching program and find your coaches are struggling, these competencies may be useful in identifying where additional learning would be helpful.

If districts or other organizations wish to have staff members become trained as credentialed, professional coaches, they should expect to invest between $5,000 and 10,000 per person, not including travel costs. It will take between six months and two years to complete a professional coach training program. The various coach training programs differ in their approaches, methodology, and terminology, but all ICF-credentialed programs focus on the 11 competencies.

SUMMARY

Coaching is not a walk in the park. Coachees work hard. When successful coaching happens, there may be very little that has *not* changed in the way coachees see themselves and their world. Coaches are success partners who inspire and encourage their coachees during times of doubt and stress. The coaching process is successful in helping individuals and organizations *through* change. It provides ongoing, customized, personalized support to people and systems. Coaches keep people encouraged and engaged. They hold them accountable and inspire them when they want to fall back into old patterns.

Coaching sessions will often float between exploring the inner selves of coachees and the outer results they're attempting to produce. Coaches help bring to life the inner persons aligned with their outer worlds. They help coachees identify their values, priorities, and goals and make choices that support them. Adopting a coaching mindset will help coaches view people from a consistent vantage point, without judgment or personal opinion. The relationship that develops between a coach and a coachee is one in which the person feels heard and understood. It becomes a safe haven for sharing and dealing with the challenges that busy educators face.

The 11 Professional Core Coaching Competencies provide educators with a baseline of essential knowledge and skills to be successful in a coaching role. Every educator-coach should become familiar with these core skills when developing a district coaching program.

You never finish learning to be a great coach. It's an ongoing process of learning about human behavior and motivation and cultivating deep change in people.

Reflective Questions

- What do you need to stop thinking, or let go of, to adopt a coaching mindset?
- How can you familiarize your staff with the ICF Professional Coaching Core Competencies?
- How would your district coach training program need to change to become more aligned with the ICF Professional Coaching Core Competencies?

Core Coaching Competencies 1–4

It takes two to speak the truth—one to speak and another to listen.

—Henry David Thoreau

It's an enormous honor to be engaged in a coaching relationship with another human being. Being witness to the inner and outer changes a coachee makes is an exciting experience. The relationships formed between educators and their coaches are unique and possibly among the most intimate, honest relationships they've ever had. When planning for long-term success and healthy, lasting relationships with coachees, professional coaches do well to adhere to a common set of standards of professionalism. These standards define how coaches interact with coachees, and they delineate the boundaries and acceptable behaviors coaches demonstrate. Staff developers may wish to examine these professional standards and align their coaching program as closely as possible with them so there is clarity and mutual understanding of what coaches can and are expected to do and what they will not do.

Let's look at another emerging profession. In the past, there was no such occupation as certified financial planner. Then, there was one. A new field emerged with a clear set of knowledge, skill, and expertise necessary for practitioners to help coachees master their financial lives. Without credentials, everybody who wanted to could call him- or herself a financial planner. Would you want to trust your financial life, your future, security and retirement to someone who has a few skills and a smattering of knowledge? I don't think so.

The same is true for coaching. As the profession becomes more mainstream and established and as more and more school systems use coaching, it becomes increasingly important that educator-coaches have a deep understanding of coaching and have sufficient knowledge and skills to be successful in this role of change agent. As said previously, creating change in organizations is first about creating change in individuals. It's a delicate process. Just like certified financial planners, credentialed professional coaches have high levels of training and skill in helping people and organizations change what they think, believe and do, to achieve peak performance and boost results.

CORE COACHING COMPETENCIES

Whether you are just beginning to develop a coaching program or seeking ways to improve a current one, carefully consider the competencies in the next three chapters to determine whether your district is aligning as closely as possible to professional standards for coaches. Chapters 3–5 focus on specific competencies necessary for successful coaching. They describe and discuss the 11 Professional Coaching Core Competencies developed by the ICF, which form the cornerstone of credentialed coach training programs (see Resource C for a one-page listing). They ensure that coaches uphold high standards and accountability for this growing profession. They can be used as guides for professional developers to determine if their training includes them and to assess whether coaches possess sufficient knowledge and coaching skill. They're broken into four main categories, and each competency has a number of subcompetencies:

Setting the Foundation

1. Meeting Ethical Guidelines and Professional Standards
2. Establishing the Coaching Agreement

Co-Creating the Coaching Relationship

3. Establishing Trust and Intimacy With the Coachee
4. Coaching Presence

Communicating Effectively

5. Active Listening
6. Powerful Questioning
7. Direct Communication

Facilitating Learning and Results

8. Creating Awareness
9. Designing Actions
10. Planning and Goal Setting
11. Managing Progress and Accountability

This chapter focuses on the first Coaching [?] two competencies: Setting the Foundation and Co-Creating the Coaching Relationship; Chapter 4 focuses on Communicating Effectively and Chapter 5 on Facilitating Learning and Results.

While Chapters 3–5 do provide practical knowledge to help prospective coaches learn the skills, reading about them is a good start for developing awareness and ensuring that these competencies are incorporated into learning programs. Experience and confidence as a coach cannot be learned from a book or in a one-day or weekend workshop. Skills, competencies, and techniques are best learned in small doses and by using them with actual people dealing with actual concerns.

COACHING TIPS:

❖ Review the competencies in Chapters 3–5.
❖ Identify missing skills in your coach training.
❖ Allow for ample practice and demonstration.

SETTING THE FOUNDATION

Core Competency 1: Meeting Ethical Guidelines and Professional Standards

As an emerging and rapidly expanding field, the coaching profession has evolved to one with a set of ethical guidelines and standards to which professional coaches are accountable. A credentialed coach knows and upholds them and is an advocate for maintaining them and strengthening the credibility and growth of the field. Implementing a coaching program or a coaching relationship represents a major shift in how the individual or organization communicates and acts to attain high levels of performance. It's important to map out an overall plan and a rationale for using a coaching approach and discussing how the movement toward excellence will be carried out within the system.

A Coach Understands and Exhibits the ICF Standards of Ethical Conduct

Certified, professional coaches uphold the standards developed by the ICF. There are 28 standards that focus on

- Professional conduct
- Confidentiality and privacy
- Conflicts of interest

A full listing can be found in Resource D. Educator-coaches may or may not hold a professional coach credential. Although some of the standards pertain to external coaches relative to their business interactions, it is useful to know and understand the ethics that coaches uphold. Customers of coaching would be wise to contract with credentialed coaches who maintain and uphold themselves according to the standards of the profession. School system leaders may wish to explore a potential coach's background, training, and experience to assess the quality of work they can offer.

A Coach Communicates the Distinctions Between Coaching, Consulting, Therapy and Other Support Professions

Although coaching was defined in Chapter 1, this section clarifies the role even further and helps distinguish it from other common helping roles in school systems. It is critical for the success of the coaching relationship and your coaching program that there's mutual understanding between the coach, the coachee and the organization before coaching begins. Doing so will ensure that there are appropriate expectations and help build the necessary trust needed for successful coaching.

Coach

Training to become a coach or in coaching skills is a different learning experience than that of mentor, trainer or facilitator. Without sufficient training, it is likely that successful coaching will not occur. Coaches hold the belief that the person they're coaching is competent and capable of generating their own solutions to reach their goals. The skilled coach provides a learning process founded on self-discovery as a means to identify inner beliefs and self-limiting doubts that inhibit coachees' progress toward their goals.

While the roles of coach, mentor, consultant, therapist, sports coach or even friend are helpful ones, each is a *different* role. For coaching to be successful and for participants to have clear expectations, it is critical that both coaches and coachees have a deep understanding of the role of coach and how it differs from other roles commonly found in schools. Coaching is a personal change management process. The partnership and process create new outcomes for the individual, work team or organization.

Since it is a young profession, it is easy to understand why coaching can seem unclear. If you've never been coached, you are likely to misunderstand the power and potential of the relationship and process or confuse it with other helping roles.

What a Coach Does

- Communicates in a nonjudgmental manner
- Asks empowering, probing and reflective questions
- Leads a change process
- Deeply listens
- Takes a neutral stance
- Follows the coachees' agendas
- Inspires the coachees
- Maintains the bigger picture
- Probes for possible solutions

- Creates awareness
- Creates a safe, trusting environment
- Challenges thinking
- Inspires coachees to reach new levels of accomplishment
- Offers feedback
- Keeps coachees in action
- Maintains an eye toward the future
- Helps coachees visualize new possibilities
- Helps coachees create conditions for success
- Gets to the heart of an issue
- Summarizes and paraphrases what coachees say
- Accepts where coachees are in their lives
- Respects coachees' present mindsets
- Allows silence and space for reflection

What a Coach Doesn't Do

- Tell coachees what to do
- Disapprove of coachees for their thoughts or beliefs
- Focus on the past
- Pass judgment

Mentor

Mentors guide from their own experience. Mentoring is often confused with coaching. Mentoring matches a novice with a person experienced in the same role. The purpose of mentoring is for mentors to share their expertise with novices, to help the novices be more comfortable and secure in their new roles. Mentors are not typically trained to work with the inner self, as coaches are.

There may be situations when a mentor is more appropriate. Suppose you're a new principal and never prepared a budget or a new staff developer who's suddenly faced with the challenge of writing a major grant application. A mentor may be more useful in these situations. However, a solution that may have worked for the mentor may not be the ideal solution for the novice. Coaching and mentoring differ in this regard: A coach would explore the range of options and choices available to the coachee. Having both a mentor and coach can be helpful, since each provides a different kind and level of support. Sometimes, the same person can be both mentor and coach.

Consultant

Consultants are hired to share their specialized expertise in a certain area or field. While consulting approaches vary widely, consultants usually work with systems to diagnose problems and make recommendations.

They help organizations solve problems and work with them for a specific period of time about a specific issue. Like mentors, consultants share their expertise and knowledge and frequently make specific recommendations.

Therapists

Coaching can be distinguished from therapy in a number of ways. Coaching is focused on the future and the attainment of meaningful goals. Therapy deals with healing personal pain, dysfunction, and conflict. The focus is often on resolving difficulties from the past that hamper an individual's emotional functioning in the present, improving overall psychological functioning, and dealing with present life and work circumstances in more emotionally healthy ways. Therapy outcomes often include improved feeling states. While positive emotions may be a natural outcome of coaching, the primary focus of coaching is on creating actionable strategies for achieving specific goals in one's work or personal life. The emphasis in a coaching relationship is on action, accountability, and follow-through.

Trainer

Training is based on the acquisition of certain learning objectives as set out by the instructor. Though objectives are clarified in the coaching process, they are set by the individual or team being coached, with guidance provided by the coach. Training also assumes a linear learning path that coincides with an established curriculum. Coaching is less linear, without a set curriculum plan.

COACHING TIPS:

- ❖ Thoroughly explain the differences between coach and mentor, coach and consultant, and coach and trainer. Do this at the beginning of your coaching relationship.
- ❖ Don't wait until there's confusion or false expectations. For example, many people think coaching is more like mentoring. Make sure coachees know you won't be telling them what to do when you're coaching. You will be working together to identify what works best for them.

Athletic Coaches

Though sports metaphors are often used, professional coaching is both similar to and different from traditional sports coaching. Athletic coaches are seen as experts who guide and direct the behavior of individuals or teams based on their greater experience and knowledge. Athletic coaches help individuals strive for peak performance, attain very challenging goals, and surpass current levels of performance. They utilize mental strategies to achieve greater physical results. Professional coaches employ similar techniques, but their interactions are based on the experience and knowledge of the individual or team they are coaching, and that determines the direction. In addition, professional coaching, unlike athletic development, does not focus on behaviors that are being executed poorly or incorrectly. Instead, the focus is on identifying opportunities for development based on individual strengths and capabilities.

COACHING TIPS:

❖ When training potential educator-coaches, request that they each choose at least two people to practice their new skills with—an educator and a non-educator. They quickly learn to maintain clear coaching roles when working with noneducators. It's easy to jump into a mentor or consulting role when you coach someone in your field.
❖ Notice the difference.

It is not unusual for some roles to be combined. It's possible to merge coach and mentor roles *if* there is adequate training. Without enough coaching know-how, there is sure to be more mentoring than coaching. When setting up an educator-coaching program, there are several options available to ensure that sufficient coaching takes place:

• Agree to work only with credentialed coaches.
• Provide a minimum of 60 hours of coach-specific training, including 30 hours of practice coaching sessions.
• Ensure the availability of an internal or external certified coach to support district coaches.
• Use different individuals as coaches and mentors, when appropriate.

To clarify how conversations might differ depending on the role of the resource person, let's look at a scenario. Assume you're a principal with a fairly veteran staff. You're struggling with resistance from several staff members regarding a new districtwide social and emotional learning program being implemented this year.

Principal:	I'm finding it a huge challenge to get this program off the ground. It's a great program, and teachers supported it in the beginning. They just aren't implementing the daily lessons.
Mentor response:	I had a similar experience with a nutrition program a few years ago. What we did was. . . .
Consultant response:	What they need to do is . . .
Trainer response:	Perhaps they're not comfortable with the curriculum. When can we schedule some more training?
Coach response:	What's getting in the way? What are they resisting?

I don't wish to suggest that one role is better than another. Each is different and is likely to yield a different result.

Many people hold a belief that a coach needs to have similar professional experience as does the coachee. While it may help the coachee feel more connected to the coach, it is *not* necessary. A certified, credentialed coach can help anyone. School system leaders or professional development planners should be looking for coaching experience, high levels of skill, and credentials when they are looking for professional coaches.

Because coaching is a new and growing field, most people have never had a coaching experience and don't know what to expect in the beginning. As mentioned, it's important to clarify all the helping roles when beginning any kind of supportive role. Doing so creates realistic expectations and sets up potential coachees and program implementation for success.

Referring Coachees to Other Support Professionals

Coaches should feel free to refer coachees to other professionals, such as mentors and trainers, when those approaches are deemed more appropriate by the coach and coachee together. Coaches should be aware that there can be instances when referring a coachee to a mental health professional is necessary, such as suicide threat. Coaches can also work in partnership with mental health professionals.

Core Competency 2: Establishing a Coaching Agreement

A successful coaching experience is one in which the coachee's expectations and goals have been met. Accurately outlining and clarifying expectations and describing the service and responsibilities of each party up front lay the groundwork for a successful coaching relationship.

A Coach Defines Boundaries and Guidelines

At the beginning of the coaching relationship, the coach and coachee need to discuss and agree on many specifics. Where will you conduct your coaching sessions? Who else will be present, or will you meet in private? How long will the sessions be? If you are engaging in telephone coaching, determine who will initiate the phone call. Be sure the coachee is agreeable and comfortable with the arrangements. Make every effort for the coaching sessions to be private, away from the eyes and ears of students and other teachers and administrators. Be sure there is an understanding of cancellation and payment policies.

Confidentiality is a vital element in the success of a coaching relationship. Refrain from starting coaching sessions until key stakeholders understand the importance of maintaining confidentiality and agree to uphold it. In the privacy of the coaching relationship, coachees can reveal themselves unconditionally and experiment with new behaviors without repercussions.

Because anything can come up during coaching, a coach may want to discuss areas that are *not* coachable. Perhaps there are sensitive areas or topics the coachee does not want to discuss at the time. Often, as time goes by and deep levels of trust develop, the coachee may be willing to delve into sensitive areas of their lives. Coaches should respect the coachees' preferences.

A Coach Clarifies Responsibilities

Be sure that your new coachee fully understands the role of the coach and the positive, collaborative nature of the relationship. You are likely to be successful when both parties fully understand what to expect. Since coaching is so new you may find some apprehensiveness or defensiveness at first. Invest additional time in clarifying the role, the relationship, and the process. Outline each person's responsibilities at the onset of coaching.

A coach will

- Collaborate with coachee to identify goals, challenges, obstacles and actions
- Follow up on promised action steps
- Negotiate through obstacles that appear to prohibit forward movement
- Maintain confidentiality

- Adhere to the coaching schedule
- Listen deeply to goals and concerns
- Inspire coachees to achieve and surpass their goals
- Be fully present
- Stay focused
- Stay attuned to the coachee's agenda

The coachees are responsible for

- Being open to learning about themselves and their professional practice
- Taking the promised action
- Speaking their personal truth
- Reflecting on their actions or lack of action
- Engaging in a collaborative process
- Being on time and keeping appointments
- Notifying the coach in advance of cancellation

A Coach Determines an Effective Match and the Needs of the Coachee

In the ideal situation, there would be a number of experienced, trained coaches available to work with educators, and there would be a choice. Just as in a mentor relationship, the coach-coachee relationship will be successful when there's a good match, which can be a matter of training, focus, personality, rapport, trust, or past history. There are also numerous specialties in the coaching world—executive coaches, life coaches, spirituality coaches, instructional coaches, entrepreneur and business coaches, parent coaches, and so on. However, specializing in specific areas is more a matter of preference and experience than preparation, although there are many advanced coaching programs that go beyond basic coach training.

The ultimate goal of coaching is for a new result to emerge from the relationship. The coachee must be open and willing to be coached and to be coached by the person offering the coaching.

A Coach Creates Win-Win Coaching Relationships by Offering Choices

If the coach notices there is no progress or insufficient progress being made toward to coachee's goals, the coach would be wise to discuss it with the coachee and determine the cause. Sometimes the coachee isn't making progress for a number of reasons:

- The coachee does not agree with or support the organization's goals for coaching.
- The coach has an agenda; the coachee is resistant.
- There is a lack of commitment.
- There are too many goals.
- There is a lack of trust.
- The coachee is unwilling to be coached.
- There is a mismatch between coach and coachee.

Also, it's important to consider the preferred style of the coach. As coaches develop their skills, they're also bringing to the coaching experience who *they* are, their personalities, their personal passions and the sometimes invisible quality one may have that creates a meaningful connection. Some coaches are more intuitive or more creative or spiritual.

Coaches should be open and reflective of their coaching personalities and styles and determine if the partnership is working. Discuss it and determine if referral to another coach is best for the coachee.

For Example

I was referred to a multistate region of churches to provide leadership coaching for new ministers. During one preliminary session, I learned that the pastor I was initially working with was fluent in Spanish, and English was her second language. I knew she would have a better coaching experience if she worked with a Spanish-speaking coach. I offered a reference to a colleague.

CO-CREATING THE RELATIONSHIP

It's critical that the coaching relationship gets off to a good start. Think of it as a three-way relationship: There's (1) the coach, (2) the person receiving coaching, and (3) the relationship between them—the powerful success partnership that develops over time. It has been called a *designed alliance*. "The relationship is designed because it's created to meet the specific needs of the coachee. It's an alliance because both the coach and coachee are involved in making it successful. It's created by both participants. Coachees are empowered by the relationship to take charge, to change their lives (personal or professional)" (Whitworth, Kimsey-House, & Sandahl, 1998, p. 13). The coach-coachee relationship is a collaboration, the ultimate continuous learning process. Both parties give and both receive. The whole is greater than the sum of its parts, and together, the coach-coachee team creates a reality larger than the individuals.

Figure 3.1   A Birds-Eye View of the Coach-Coachee Relationship

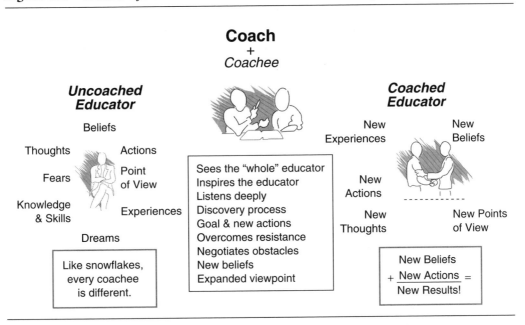

Successful coaching happens when coachees experience something powerful that has great meaning for them. I can't underestimate the power of the partnership that develops and emerges.

Figure 3.1 demonstrates the transformation that occurs within the coachee by collaborating with a coach. Coachees come to the coaching process with their current or collective thoughts and beliefs that have been developed over their lifetimes. In the space of the coaching relationship, the coach and coachee explore those thoughts and beliefs and how they impact the coachee, in his or her professional or personal life. With new awareness, specific goals, and bold, new actions and support, the coachee

> *As I wander confidently towards the realization of my dreams, I am wondering who will be by my side.*
>
> —Anonymous

moves forward toward a new future. With new attitudes, thoughts and beliefs, the coachee sets new, higher goals. The coachee becomes more confident and optimistic. The cycle continues as coach and coachee formulate continuously higher goals; the process becomes an ongoing success loop (see Chapter 7, Phases of the Coaching Relationship).

Core Competency 3: A Coach Establishes Trust and Safety

The beginning of the coach-coachee relationship is about establishing a connection, creating a special relationship that will encourage the coachee to reveal his or her innermost self to the coach. When there's a high level of trust between the coach and the coachee, there will be a successful coaching relationship. It's critical for there to be both a good match, as stated earlier, and a deep connection and sense of safety that the coachee feels right from the start.

Creating a mutually trusting relationship should be the highest priority at the onset of coaching. You'll be laying the foundation for the future.

If you're an external coach, you have a clean slate to begin a new relationship, although it may take time for the coachee to come to know your integrity and honesty. If you're an internal coach and you already know the coachee, this relationship becomes one in which the coachee reveals himself or herself in new ways. This new relationship is based on the coach's sincere efforts in supporting the educator through the rough period of personal and professional change. The coach should be consistent and always upfront with the coachee.

When commitment to confidentiality is a district policy, trust will be expedited. Without trust, the ability to communicate openly evaporates, and the coaching partnership suffers. Trust is based on shared experiences, credibility and keeping commitments. To establish trust with a coachee, coaches should

- Maintain confidentiality at all times
- Keep promises
- Be honest
- Be on time, keep appointments
- Follow up on coachees' action steps
- Be committed

A Coach Shows Concern for the Coachee

Remember: The focus of a coaching relationship is on the *coachee.* In the role of leadership or school-based coach, coaches come to know the people they're working with in new ways, in ways very different from a traditional work relationship. They learn how coachees think; what they fear; what makes them happy; and about their talents, goals, and dreams.

Remember also: In school systems, there will be externally focused goals that the organization wants to accomplish, such as higher test scores, lower drop-out rates, increased attendance rates, or other important goals that may be the catalysts for coaching. There may also be goals that the coachee wants to accomplish—both professional goals and personal ones.

The coach is the intermediary between what the organization wants or needs to achieve and the coachee. When you're coaching someone, maintain your focus on the *coachees* and what *they* need in order to achieve those goals. Coachees may initiate their own goals that appear to be unrelated to the organization's goals. A wise coach will be OK with that. In the long run, an eager employee will produce better results for the district.

For Example

I once coached a director of staff development who had numerous business ideas in addition to issues around developing funding sources and interpersonal communication in his agency. He had invented a product and wanted to bring it to the marketplace. The goal had nothing to do with his salaried work. It would be easy to dismiss it as unrelated and focus only on his work goals. However, he was so excited and passionate about his product and derived so much positive energy talking about it that we kept that goal in our coaching plan. Because the coaching was about the coachee, his well-being and his future, the benefit of maintaining the goals he had chosen also benefited the organization. His increased energy, specific goals, weekly actions and bias toward "doing" helped him remain focused and self-motivated.

COACHING TIPS:

What are some ways to specifically demonstrate your concern for your coachees? In my coaching practice, I invite coachees to communicate with me between sessions. It's helpful to them to know I care, that I'm thinking of them all the time. I want to know the outcome of their intended actions or how successful they were confronting a challenge. Usually they'll send me a quick e-mail message, and I'll respond. Sometimes they'll call me and share what has happened. They know I'm there for them, thinking of them, and cheering them on.

Happy, energized employees have an abundance of positive energy that spills over into other areas of their work. When someone feels "I can do it" about one area of his or her life or work, it's likely the enthusiasm will affect other areas. I've seen it happen many times.

When coaching addresses the professional *and* personal aspirations of the coachee, the person is more focused, more attentive and interested, more open to introspection, and feels more supported by the coaching process. I find a good way to approach this, in my coaching practice, is to identify the organization's goals with the coachee. And with those in mind, we create a set of goals that addresses *both* the goals of the district and the personal goals of the coachee. Everyone wins.

A Coach Respects Perceptions, Learning Styles and Personal Being

Coaching is all about expanding and reaching full potential. During the early phase of the coaching relationship, the coaches learn all about the coachees: how they see the world and how they view themselves. Coaches always demonstrate high regard and acceptance for their viewpoints, how their life journeys have created their perceptions and current realities. Treating the coachees in a neutral manner enables them to be more open and reflective. Coaches don't need to agree but to accept. The coachees feel accepted, strengthening the coach-coachee relationship. Treating coachees in a nonjudgmental manner builds trust and enables the coachees to be more open and reflective.

Begin *wherever the coachee is,* without judgment. When you begin in neutral, acknowledging and respecting the coachees' viewpoints, you create a relationship in which the coachees can be themselves. They'll feel truly accepted for their values and perspectives and are more likely to open up and reflect on their points of view.

A Coach Champions New Behaviors

Coaching is highly effective in helping coachees reach goals previously thought out of their reach or too challenging. It can be so easy to talk oneself out of stepping into new turf. It's a huge act of courage to actually be in action, taking a step, especially the first step toward a scary goal.

As a coach, you believe anything is possible for the coachee to accomplish, and you communicate that to him or her. Imagine what it would feel like to know there is someone who totally believes you can do it. Just as effective teachers inspire their students, effective coaches inspire their coachees to bring forth the potential within them. As a coach, you "see" the coachees as completely capable of anything. Nothing is impossible. You know that there is greatness within them, and by inspiring them, you encourage them to step beyond their comfort zones, take new risks, and achieve goals beyond their imagination.

Become their cheerleader. Inspire them to keep going, to keep moving toward their goals. Being inspired lifts the level of energy in the coachee. Your inspiring comments should focus on the *person,* not the task. It helps them believe in themselves and erases self-doubt. Coaches see the absolute best in the coachees and tell them directly how great they are. Be sure to always be authentic in your comments.

For Example

Coachee: I'm not very creative.

Coach: I hear you create ideas all the time. You're like an idea machine.

We've become too accustomed to stay small. And by doing so, we rob the world of our potential. Often, we're given messages as children that remain with us as adults, things like, "Who do you think *you* are?" "Don't get too big for your britches." We stop stretching ourselves, we stop trying, and too often our dreams fade. A great coach is a great cheerleader that elicits the greatness within the coachee.

A Coach Asks Permission

Coaching isn't a process you sneak in or dump on someone without his or her knowledge or consent. Whether you're engaged in full-fledged coaching or using a coaching leadership style, whenever you engage in coaching, be sure the recipient knows about and agrees to be coached.

Because of the intimate nature of the coaching relationship, people are likely to open up and begin looking at all areas of their lives. As mentioned earlier, it's a good idea in the beginning of the coaching relationship to ask if there are sensitive areas that the coachee is not willing to talk about. When the coachee brings up an issue, or you sense there's more to be revealed, ask for permission to coach in that area. Confronting a sensitive area during coaching is a process, like peeling an onion. Respect the wishes of the coachee as the relationship moves forward. In my coaching practice, I find that although some people resist an issue in the early weeks of coaching, they're often ready later on. They'll let you know when they're ready to "go there."

Here are two suggested approaches:

"Would you like some coaching on that?"

"How ready are you to address that issue?"

For Example

I was coaching a superintendent whose initial goals were about making a decision to move on to a more challenging role. She was in a small district and felt she'd made enough of a difference and wanted more challenge. As we progressed, it became clear that her marriage was in trouble. Initially, we talked

> about everything *but*. However, it became evident that the decision to stay or go relied on the outcome of her marriage issues. Although she tried to avoid the issue, there came a time that she was ready and willing to confront it.

When dealing with emotionally difficult issues, even though the coachees are ready to deal with them, be aware that they may move slowly and need a higher level of support from the coach.

Core Competency 4: Coaching Presence

This competency describes the ability to be fully conscious and create a spontaneous relationship, employing a style that is open, flexible and confident. As new coaches gain experience and confidence, the coaching relationships become comfortable and intuitive. Coaches learn to let the coaching sessions follow the direction that emanates from the coachee. There's no curriculum or rigid scope and sequence. An experienced coach can respond with astute awareness of what the coachee needs at the time.

A Coach Is Present and Flexible

What does it mean to be "present" as a coach? It means to be fully focused and available for the coachee. Enter your coaching session without your own stuff getting in the way. Let go of any stress *you* are dealing with so you can focus totally on the coachee. Think of the time you spend with the coachee as a gift of your presence. How can you enter a session with an attitude of "I'm here for you"? How can you prepare yourself as a coach, to ready yourself for the session?

With experience and skill as a coach comes the increased ability to "go with the flow." Preparing for a coaching session is vastly different from preparing for a training session or a workshop. Once again, in coaching, the agenda is the coachee's. Though certain goals have been

---

COACHING TIPS:

- ❖ Take a few deep breaths.
- ❖ Release any tension you're holding.
- ❖ Let go of your own mental chatter.
- ❖ Review notes from your last session.

set, something may come up on any given day that needs to be focused on instead. Be willing to follow the coachee's lead while keeping the bigger picture in mind. Each coaching session should ideally end with the coachee feeling fully helped and supported in what's *important to him or her.*

To give a spin to the famous phrase, "many roads lead to Rome." There is usually more than one way to achieve a goal, more than one strategy that will be useful to the coachee. In addition, every person will have good days and challenging days. An approach you take with a coachee on Monday may not work as well on Friday. If you sense a high level of anxiety or stress from a coachee, you will be more successful by being flexible and addressing the coachee's issues of the day.

> *Coaches instead see themselves as part advisor, part sounding board, part cheerleader, part manager and part strategist.*
>
> —Karine Michael (2000, p.2)

A Coach Is Intuitive

As coaches become more experienced and skilled, they begin to rely on their intuition. Coaches always listen deeply to what's being said and are comfortable letting the coaching session follow the path the coachee is taking. Astute coaches are listening "between the lines" and will give feedback to the coachees based on their perceptions and instincts. Being intuitive is about going with one's gut, then acting on it. With no scope and sequence for coaching; experienced coaches are confident in their ability to let sessions unfold and determine the supports the coachee needs.

A Coach Is Comfortable With Uncertainty and Risk Taking

While there's no curriculum to follow and no lesson plan for coaching, there is a suggested model to address key elements of a coaching session (see Chapter 7), coaches should be comfortable with uncertainty. If a coach is focused on a specific outcome, there may be a hidden agenda. Remember: With no preconceived outcome, anything is possible. Coaching is a discovery process for both the coach, and the coachee. It's typical that unforeseen outcomes emerge as the result of coaching, even when the coachee has specific initial goals. It's an exciting adventure that can lead to results far beyond the original intent.

Good coaches are willing to take risks in their own lives. Doing so inspires others. It's when one takes a risk and takes an action into the discomfort zone that meaningful and lasting change occurs.

A Coach Uses Humor to Create Lightness and Energy

Coaching is a lot more effective and fun for the coachee if the sessions aren't "heavy" and serious. There's nothing wrong with creating a lively and fun atmosphere; in fact, it's recommended. It's especially important when new tasks feel intense for the coachees. Remove the pressure by helping them see that change can actually be enjoyable.

Taking new steps or risks feels uncomfortable in the moment. It can produce anxiety and stress and be a generally unpleasant experience. It can be emotionally demanding to make changes in behavior. Humor lightens the atmosphere and can change the energy from negative to positive.

A Coach Is Confident Working With Strong Emotions

Often, the goals a coachee wishes to bring into the process can trigger deep feelings and unpredictable emotions. A coach should be prepared for this possibility and be comfortable dealing with them and helping the coachee to work through their feelings.

There are a number of coaching skills and techniques, such as venting, visualization, and reframing, that are helpful when a coachee is in a highly emotional state.

For Example

Two months into a coaching relationship, a coachee developed a new goal to seek another position with a substantially higher salary. Upon probing and questioning his motives, he became silent. His voice dropped to barely a whisper. He talked about providing for his family "when something happens to me." Two years earlier, in his early forties, he had had a heart transplant and feared he'd live a short life.

The coaching process touches the hearts and souls of coachees. It is very common for pent-up emotions to come to the surface, especially as coachees discover or rediscover buried wishes, fears, hopes, and dreams. Coaching taps into the very depths of what it is to be human and live a purposeful, meaningful life. Coaches should not be surprised when deep feelings surface. They should develop a level of comfort in helping coachees recognize their significance.

SUMMARY

A coaching relationship is a unique relationship between two people. For the relationship to thrive and be meaningful to coachees and to their organizations, pay careful attention to your preplanning and start-up conversations.

The ICF has developed and provided a set of Professional Coaching Core Competencies that all successful coaches strive to master.

Make sure that the coaching role is fully understood by everyone before beginning the coaching relationship: coach, coachee, principal, central office, and school board members. Spend the necessary time explaining to potential coachees what they can expect and what they'll be doing in the relationship and when and where coaching will occur. Strive to protect the privacy and confidentiality of the relationship. Also be sure that coaches are aware of the warning signs when another professional, such as a counselor or therapist, may need to intervene.

Develop a system of matching coaches with coachees. Pay attention to each match, and if possible, have several coaches available to ensure that good matches and lasting relationships occur.

Reflective Questions

- Does your district have or want an ethics policy related to your coaching program?
- Will you have clear boundaries on areas that are "coachable" and areas that are not?
- How will your district or university deal with having enough coaches to ensure good matches?
- What are the benefits of confidentiality in the coaching relationship?

Core Coaching Competencies 5–7

It is impossible to overemphasize the immense need human beings have to be really listened to.

—Paul Tournier (as quoted in Borisoff & Purdy, 1996, p. 4)

IN THIS CHAPTER

Active listening

Powerful questioning

Direct communication

COMMUNICATING EFFECTIVELY

Think of a time when you had a conversation with someone that was very meaningful to you. What did you notice? What did you feel? It is likely that the person you were talking to was really listening to *you*. They were tuned in to what you were saying, and you knew it.

Most of us go through our daily lives, at work and home, and feel unheard. Modern life is so overly busy that we rarely take the time to listen to one another. Sometimes it is difficult to tune out the demands and stresses in our lives to tune into another person. Most of the time, all we want is someone to listen. We don't always need or want a response or reaction—just the aching desire to be heard, to be understood. We want to know that someone gets it; they get what we're feeling. We crave that kind of connection.

A great coach is a skilled communicator. A great coach listens deeply to what the coachees are saying, how they are saying it, and what thoughts and belief systems lay behind the spoken words. Effectively communicating creates the kind of relationship that is sorely missing from most of our lives—a true listening partner. Coaching provides that partnership. Professionally trained coaches spend months learning and practicing effective listening and communication skills.

Most states now include "speaking and listening" in their literacy standards for students. Yet adults must improve techniques for doing so, too. Listening well and deeply is one of the critical skills for successful coaching. In addition, there are dozens of other skills that make for a successful coaching experience. Masterful coaches blend various kinds of questioning techniques with paraphrasing, summarizing, brainstorming, reframing, use of metaphors, and others, as appropriate.

Core Competency 5: Active Listening

This competency is all about deeply listening to the coachees. A great coach develops the ability to focus completely on what the coachees are saying and not saying, to understand the meaning of what is said in the context of the coachees' desires, and to support their self-expression. In this section are specific skills and subskills that will produce insight and purposeful action.

A Coach Focuses on the Coachee's Agenda

Coaching focuses on the coachees: *their* agendas, beliefs, actions, attitudes, interpretations and perceptions versus that of the coach. Remember that the core of

When I ask you to listen to me
And you start giving advice
You have not done what I asked.
Listen! All I asked was that you listen.
Not talk or do—just hear me.

Advice is cheap: A quarter will get you both Dear Abby and Billy Graham in the same newspaper. And I can do for myself. I'm not helpless; maybe discouraged and faltering, but not helpless.

So please, listen and just hear me, and, if you want to talk, wait a minute for your turn; and I'll listen to you.

—Anonymous

coaching is about helping people view themselves and the world in new ways, which in turn enables them to change their thoughts, beliefs and actions to yield different results. There must be willingness on the part of the coachees—they must be open to coaching and open to changing. When the coaching sessions and relationships are solely focused on the coachees, they will become more open, motivated and willing to change.

This may spark some controversy and lively discussion. After all, if educators are being coached to improve their school, district or classroom, how can it be good or preferable to enable the coachee to choose the focus? How and why is it helpful for the organization? Ideally, this is exactly what should happen in a pure coaching situation. People are motivated to do what is valuable to them, what is satisfying and meaningful. Goals that have descended from an external source may have little meaning. When you free people to discover their own way, path, goal, and purpose, they will be motivated to persevere—to maintain momentum and persist through the rough waters of change. We require choice. Telling someone what to do limits choice, diminishes creativity and causes defensiveness. You can disempower someone by giving them your goals, your solutions, your methods.

For Example

You're a principal or instructional coach and observe several opportunities for improving the learning environment in a classroom you're visiting. Although you could easily suggest a number of goals, a coaching conversation without an agenda might sound like this:

Coach: You seem stressed.

Coachee: Yes, my students are often out of control.

Coach: Sounds like you'd like to feel more in control.

Coachee: I really would. Seems nothing works with some kids.

Coach: I hear you'd really like to focus on this now.

Coachee: I would. It'll be great to have my classroom more orderly.

Coach: Great, let's start working on that goal.

Notice in the foregoing example, the coach did not specifically bring up the issue of classroom chaos. The coach helped the teacher identify a goal important to her. The teacher acknowledged the problem and voiced her frustration. She was ready and willing to deal with it—a great opening for coaching. Imagine, instead, the coach offering up opinion and advice. The result would likely be defensiveness and little movement or enthusiasm toward a goal.

COACHING TIPS:

- ❖ Notice if your coaching interaction is focused on what you want to accomplish or what the coachee needs or wants.
- ❖ Be acutely aware of the focus of your attention during coaching sessions and shift your focus to the person being coached.

If you're brand new to coaching, trust me on this for a while. See what happens when you let go of your agenda or your school or district's agenda. Notice what happens when people become empowered. They soar!

On the other hand, when districts invest in coaching, they want to be assured of improved results for the organization. Coaches would be wise to strike a smart balance, acknowledging the district's goals and allowing freedom for the coachees to add their own.

A Coach Listens Deeply

Masterful coaching occurs when coaches are acutely and deeply listening—a forgotten skill in our hurry-up world. There are varying levels of listening, from superficial to deeper listening, where the coach is really "with" the coachee. Skillful listening is the heart and soul of successful coaching and is key to truly connecting on a meaningful level with a coachee. A coach spends far more time listening than speaking. There's a goldmine of information in the coachee's spoken words and the coach is mining for the gold during the coaching conversation.

Having a trusted coach who listens to your deepest dreams, desires, and goals can be a profound experience for many people. For some, it may be the only relationship, or the first, in which they feel truly listened to. Silence is common, and tears are not uncommon, especially when the issue at hand touches the soul of the coachee.

Let's look at three levels of listening. The first level should *never* be part of the coaching conversation. It is included to examine the difference between it and deeper, more effective levels.

Superficial Listening

This level is subjective. The listener brings the focus of the conversation to him- or herself instead of on the person speaking. It usually leaves the speaker feeling disconnected. It is the kind of listening in "normal" conversation. What is said is filtered by the experience of the listener. It is often dissatisfying to the one who's talking. Think of superficial listening as cocktail party conversation. Notice in the following example how the focus shifts to the listener.

> ### ⌐ For Example
>
> *Speaker:*   My office is a horrendous mess. I'm so busy I can't seem to get it organized.
>
> *Listener:*   I know what you mean. Mine's a mess, too. I can't stand it.

Most people are very familiar with this shallow level of listening. It is not very satisfying for the speaker, who may be looking for feedback, assistance, or empathy. When we're in superficial listening mode, we're not really paying attention to the speaker. We're having an internal conversation with ourselves, relating what is said to our own lives. Perhaps we're making judgments and forming opinions, none of which is helpful to the speaker.

Listening at this level has no place in a coaching conversation. Nothing will be accomplished and no one wins. There's no benefit to the coachee and frustration and impatience will be high. Well-trained coaches listen at a deeper level, enabling them to connect more meaningfully with the coachees and assist the coachees in exploring their inner selves.

Objective Listening

In objective listening, the listener's focus is on the person speaking. The listeners, the coaches, make a connection. They may make eye contact, lean forward, or make gestures that demonstrate that they are engaged with the speakers. If coaching occurs on the telephone, the coaches tune out distractions and are totally aligned with the conversation. They tune out thoughts that are not pertinent to the conversation and are completely focused on the speakers. The listeners aren't relating *their* experiences; they're focused on the *speakers'* experiences. The listeners are focusing on what is and is not being said.

Among the things a coach listens for are

- Values
- Self-doubts
- Assumptions
- Fears

- Limiting beliefs
- Judgments
- Interpretations
- Passion
- Energy
- Enthusiasm
- Boredom

The skilled coach has awareness of this level of listening and its impact on the coachee. Notice the difference in the following example, the shift and depth in this conversation, versus the previous example of superficial listening.

For Example

Coachee:	My office is a horrendous mess. I'm so busy I can't seem to get it organized.
Coach:	Sounds like it is important for you to get it organized.
Coachee:	It is. I want to feel together and settled into my new role yet don't want to neglect my piles of work. I feel so overwhelmed.
Coach:	I hear that the clutter is draining your productive energy. How can you deal with it and still maintain your enthusiasm?
Coachee:	I don't know. I just don't have the time.
Coach:	What *do* you have time for?
Coachee:	I wish I had a whole day to devote to organizing.
Coach:	What can you do instead?
Coachee:	I guess I could spend 15 minutes a day.

Coaching should always occur at this level, *at a minimum.* Coachees sense they are heard and that the coach is right there with them. During objective listening, coaches are detached from any agenda, opinions and their own thoughts. Coach and coachee are connected on a deeper level than in superficial listening. When coaching at this level, coaches rely on what the coachee says to determine what to say next. Objective listening is a far better means of communication than superficial listening; however, it doesn't always get to the heart and soul of the coachee.

Intuitive Listening

This is the most powerful form of listening. Masterful coaching takes place here. The coach is really connected to the coachees, and they feel it. The coach is probing further, based on what the coachees are saying. Most people never listen at this level, and most people are never heard at this level. In my experience, when coachees experience this deep level of listening, they are often overwhelmed. Sometimes they'll cry. When coaching at this level, you may hear long periods of silence during the session. That's a positive sign that the coachee is touching on something profound. Be okay with the silence—it is powerful. It is a sign of a breakthrough and the opening for deep change to occur.

For Example

Coachee: My office is a horrendous mess. I'm so busy I can't seem to get it organized.

Coach: How important is it to you to get organized?

Coachee: Very. I'd be far more productive. I really want it to be orderly.

Coach: What's that about? You sound agitated.

Coachee: The stuff is in the way all the time. I can't get around it and move freely.

Coach: I sense there's more to this. What do you need to let go of to clear the way?

Coachee: You may be right. I'm holding on to the old, actually an old relationship that's gone sour. It has nothing to do with my job, but the stuff may be symbolic.

Coach: What do you want to do about that?

Coachee: Avoiding it isn't exactly working. I guess it is time to deal with it.

Master coaches are highly intuitive; they listen as if they were collecting and noticing everything. They'll synthesize what they hear and use their intuition and skills to move the coachees forward. When coachees feel truly listened to, they will be more open to exploring their issues. You and your coachees will be deeply connected, opening up a trusting space for greater awareness and purposeful, personal growth.

Often the coachee doesn't see the big picture. Fears and doubts intrude. Coaches "read their audience" as a performer or politician might and adjust their feedback or next steps accordingly. Aim for coaching to occur at this level. This is where coaching magic happens.

A Coach Listens for Emotion

A good coach also distinguishes between the spoken words and the level of emotion they hear. It is part of the listening and learning process—listening for feelings and moods, the emotions that lay behind the words. Listen for tone and pace of the speaker and noticing if there's a disconnect between what is said and the coachee's emotions.

You can easily tell by the level of energy in the voice if someone is bored and disinterested or excited and passionate. When coaching occurs on the telephone, common in executive and leadership coaching, a coach develops a highly tuned ability to detect alignment between the words and feelings and between feelings and action.

For Example

I clearly remember when I was undecided about forming my consulting company or looking for another position. My coach responded by saying, "You sound so excited when you talk about starting your own business. When you talk about job hunting, I can hear your voice go flat."

She was right on. She could hear my hidden desire. For 20 years, I had secret dreams of having my own business and didn't have the courage or support to pursue it. The feedback she gave was powerful. It helped me garner the courage I needed to take my life in a new direction.

A Coach Summarizes and Paraphrases to Ensure Understanding

Typically, the coachee does far more talking than the coach and the coach is doing far more listening. Summarizing and paraphrasing are essential for both the coach and coachee. The coach moves on during the session based on what is already said; therefore it is very important for the coach to clarify what the coachee is thinking, what is behind the words. And the coach can proceed with a clear picture and assurance that the flow of the session, the next step, is following the coachee's needs.

Taking time to review and recap what has already been said communicates to the coachees that the coach hears them clearly and knows and understands what they are dealing with. These skills and competencies also create a closer relationship between the coach and coachee and are essential techniques for a coach.

┌─ For Example ─────────────────────────────

Coachee: I'm uncertain about leaving my position for another one. I have several principals in my district who seem to think they're running their own show without the district office being a presence at all. They don't get along with each other and are not functioning as a team. I get the feeling they're very competitive with each other.

Coach: You seem to have several issues here. Sounds like you're in conflict about staying or leaving your current position. And you've got some serious challenges with staff.

Coachee: Those are the two main issues right now.

Coach: You've got three principals not getting along very well right now, and you want them to work together.

Coachee: That's right.

Sample approaches:

"What I hear you say is . . . "

"Am I hearing you correctly?"

"So in other words . . . "

A Coach Encourages Expression of Thoughts and Beliefs

A coach is like a detective, getting to the heart of issues important to the coachee and to the organization. A good coach is nonjudgmental, always accepting the coachee's outlook on life. It is important for coaches to acknowledge and validate people's opinions, feelings and beliefs. You don't have to agree with them; simply accept them.

Coaches want to keep the coachee talking. It is part of the exploratory learning process for both parties. The more the coach probes, the more both are learning about each other. Encouraging the coachees to voice their beliefs, concerns and perceptions brings them out into the open and into the coachees' consciousness. People can't change what they don't recognize. It is only with the coming of awareness of something that the change process can start.

It is helpful in the coaching conversation to *acknowledge* the coachees' thoughts, beliefs, and experiences. Acknowledging is letting the coachees know you hear what they're saying. The coach simply states what is. Acknowledging is important because it helps relieve the stress the coachee may be feeling. This skill is most often used in the beginning of a coaching session, when a high level of stress is heard in the coachee's voice.

For Example

Coachee: It seems that no matter what I try, my classroom is out of control.

Coach: Sounds like you're putting in the effort and not getting the result you want.

Other approaches:

- That can be challenging.
- That sounds like a difficult situation.

Another helpful method of encouraging and furthering the coaching conversation is *validating*. Validating let's the coachees know not to feel guilty for how they feel. It is okay for them to feel the way they do. There is no judgment. The coaches simply let the coachees know that they see things from their perspective. It normalizes the coachees' feelings. Validating and acknowledging are often used together, although they are not the same skill.

For Example

Coachee: I am so upset that the parent was screaming at me on the phone.

Coach: I can certainly see how that would bother you.

Other approaches:

- It can be upsetting when that happens.
- You have a right to feel that way.

A Coach Integrates and Builds on Ideas

Coaching is an accelerated change process. The coach is a vast receptacle, collecting all of the information the coachee shares with the coach. The coach synthesizes it and offers it back to the coachee in the form of feedback and insights. The wise coach listens for openings, for moments when coachees have a spark, an idea they're willing to explore and incorporate it into their action plans. The coach is actually facilitating a process. This is where coaching and consulting and mentoring are so different. Coaches respect the coachees' capacity to develop their own solutions and help them progress in the direction of their choices.

For Example

Coachee: I want my faculty meetings to run more smoothly and be more productive.

Coach: What has worked for you in the past?

Coachee: Well, I remember some meetings that went well and others that didn't.

Coach: What did you learn?

Coachee: They seem to go better when I plan the agenda to include time frames for each item as well as who will lead the discussion for each one. A few people thought that was too rigid, but now that I think about it, I see those were the best meetings. We really accomplished our goals.

Coach: How does that help you plan for next week's meeting?

Coachee: I guess I should continue, and I'll talk to the principals about their concerns.

Notice that the coach extracted the ideas from the coachee by asking questions and by building on what had worked in the past. To repeat a comment earlier in the book, coaches know that the answers to coachees' concerns are usually within the coachees. They are able and capable of devising their own solutions. The coaching conversation leads the coachees to discover the solutions and by doing so, they are committed to implementing the steps to accomplish them.

A Coach Gets to the Bottom Line

A successful coaching conversation is not a gripe session or a pity party. It is a productive, focused conversation aimed at producing a successful result. Often, time is scarce for lengthy coaching conversations. Coaches need to become comfortable with strategies that will enable them to "cut to the chase."

When you enter coaching sessions and sense high levels of tension and stress, you can easily anticipate that the coachees have a need to be heard and time to vent. However, since your goal as coach is to ensure that the sessions are successful and meaningful for the coachees, you must strike a balance between allowing them some time to "get it off their chests" and interrupt so they can progress.

People frequently come to a coaching session scattered. They may ramble on and on about what's going on or what's going wrong. Often a coachee will go off on a tangent as a clever way of avoiding or confronting something else. Or the coachee is simply spinning out of control. Sometimes a brief period of venting is necessary before the air is cleared so that a useful coaching session can occur. A masterful coach, always holding the coachee's original agenda, steers the coaching session toward achieving it.

For Example

Coachee: I just don't see how I can get my office organized. I've got meetings morning, noon, and night. And teachers coming into my office any time they have a problem. Parents are constantly calling, and central office has too many reports for me to do. I just can't get to it. I don't have a minute to breathe, let alone clean my office. Just today, I had PTA, a book sale, teacher observations, and the new-teacher program. The new teachers need lots of help and there's only me to give it and . . .

Coach: You have a lot on your plate and sound overwhelmed by it all. How about taking a few deep breaths before we begin.

Coachee: Good idea.

Coach: So what would be most helpful to focus on today?

The coach intrudes to get to the bottom line in order to focus the coachee and move the coaching session along. It is human nature to tell stories, yet as a coach, you need to limit rambling. It may feel rude to intrude; however, if the entire coaching session rambles on, the coachee will not feel helped or served.

COACHING TIP:

It is helpful in the beginning of a coaching relationship to tell the coachee that there may be times you need to intrude during a session.

A Coach Allows Venting

A coach might be inclined to completely eliminate the long stories and ramblings of a coachee. I don't recommend that. In order for successful coaching to happen, the coachee needs to be clear and ready for a quality session. A lot can happen between coaching sessions or on the day the session takes place. If a coachee arrives at a session stressed out and upset about something, the wise coach will refocus the session on the issue at hand *for a period of time.*

Unless the coachee has a means for releasing negative energy, good coaching won't take place. Express to the coachee that you hear the concern and you understand. You will likely hear the level of stress decrease when he or she feels heard. Venting frees up energy and creates space for coaching to occur.

For Example

While conducting a leadership coaching session, my coachee arrived at the session with news of her father's sudden illness. Because I follow the coachee's agenda, I spent about one-quarter of the session listening. Once I sensed that her stress level had lowered, we were able to proceed.

Core Competency 6: Powerful Questioning

You may have noticed in the brief examples used throughout the book that the coach is mainly asking questions—very specific questions—that are designed to reveal information about the coachees to themselves. Asking questions uncovers what lies behind the words and what motivates the coachees. Let me repeat: The coaching conversation is based on an open dialogue that leads to creative approaches to the problems and issues of the coachee or the organization. The coaching conversation is less about telling the coachee what to do or how to do it. It is more about asking, learning and discovering the potential within the coachee that is waiting to emerge. Just as good teachers ask open, probing questions with students, good coaches use questioning techniques to understand what lies beneath the performance of individuals.

The coaching process is based on curiosity, for a purpose. Coaches ask questions to spark the coachees to think in new ways. Coaches don't want to be quizzing them, but they are inquisitive, leading the coachees to explore and challenge their thoughts and belief systems. Therefore, a good coach needs to be very skilled in various types of questions that will yield "aha" moments. It is those moments that reflect that a great learning or insight has occurred and new actions can be taken.

A Coach Asks Questions That Reflect Active Listening

Listening and questioning are directly linked in the coaching process. One flows from and into the other. The questions the coach asks are derived from the coaching conversation. It is like a dance. The coachees lead by offering their comments; the coaches respond by offering new questions based on those comments. It becomes a pattern. The coaching session flows.

> *The problem in life isn't in receiving answers. The problem is in identifying your current questions. Once you get the questions right, the answers always come.*
>
> —James Redfield (1993)

For Example

Coachee: I've been in this district for five years, and I think it is time to move on. I'll be retiring in a few years. And to be honest, I'm getting a little bored in this small district.

Coach: I'm hearing two different things. You're thinking about planning for retirement and you want more challenge.

Coachee: Yes, I do want a more challenging position, and I have my eye on the future and wouldn't mind an increase in salary.

Coach: Sounds like two important values are surfacing. Let's explore. Which one is the driving force?

Sample reflective questions:

Why do you think that worked?

What's another way of looking at that?

What's stopping you?

Why do you want that?

A Coach Asks Open-Ended, Thought-Provoking Questions

Coaching is a discovery process that helps coachees learn more about themselves, what they want, why they want it, and what may block them from achieving it. A coach asks deeply probing questions that challenge the coachee's long-held assumptions and beliefs. When an important new insight is

> *It is not the answer that enlightens but the question.*
>
> —Eugene Ionesco

made, you can hear the "aha" from the coachee. A breakthrough has been made. It is a magical moment in coaching.

Open-ended questions begin with "how," "why," and "what." Open-ended questions cause the coachees to stop, explore, reflect, and deeply think about the questions. Although coaches don't have specific agendas, they do want to move the coachees to action toward their goals in *every* coaching session. The coaches craft questions that help the coachees see from new perspectives and create opportunities to attain new results.

Sample questions:

What did you learn from that?

What is really bothering you about that?

Why is that important to you?

What does your intuition tell you?

A Coach Asks Empowering Questions That Lead to Action

Masterful coaches ask lots of empowering questions. As already stated numerous times, coaches refrain from telling coachees what to do or what to think. Skilled questioning techniques help the coachees go to a deeper level to uncover patterns of thinking, limiting beliefs or fear that impede their success or prevent them from performing at their peak. Asking empowering questions helps the coachees create new ways of thinking and thus create new opportunities and new possibilities.

Empowering questions cause the coachees to reflect, think, and respond. They inspire the coachees to take new actions. Like all questions asked in coaching, empowering questions don't have "yes" or "no" answers. They enable coachees to think about possibilities, explore the unknown, elaborate or expand their thinking, and see with new eyes. Coaches avoid asking questions that would elicit a "yes" or "no" response, which would shut down the conversation. The goal of asking empowering questions is for the coachees to think deeply about their own beliefs.

There are no right or wrong empowering questions. Use your intuition; ask the questions that lead your coachees to think and look at their situations, their goals, dreams, and challenges in new ways. This process helps coachees "see" their thoughts and new ways to think. Accomplishing challenging goals requires new ways of thinking. It requires letting go of old thinking habits and adopting new, positive ones. That is the heart of change and the heart of coaching.

Sample questions:

How can you find out more?

What will you do about that?

How will you know when you're successful?

Which day works better for you to walk those five miles in the morning, Thursday or Friday?

When can you write the draft plan this week?

How can you communicate your concern?

Coaches ask questions to understand what the coachees think or believe, to help the coachees gain insight into their own thought patterns and to create momentum. They help coachees explore all the possibilities and choices available from which the coachees choose the actions they're willing to commit to. In Chapter 7, readers will find a structured coaching model to follow in coaching sessions of any length. Since all coaching sessions are expected to result in action, a coach needs to learn questioning techniques that lead to decisions about what specific steps the coachee is willing to take next.

Another effective technique for gaining commitment to goals or tasks is to ask scaling questions. Scaling questions enable coachees to evaluate the level of importance or commitment they have to something. It is important for both the coach and the coachees to rate or rank their interest in taking on a goal or action steps. Scaling can be an indicator of their motivation and the likelihood of taking the necessary steps.

Sample scaling questions:

On a scale of 1–10, how ready are you to put your energy into that goal?

On a scale of 1–10, how important is it to you to confront that situation?

On a scale of 1–10, how likely is it that you will work on that plan this week?

Scaling questions are best used when identifying goals and determining how committed a coachee is to accomplishing them or when designing actions, especially those that are challenging or perceived as difficult.

Let's look at a sample scenario during a leadership coaching session that incorporates various questioning techniques. Coach Paul is meeting with Jane, an assistant superintendent in a new district with a new superintendent as well. She is dealing with a personnel issue and quite stressed about it.

Paul: Hi Jane. How are you doing today?

Jane: I'm kind of upset. I have a meeting in an hour with a colleague whom I have to write up on a personnel issue.

Paul: That can be rough. I can see why you're stressed. What is upsetting you so much?

Jane: Well, I'm stunned and surprised that Cindy completely ignored what I've asked her to do. Several weeks ago, I called her into my office and advised her that she needed to clean up her office. The piles of papers everywhere are causing embarrassment for the superintendent when visitors walk by her office. She completely ignored my request, and I have no choice but to submit a reprimand in her file.

Paul: You always have a choice. Sounds like you're in the middle of this issue—that the request is from your supervisor, and you are the messenger.

Jane: Exactly; actually I've been told I need to let her go by the end of the year. I've never done that before. I don't like the mess, either, but I doubt that I'd fire her because of it, if it were up to me.

Paul: So you will be the bearer of bad news. I get that you're pretty uncomfortable. What I hear is you're very upset that she disregarded your request to clean up the office. In one hour, you will be having a tough conversation with her. I hear you're angry, but I also sense that you wish you could handle the situation differently.

Jane: Yes, I can see a few options—maybe move her office.

Paul: Let's brainstorm about this a little. Why do you think Cindy ignored the request?

Jane: I think she was being passive-aggressive about it.

Paul: What are some other possibilities? What could be going on for Cindy that she didn't comply with your request?

Jane: Well, I assumed she was just being defensive and chose to ignore me. I have to think about this one. Maybe she was really busy. It is the beginning of the school year. Maybe she isn't an organized person or didn't realize how important it was. Gee, maybe she just doesn't know how to organize her office! I hadn't really stopped to think about it.

Paul: How can you learn more about this issue?

Jane: When she arrives in my office, instead of scolding her about not doing it, I guess I can talk to her and ask her what support she may need. Wow, that feels better. Thanks Paul. I can see the situation differently now. This session has been really helpful.

In this situation, the discussion between Jane and Cindy might have been a hostile one. Instead, with the opportunity to probe into the issue and brainstorm with the coach, Jane was able to think through the problem and discover a solution. She faced the discussion with a new attitude and confidence. Instead of finger pointing, she talked with Cindy about the value the new superintendent places on an orderly workplace and how she wanted community members who passed by to perceive the district office as being organized and well run. She also honored Cindy by approaching their talk with openness and a supportive attitude instead of being blaming and punishing. She treated Cindy with understanding and grace. The result was positive. Cindy simply hadn't realized the importance of the request. Her office has been neat and organized since their discussion.

Core Competency 7: Direct Communication

I could probably describe coaching in a nutshell as good communication that produces extraordinary results. Good coaches have dozens of specific skills, techniques and tools in their toolboxes to help coachees make progress. In Chapter 1, I described coaches as vehicles. Utilizing their collective skills and techniques, coaches facilitate a communication process that moves the coachees or the organizations from Point A to Point B. They provide concrete information in the form of observations and feedback that leads the coachees on a journey of professional and personal growth.

A Coach Provides Clear Feedback

Few of us enjoy receiving negative feedback—or giving it. In the safe space created by the coaching relationship, we can be open to receiving supportive feedback. Providing direct, honest feedback is a powerful gift from coach to coachee. We don't always see ourselves as others see us. We see the world as we are, and sometimes that view is foggy. Most people want to do their best and need concrete, specific knowledge in order to improve or change. Too often, we don't receive that kind of information, especially in our professional work, until it is too late.

Coaching sessions usually take place in an hour or less. A well-structured session is one that is meaningful, productive, and insightful and results in action. Coaches need to develop their skills in communicating clearly, crisply and directly, eliminating extraneous discussion. Doing so eliminates guesswork and vagueness and helps the coachees receive direct information.

Without feedback, people live with their self-doubts, interpretations, and assumptions. Giving feedback can cause discomfort for the coach and receiving it can cause defensiveness for the coachee, if not done with care. Inside a positive coaching relationship, however, feedback is expected and received as positive and necessary for achieving peak performance. Coaches give feedback continuously.

How to give useful feedback:

- Be sincere and avoid sugarcoating your comments.
- Focus on positive attributes before areas for improvement.
- Be descriptive instead of judgmental.
- Focus on behavior and performance versus the person.
- Turn negative feedback into a new goal or challenge.
- Deliver feedback in an encouraging, supportive manner.

Coaches provide feedback as part of the ongoing learning cycle. The open, confidential environment in a coaching relationship provides the opportunity for meaningful learning about oneself to occur.

A Coach Reframes for Understanding

If I had to choose one skill that would have the biggest impact on a coachee, my vote is for the powerful skill of reframing. A masterful coach helps the coachee see situations, beliefs and thoughts in new ways. Coachees may see situations, programs, projects or ideas in a negative light, stemming from years of limited thinking or deeply ingrained beliefs. Or they have just never considered other possibilities and have been stuck in one way of thinking.

Reframing shifts thinking patterns from the negative to the positive. Reframing empowers the coachee to be more positive, to change from "I can't" to "I'll consider that" to "I choose to." Believing that problems are opportunities, a coach will lead the coachee to see the many possibilities in any situation.

For Example

Coachee:	I'm stressed out over the presentation I have to make next week. I'm not a good speaker.
Coach:	Most people feel that way. Where is the opportunity here?
Coachee:	Well, I wasn't seeing it that way. I guess it is time I look at it as a chance to improve myself, now that I'm a principal.

Other approaches:

What's another way of looking at that?

How can that work for you?

How can that help you?

What other options exist?

How can you reframe that thought?

A Coach Explains Objectives and Techniques

Every coaching session should have a specific purpose. While there will be short- and long-term goals established early in the coaching relationship that will stretch over many months, coaches can also acknowledge the purpose of each coaching session. It is perfectly okay to communicate to the coachee, at the onset of the session, what the plan is that specific session and how it may be connected to the long-term goal. On occasion, an isolated session may diverge from the long-range plan to address a current issue of importance.

A coach may use one or more specific techniques. There are no secrets in coaching. Coaches should feel free explaining a technique and why they've chosen to use it at a particular time.

Sample approaches:

In today's session, let's look at that obstacle and figure out how you can overcome it.

Let's examine your beliefs that cause you to think that way.

Let's brainstorm for a while and look at all the options available to you.

A Coach Uses Metaphors to Paint a Verbal Picture

There are no two people alike, no two situations alike, and well-trained coaches have numerous techniques, tools, and strategies to help their coachees move toward their goals. Using metaphors can be a powerful strategy to help create understanding. They help create images that remain long after the conversation is gone. Earlier in the book, I compared a coach to a chiropractor, a metaphor for creating alignment. Metaphors are useful in helping people who are predominantly left-brained, more logical, concrete and linear, to visualize something and utilize their right brain, the more creative side. Metaphors help clarify a vague concept or help some coachees open up to a new idea. Some personality types relate to metaphors more than others. Since coaches need to be knowledgeable about numerous strategies, it's important for them to know how helpful metaphors can be in visualizing new realities.

For some people who may not otherwise visualize a goal as being possible, metaphors enable them to see the potential more clearly. Visual images are stored in the subconscious mind, the same place dreams and hopes for the future are stored.

┌─ For Example ─────────────────────────────┐

Buried in a mountain of paperwork

Strong as an ox

Stuck in the mud

└──┘

SUMMARY

In our hurried world, people feel detached and isolated and hungry for meaningful connection with others. Listening is fundamental to coaching. Coaches are always listening *for something* that will help the coachees make steady progress. They listen for clues, for signs, and for resistance. They use that information to probe, to help the coachees reach deeper levels of understanding and construct plans for developing the performance and results they are seeking.

Coaches combine all of their highly developed communication skills—employing deep levels of listening, skilled questioning techniques, and delivering feedback—for the purpose of achieving breakthroughs and forward action for the coachees.

Reflective Questions

- Think of one truly meaningful conversation you've had. What indicators did you have that someone was truly listening?
- Notice how you listen to others. Change how you listen to a deeper level and notice the difference in the relationship.
- When asked for advice, respond instead with a powerful question. Notice the difference.

Core Coaching Competencies 8–11

Never mistake motion for action.

—Ernest Hemingway

FACILITATING LEARNING AND RESULTS

Superficial, temporary results are not what we're after when we're coaching. We're looking for deep, lasting change and extraordinary results. We want to reach those goals that have frustrated, paralyzed, eluded, or mystified us. There will be no change, no growth, and no improvement until something new happens. It is only then that the power of coaching is felt and witnessed. A different result emerges for the individual, the team, the student or the organization when new behaviors are implemented.

Why is change so challenging? What is it that causes us to stay stuck even when we want to grow? What holds us back? How can we get to the core of the issues that keep us small and inhibit us from reaching our full potential? We talk about students reaching their full potential all the time, and for educators, that's a priority.

What about the adults in the system? Staff development and professional learning opportunities that address external knowledge may be helpful, but may not address what individuals actually need to progress. Often the inhibitors are internal. During the coaching process, coachees are engaged in profound learning about themselves.

Chapter 6 delves into resistance and helping new coaches overcome it. This chapter focuses on the expertise and skills coaches develop related to helping coachees learn about themselves, creating breakthrough thoughts, intentional actions, and higher levels of performance.

As mentioned in the last chapter, we humans are unable to change what we cannot see. We have to notice that something exists before we can do anything about it. Coaches help coachees create awareness of themselves, their environments and how they move through them. With that knowledge, once we see how we think and interact, there's unlimited capacity for growth and achieving peak performance.

Core Competency 8: Creates Awareness

While awareness includes seeing and hearing in the workplace, it encompasses much more than that. It is the gathering and the clear perception of the relevant facts and information, and the ability to determine what is relevant. That ability will include an understanding of systems, of dynamics, of relationships between things and people. Awareness also encompasses self-awareness, in particular recognizing when and how emotions or desires distort one's own perceptions.

—J. Whitmore (2004)

Another very important function of coaching is to help coachees raise their levels of awareness to a new height, where they can see and learn about themselves from a new perspective. It is from that new perspective that they're able to see what is possible. With another viewpoint and new information, coachees are more willing to take new steps. Awareness and feedback are related. Within this section are insights into how coaches can develop their skill in creating awareness.

The exploratory nature of coaching greatly expands the coachees' awareness of themselves, their inner thoughts, intentions, emotions, conflicts, and beliefs. Expanding awareness is also about observing the world around the coachees, the environment, relationships, other organizations, people, and other aspects of their lives. Expanding awareness is a process for making sense of all of the coachees' worlds, inner and outer.

A Coach Goes Beyond the Spoken Word

Because coaches have a sophisticated ability to listen deeply, they're listening between the words for inferences and underlying doubts. Coaches go beneath the surface level of the spoken word. Successful coaches have genuine curiosity about the coachees. They want to know more. They want to know why. They're seeking causes and uncovering stale belief systems.

People can be very clever and sophisticated in covering up issues they don't want to address. Unless there's a specific agreement to avoid a certain aspect of their lives, coaches will query them and allow the coachees the chance to bring to the surface difficult or challenging issues.

⌐ For Example ⎯⎯⎯⎯⎯⎯⎯⎯⎯⎯⎯⎯⎯⎯⎯⎯⎯⎯⎯⎯⎯

I was working with an education consultant, coaching her to grow and expand her work with school systems. She was having a hard time managing her time to accomplish her goals, to create and distribute publicity for an upcoming training event.

Coachee: I need to get the flyer designed, developed, and in the mail in the next two weeks. I hope I can pull this off.

Coach: Of course you *can*. Something tells me there's more going on.

Coachee: Well, I share my office with my husband, as you know. He needed my help with one of his projects. So I seem to end up spending more time on his stuff than mine.

A Coach Invokes Inquiry

Great coaches are insatiably curious. Through targeted questioning techniques, coaches continually probe, question and inquire, helping the coachees become conscious, themselves, of how and why they believe or behave as they do. An important part of the discovery process, being curious acknowledges that coaches don't have the answers. Coaches know that within the coachees is an inner knowing that emerges. "The information is inside the coachee. Your curiosity allows the coachee to explore and discover. It opens a wider range of possibility by being more flexible. Curiosity invites the coachee to look for answers" (Whitworth et al., 1998, p. 65).

Sample approaches:

Why is that important to you?

How will you feel when you do that?

What stops you?

A Coach Differentiates Between Facts, Interpretations, and Action

A coach notices gaps between what people say they want and actions they're taking or avoiding. The coachees often miss the connection or fail to notice that their actions are not in synch with their goals. Often, there are underlying beliefs that have been held onto since childhood that hold people back as adults. Most people have formed beliefs about themselves that determine how they live, what they think they can do and cannot do, what they deserve to have or not have, and what is possible for them and what is not.

There really are no limits to what's possible, other than those we impose on ourselves or those we've been told throughout our lives and have adopted as truth. Coaching helps to break down those limiting thoughts and our interpretations of them.

For Example

One coachee was sure he needed to find another job, one that paid a lot more money. He was certain he'd never have enough, especially as he looked toward the future. He was a superintendent and was well paid. I noticed a giant gap between his economic reality and his deeply held belief that there'd never be enough for him. As a child, he was the caretaker, the doer. The messages he received in childhood were about lack. There would never be enough: enough food, enough money, enough time, enough attention. Bringing it to the surface was a huge awareness for him. As he considered his definition of enough, he realized he already had it—a huge shift that greatly affected his plan.

A Coach Helps Discover New Thoughts, Beliefs, and Perceptions

The enormous power in the coaching relationship stems from the coach's ability to help the coachee adopt new thoughts, viewpoints, perceptions, and attitudes. Once people realize they actually have a choice about what they think and believe, they're well on their way to creating change. People can make choices about what they think the same way they choose what to wear. Just try on a new thought . . . and see what happens.

> *The greatest discovery of my generation is that people can alter their lives by altering their attitudes of mind.*
>
> *—William James, psychologist*

Circumstances may often be out of our control, but how we approach them through our thoughts, outlooks, and beliefs determines the outcome. A positive outlook and healthy attitude make all the difference between viewing a new initiative for your school as a chore or an exciting challenge. "In our eighteen-year study of outstanding performance, scores of teams have validated that attitude in by far the dominant factor separating high performance Creative Thinkers from their less productive Reactive Thinkers" (Oakley & Krug, 1991).

Sample approaches:

How else can you think about that?

How does that thought hinder you?

A Coach Communicates Broader Perspectives

When I started coaching, one activity I conducted with a group was to think about the difference they wanted to make in the world, to consider how they wanted to be thought of and remembered 100 years from now. I was stunned at the responses, which ranged from confused stares to tears. For many, it was the first time they had thought about themselves as having the capacity to make a bigger impact on the world.

> *Great minds discuss ideas. Average minds discuss events. Small minds discuss people.*
>
> *—Eleanor Roosevelt*

Coaches help coachees see a bigger picture in the situations they're dealing with. With a fresh outlook, the coachee can see the issue from another view and take different actions accordingly. "The coach triggers the formation of different interpretations and new meaning by the coachee. Different perspectives reveal new possibilities for participating in the world differently. The coachee is able to view him or herself and the world differently, so that new possibilities and avenues for creating a better life open up" (Seiler, 2003, p. 33).

┌─ **For Example** ─────────────────────────────────

Coachee: I had a parent hang up the phone on me today. I'm outraged she did that.

Coach: Tell me more about that.

> *Coachee*: She was screaming at me, upset about her child's teacher. Her daughter came home in tears, feeling embarrassed about something the teacher said. She wanted me to do something about it. I tried to talk and reason with her, but she just yelled and yelled and then hung up.
>
> *Coach*: I can see how that could be upsetting. What do you think was going on for the parent? Sounds like the parent was doing what most would do—protecting her child. While her behavior was difficult to deal with, how else could you have reacted if you realized it wasn't a personal attack?
>
> *Coachee*: I guess any parent would do that. I could have been more understanding or invited her in to meet with me.

We often get in our own ways and become our own worst enemies. By that I mean we can get stalled by beliefs we've so internalized, we don't see another way. A coach senses when a coachee is stuck. A good coach knows it's usually an internal shift that needs to happen for any external change to occur.

For Example

> *Coachee:* I don't think I sound professional when I speak.
>
> *Coach:* What exactly are you questioning?
>
> *Coachee:* Well, I know my stuff. I know the content. But I don't I think I come across as if I do.
>
> *Coach:* What makes you think so?
>
> *Coachee:* Well, I've actually had good feedback from others about how I come across. I guess it comes from me.
>
> *Coach:* I know this position is new for you. When you begin to *see* yourself as professional and stop doubting yourself, you'll *feel* professional. What will it take for you to feel professional?
>
> *Coachee:* Well, since I know my material, I guess I have to develop my confidence and feel more assured when I'm speaking to a group.
>
> *Coach:* So, it's a self-confidence issue! Let's get started working on that.

A Coach Helps See Interrelated Factors

Coaches know that everything is connected; that our home life affects our work life, that our energy level is affected by our health, that our moods and feelings are affected by our outlooks. When we neglect important aspects of our work or life, other areas may suffer. When we pay attention to the neglected areas, others improve.

Just as school systems are complex organizations, every individual is a complex, interrelated set of systems. We are a composite of our histories, family values, feelings, thoughts, attitudes and aspirations. As a customized, individualized process, coaching looks at people from a holistic perspective—what are all the parts that equal the sum?

We strive to have it all and be in balance in important areas of life: work, family, relationships, recreation, physical health, finances. We all want to be successful in our work and achieve results for our organizations. A coach sees the big picture and calls attention to how the parts relate to the whole.

A Coach Expresses Useful Insights

I once thought of myself as the most uncreative person on the planet. I can't sing or paint and have never succeeded in anything artistic. I remember being told to just mouth the words when I joined a school chorus. And today, my drawings still look like those of an eight-year-old. When questioned by my coach about my creative side, I realized I was holding onto childhood feedback that I couldn't do anything creative. I adopted the belief that creativity was an area off-limits to me. However, as an adult, I hadn't tried. I'd given up. I was so sure I couldn't.

When I realized a part of me had died, I began to explore my creative side. When my coach gave me feedback and said, "You are very creative. You create ideas," I literally broke down and cried. That reaction opened up a whole new world. I started writing and acting. And I wonder what I'll do next. It's enormously powerful to let go of a long-held belief.

A Coach Identifies Strengths and Areas for Growth

Discovering and uncovering opportunities for personal and professional growth are the gems that emerge from the coaching relationship. If we accept, acknowledge and are open to being continuous learners, we need a method of knowing specifically and exactly where we need to grow. We want to identify our growing edges. In the safe space of the coaching relationship, we come face to face with our reality. We can more easily identify the areas in which we shine. We may be great at interpersonal communication and building teams that work well together. We know if we're risk takers.

Often, we don't have a means for learning, very specifically, where and how to improve our performance, our interpersonal communication, or how we manage ourselves or our time. In a supervisory mode, we can easily get defensive. In a coaching mode, where continuous growth and improvement are a given, we're more open to receiving feedback and concrete knowledge about where we need to grow to improve who we are and how we conduct ourselves at work.

So how does a coach help determine areas of growth? One way is by observation, helping the coachees see themselves and how their thoughts and beliefs impact their success or lack of it. Another is observing outcomes of changed behavior, witnessing the difference a change in behavior or action can make. One small change usually has a tremendous impact. Another method of identifying areas of growth is through formal assessments. Many organizations use assessments to identify one's personality and how it affects team functioning. Leadership assessments are commonly used by coaches to determine areas of growth (see Using Assessments in Coaching in Chapter 7).

> *Coaching people to unleash their aspirations, move beyond what they already think and know, and maximize their results is one of the highest aspirations of what it is to be a human.*
>
> —Robert Hargrove (2000)

For Example

I conducted a leadership assessment with an assistant superintendent who had set her sights on obtaining a superintendency in a few years. She was strong, confident, and determined. Her assessment led to some helpful knowledge. It actually affirmed that she had *almost* all of the necessary leadership attributes to be successful in any leadership position and particularly at a high level. It identified very specifically areas in which she needed to grow, particularly in the area of decision making. Although she was decisive and did her research and homework on pending decisions, she was more likely to surge ahead without taking the necessary time to gain support from others. She fully acknowledged her tendency to go too fast. She knew that that could potentially derail her, and we began to focus our coaching sessions on how she could bring others along.

Core Competency 9: Designing Actions

Everyone has a never-ending to-do list in their mind. Usually, we have so many items on the list, we feel overwhelmed and can never accomplish all of them. Sound familiar? In a coaching relationship, the list may quickly become shorter as coach and coachee prioritize and commit to actions that focus on the coachee's most important priorities. A sense of both calm and hope surfaces as coachees begin to see that goals are within their reach. They learn to say "no" or "not now" to items less meaningful and a definite "yes" to those most important.

Coaching is like having a school improvement plan for an individual. Most improvement plans in school systems state intended goals and actions to achieve them. It's the same for coaching. There's an individual action plan to achieve your personal and professional goals. (See Chapter 7.) Together, coaches and coachees create actions on *a regular, ongoing basis:* weekly, biweekly, or on a schedule created together.

A Coach Defines Actions That Deepen Learning

The coach is a facilitator for learning about oneself and moving along the process of learning and growing. We don't just talk about change. We work with the coachees to *implement* new actions and create opportunities to apply and practice new behaviors. Because every coaching session ends with action, the coach and coachee work together to determine an action plan each and every time they meet.

> Each of our acts makes a statement as to our purpose.
>
> —Leo Buscaglia

--- **For Example** ---

Coachee: I'd like to be more comfortable speaking up in groups. I think it holds me back from being a more effective leader.

Coach: How can you do that?

Coachee: Instead of remaining silent or listening to everyone else, I could just do it. Even though it sounds simple, I get sweaty at the thought of it.

Coach: Many people feel that way. You have a lot to contribute. How much do you believe that?

Coachee: Guess I don't. I get stuck in my throat. I'm not sure I believe my thoughts are valuable to others.

Coach: We've hit on something important. It is *that* thought that keeps you stuck. When you shift your thoughts to realizing you have important contributions, you will speak up without effort. How can you practice that this week?

Coachee: Well, I do have a faculty meeting Thursday. I will share my thoughts no less than three times.

Coach: What else can you do?

Coachee: Well, I know that being truly successful will not happen for me unless I overcome this. I've been safely avoiding it for years, but I'm not willing to do that anymore. I will look for new opportunities and ways to diminish the fear.

Coach: Many people fear speaking up. What groups or supports exist to help?

Coachee: I've heard good things about Toastmasters for years. Maybe I'll check it out.

Coach: Maybe?

Coachee: No—I will. I'll see if there's a local chapter and attend a meeting this week.

Coach: Great. So this week, you will . . . speak up, no less than three times at Thursday's faculty meeting, and you will explore Toastmasters for a group that fits your schedule.

COACHING TIPS:

❖ Notice that the coach isn't telling the coachee what to do, but together they are brainstorming possibilities and actions.
❖ There are many possible actions; however, these are the ones the coachee chose.
❖ When "forwarding the action," coachees are best served by choosing their own actions, and you, the coach, encouraging them and holding them accountable for accomplishing them.
❖ It's OK to nudge coachees along gently with inspiring support or with a firmer approach, whichever is more effective for the coachee.

A Coach Explores Alternative Ideas and Solutions

Holding the coachees' overall goals always at the forefront, the coaches and coachees move forward, focusing on how the coachees will arrive at their destinations. There are usually multiple pathways to achieve a goal.

Together, the coach and coachee evaluate the universe of possible options. Brainstorming is a common technique that coaches use to solicit ideas from the coachee. It is during brainstorming sessions that coaches can throw in some ideas and alternatives to stretch the coachees' thinking when they're stuck. Remember: It's always the coachee who chooses.

COACHING TIP:

- ❖ Use brainstorming when the coachee can't see another way.
- ❖ Create lists of ideas, then review the list to determine the best options.
- ❖ Encourage coachees to consider all the options and choose those that work for them.

For Example

You are a first-year principal and want to succeed in your new role. You have set a specific goal for the first three months of coaching: to develop confidence as a leader. Yet you have no idea how to proceed.

Coach:	What does a confident leader look like to you?
Coachee:	I think a confident leader has sufficient knowledge and confidence to enter any situation without anxiety. That's what I want for myself. I think I'm OK in the knowledge department.
Coach:	That's a great start. So how can you feel more confident?
Coachee:	I don't know. A few years of experience, maybe.
Coach:	I bet you'd rather not wait that long. How about we brainstorm some ideas so you can feel more confident now?
Coachee:	OK.
Coach:	You first. We'll just write down everything we think of. Don't limit your ideas.
Coachee:	Here goes. I can buy a new wardrobe.
Coach:	Great. What else?
Coachee:	I could stop thinking I'm not good enough.
Coach:	Great one. What else?

Coachee:	I can start thinking I have what it takes. Hmm. I can't think of any more.
Coach:	Terrific! I'll throw some out, too. You could create a time management schedule. Or ask for more help on that committee.
Coachee:	OK. That's a lot of ideas.
Coach:	Yes, we have a list. Choose three you're willing to get started on now.

A Coach Promotes Experimentation and Self-Discovery

One reason why coaching is so effective in boosting performance, achieving results and creating long-sought change is the simple fact that with it, people are in constant action toward their goals. No more thinking about it. No more wishing and hoping. Coachees are in motion, moving toward something they desire.

When goals are meaningful to the coachees, they're usually eager to get to work on them. The energy level is high; there's a sense of *finally getting there.* It's usually in the best interest of the coachees that they integrate a new action soon after it comes up: the next day, at the next meeting, during the next week.

Experimenting with new actions typically results in new levels of courage and the recognition that the coachee is capable of change. A coach continually encourages a coachee to try out new behaviors.

For Example

Coachee:	I'm getting a clear message from my principals that my faculty meetings have too much packed into them.
Coach:	What would make the meetings more meaningful to them and still accomplish your agenda?
Coachee:	Well, they want more time to talk about issues. I don't think we have time for that. There's so much to do.
Coach:	How will you get them to do all you want if they're not being supportive?
Coachee:	Well, I guess if I continue this way, they'll only get more resentful, and nothing much will happen.

Coach:	So how can you structure your next meeting differently?
Coachee:	Of course, I do need their support to accomplish our district goals. This week, I'll structure the meeting with talk time, 10 minutes for each agenda item. It'll be a long meeting. We may not get to everything. For some items, I'll create handouts.
Coach:	The next meeting is Wednesday. Sounds like a plan that will work for everyone. Let me know how it goes. Send me a quick note on Thursday.

A Coach Celebrates Successes

Coaching is no walk in the park. Coachees work hard to make changes, physically and emotionally. Seize opportunities to celebrate their success, and champion their new courageous behaviors. Although they are likely to feel ecstatic without the coaches' input, you are a team, you've accomplished success together. Encourage coaches to find ways to celebrate, to honor themselves for the growth they've made.

A Coach Challenges Assumptions and Perspectives

Assumptions can be wicked thoughts that keep us from trying something new. We assume we already know the answer, so we act accordingly. Assumptions are usually based on a past experience and can stop a person or a team from progressing. How often have you heard, "We've tried that before," "Been there, done that"? (See Chapter 6.) Coaching is about formulating and taking *new* actions. Coaches often have to delve into the coachees' self-imposed assumptions and help the coachees see that, with a different point of view, a different result can occur.

> *Hardening of the attitudes is the most deadly disease on the face of the earth.*
>
> *—Zig Ziglar*
> *(www.unitync.net/Quotes.html)*

For Example

Coachee:	I'm 58 years old and never expected to be out of a job.
Coach:	I hear that you think your age is a factor in obtaining another position.
Coachee:	Well, yes. Most people my age are retired by now.

Coach:	The way I see it, you have years of experience, and many districts would be glad to have you on board.
Coachee:	I didn't think of it that way.
Coach:	Which attitude would help you get the job: I'm too old, or I have a great deal of experience?
Coachee:	I see what you mean. I made a giant assumption. Better change my outlook.

Core Competency 10: Planning and Goal Setting

> *A life that hasn't a definite plan is likely to become driftwood.*
>
> —David Sarnoff (www.copingtoday .com/inspiration-quotes.html)

Change happens by taking small, consistent steps. A competent coach develops and maintains an effective, customized coaching plan designed with the coachee. In this section are specific skills coaches need to ensure aligned action that propels the coachees forward into their desired futures.

A Coach Establishes a Specific, Results-Oriented Coaching Plan

Just as school systems and high-achieving organizations depend on a strategic planning process for reaching goals, individuals involved in a coaching process develop similar plans for *themselves.* The coaches' role is to ensure that coachees have a guiding plan for their work together that is meaningful, motivating, and focused on results.

Educator coaches work with coachees to define success with the individual, the team or the organization. Most educators know that goal statements need to be SMART: specific, measurable, achievable, results focused, and timed. (See Chapter 7 for more on goal setting.)

> *Stretch goals hold the possibility of breakthrough in performance and development.*
>
> —Robert Hargrove (2000)

In the early weeks of coaching, as the coach and coachee learn about each other, goals will emerge. Coachees may be vague about their goals or their future or have a nagging sense of dissatisfaction in their professional or personal lives. They may need the coach to help them gain clarity about their goals or direction. An exploration of the coachees' values, purpose, dreams and passions often occurs and may take several weeks.

Or a coach may work with an organizational team to set goals and processes for the entire staff to achieve. Sometimes, specific goals are known at the beginning or are identified early in the process. Either way, a specific written plan emerges.

Sample questions to establish goals:

- How connected are the goals with the coachees' strengths, interests, and values?
- Will achieving the goals increase the coachees' level of fulfillment, personally or professionally?
- How will the goals improve performance or satisfaction at work?
- Are the goals inspiring to the coachee?
- How do the goals align with the organization's goals?
- Is the coachee seeking to develop a skill, enhance performance, or advance to a new role?
- How can the coachees integrate their interests and passions into their work?
- What behaviors will demonstrate success?

A Coach Makes Adjustments to the Plan

Coaching is a dynamic process. Although specific goals are set, coaches should be aware that anything can happen and be prepared to make necessary adjustments. Coaches should open to and be accepting of any change in direction that grows out of the coaching process. As a coach, be flexible and follow the flow and the lead of the coachee.

For Example

I recall a coachee, mentioned in an earlier example, who came to me seeking her first superintendency. Within a few weeks she decided *not* to pursue such a position, after gaining clarity about her reasons and other priorities. She realized she'd have little time for her aging father who'd just moved in with her. Instead, she found a high-level leadership position in a nonprofit organization where she could still employ her experience as an educator while paying attention to her family life. I felt successful because the *coachee* was successful in arriving at a decision and solution that worked for her life.

A Coach Identifies Resources for Learning

As a facilitator of learning, the coach acts as a resource helping coachees identify inner and external resources for their customized learning and growth. Rather than tell the coachees or enable them, the coach directs them to sources they may have neglected or simply not thought about.

Sample approach:

How can you find out more about that?

Where can you learn to be a better public speaker?

A Coach Identifies Early Successes

Enthusiastic coachees who seek coaching will jump right into the process and discover success very early in the process. They may also develop exhaustion, as it can be highly emotionally draining to work so hard and see success come so quickly and easily. A small success may go unnoticed, or it may be cause for celebration. Coaches should provide continuous feedback and congratulate the coachees for their accomplishment. Championing their success helps keep the coachees motivated and moving forward, despite their feelings of exhaustion or exhilaration.

Core Competency 11:
Managing Progress and Accountability

Holding the coachees accountable for taking actions and progressing toward their goals is the built-in success ingredient in the coaching relationship. Without it, it's just another conversation. Coachees make swift progress in coaching because of the structured yet intuitive approach to change.

Coaches help coachees be successful in a number of ways; they help coachees choose the goals and choose the action steps they'll take on a regular basis. Together, the coach-coachee team addresses obstacles in advance, anticipating them and identifying strategies to circumvent them or deal with them head-on. A weekly schedule of coaching sessions creates momentum and a system of regular accountability between the coachee and coach.

A Coach Demonstrates Follow-Through

Coaches meet with coachees on a schedule they develop together—weekly, biweekly, or monthly. Whatever they choose, there's a schedule of sessions, each ending with committed actions that the coachee agrees to take *before* the next coaching session. The coachees are always in action toward their goals. The coaching session doesn't end until there are typically three to five specific actions promised. The coachees have made a commitment and the coaches hold them accountable by checking in at the *beginning* of the next session.

Sample approach:

How did the principals react to the new agenda format?

How did you feel making the presentation?

A Coach Keeps the Coachee on Track

Coaching is becoming a mainstream process because it is effective in producing results where other strategies have not. A key element of that success is the sense of focus and determination that evolves. When the relationship between the coach and coachee is established and strong, each person is committed to the success of the partnership. The coachees know the coach is their ally, and they want to be successful for both of them. The coach is also invested in the success of the coachee and keeps the coachee focused on goals, even when the coachee slows down or strays from the plan.

Predicting obstacles in advance is an important part of a quality coaching session and helps the coachee stay on track. Obstacles will always arise, and it is in the best interest of the coachee to anticipate them and plan ways to negotiate them.

Sample approaches:

What could come up that could get in the way?

What might prevent that from happening?

A Coach Holds Coachee Accountable

A clear function and role of the coach is to ensure that the coachees take the action they commit to during a coaching session. This is a *must* for the coaching process to be successful. Accountability keeps the coaching plan alive and keeps the coaching always in meaningful action. Because obstacles are predicted in advance, the coachee is set up for success. The reasons the action wouldn't be taken are reduced, and excuses are eliminated.

It's too easy to find reasons to *not* accomplish something, even something important to us. Life intrudes, other people make demands on our time, and we too often find ourselves saying "no" to what we've identified as important. The combination of predictable, scheduled coaching sessions, ongoing action and the built-in system of accountability provides a framework for success.

Advise coachees in the beginning of coaching that accountability is a norm. It's not negotiable.

For Example

Coach: OK, you've agreed, this week, to develop your schedule for meeting with all principals, maintain your workout schedule and contact that parent. That's what I've got written down. Are these our agreements?

Coachee: Yes, I will do the schedule over the weekend, walk four times a week for five miles, and call the angry parent on Monday.

Coach: Great. How will I know you've done it?

Coachee: I'll send you a note Wednesday, before our session.

On the flip side, if a coachee does *not* accomplish the promised tasks, the coach delves into the causes, deals directly with the coachee and does not accept excuses. In a positive manner, the coach and coachee explore the issues that prevented success and work to eliminate them in the next week or before the next session.

SUMMARY

A coaching process and relationship are only successful when there are new actions that lead to extraordinary results. The coaching process provides a structured framework that, when adhered to, nearly guarantees success for the coachee or the organization.

The competencies and subcompetencies I identify and briefly describe in this chapter are essential for productive coaching. While I don't expect readers to be highly skilled in them from reading this or any book, the descriptions provide a useful start in examining skills that should be incorporated into coaching learning opportunities that will ensure a more successful program. Creating awareness, designing action, planning and goal setting, and managing progress and accountability are essential skills for all coaches to master, whether instructional, classroom-based coaches or executive and leadership coaches. Mastering these boosts their confidence and boosts results for school systems and other organizations.

Reflective Questions

- What new learning about coaching have you discovered?
- What are your thoughts about accountability in the coaching process? Discuss with your team or colleagues.
- Who would benefit from having a coaching plan?

PART III

Ensuring Success Through Coaching

Strategies to Break
Through Resistance

You are today where your thoughts have brought you. You will be tomorrow where your thoughts take you.

—James Allen (www.brainyquote.com)

The human mind processes between 50,000 and 80,000 messages per day from external sources, such as the media and news, and internal sources, such as self-talk. As much as 80% of those messages are negative. No wonder change is a challenge! Imagine what could be created in schools systems, in the lives of students and staff, if that number were reversed.

What if 80% of your thoughts were positive? What if, instead of thinking, "I'm not a very creative person" you thought, "I create ideas, dozens of them, every day." Or your students went from thinking, "I just can't understand that math problem," to "I'm finding the help I need to understand that math problem." Notice the difference.

The familiar saying, "it takes a village to raise a child," also applies to the concept that it takes a team for lasting change to happen. It doesn't happen in isolation. It takes looking at the environment in which it is to happen and ensuring that other people and systems support the change.

Coaches are positive thinkers who believe anything is possible. They believe problems are opportunities. In fact, they believe there are no problems at all—only opportunities. Coaches see their coachees as able and capable of anything they want to achieve. They hold that belief at all times when working with coachees. They hold their coachees' goals, dreams, and visions in their minds and their hearts and use all of their highly developed skills, techniques, and strategies to help their coachees move toward them.

Generating large-scale change for school systems boils down to every individual within the system committing to the internal personal change needed for the external result to emerge. Whether you are an instructional coach working with teachers to change classroom practice or an executive coach working with principals or central office leaders to implement district goals, you are likely to meet resistance. Creating change for school systems using a coaching approach offers a method and process for addressing and overcoming it.

Among the many possible, Fullan and Stiegelbauer (1991) identified the following causes for educators resisting change:

- The purpose is not made clear.
- The participants are not involved in the planning.
- The appeal is based on personal reasons.
- The habit patterns of the work group are ignored.
- There is poor communication regarding a change.
- There is fear of failure.
- Excessive work pressure is involved.
- The cost is too high, or the reward for making the change is seen as inadequate.
- The present situation seems satisfactory.
- There is a lack of respect and trust in the change initiator.

In a study of 25,000 managers and supervisors examining why employees didn't comply with their managers' requests, most of the results centered on lack of direction and lack of feedback (Fournies, 2000). Here follow some of the responses:

- They don't know what they're supposed to do or how to do it.
- They don't know why they should do it.
- They think they're already doing it.
- There are obstacles beyond their control.
- They think it won't work.
- They think their way is better.
- Something else is more important.
- There is no positive consequence to them for doing it.
- There is a negative consequence to them for doing it.
- There is a positive consequence to them for not doing it.
- There is no negative consequence to them for not doing it.
- Personal limits;
- Personal problems;
- Fear (anticipate future negative consequences);
- No one could do it. (p. 94)

Traditional supervisory relationships don't typically address the people issues that cause resistance. While feedback may be offered, without a coaching approach, there is not an effective process for getting to the heart of the changes needed for the organization. In the safe space of the coaching relationship, the coach-coachee team can explore the source of resistance and develop ways to transcend it.

CONQUERING RESISTANCE

Creating change would be a snap if there weren't any resistance. Even people who want and seek change will confront resistance at some level and at some point during their transformation. Coaches can guide them through it, providing support and encouragement, holding onto their goals and dreams, always envisioning the coachees successful.

> *Obstacles don't have to stop you. If you run into a wall, don't turn around and give up. Figure out how to climb it, go through it, or work around it.*
>
> —Michael Jordan (www.imdb.com)

Successful change would be easily within reach if all people were open, willing to be coached, and willing to change. The reality is, not everyone who could benefit from coaching is eager or ready to change how they think, what they believe, or what they do. This section identifies strategies to help coaches overcome the resistance they may face. Among the sources of resistance are the following:

- Limiting beliefs
- Assumptions
- Fear
- Judgments
- Obstacles

Think about resistance to change you may have witnessed in your district. Think about the change efforts you have seen come and go. Coaching supports individuals and organizations *through* the resistance period and ensures that people making change remain focused on the goal, and navigate through the rough periods. Making any change requires a letting go of something in order to make room for the new. There are endings to consider, a transitional phase when the future appears uncertain, and stamina is necessary to stay the course until a new outcome is realized.

Ask anyone, anywhere, if they like or seek change. Most people will say "no way." People tend to like the tried and true, to stay in their comfort zones and shy away from change. Even people who want change in their personal or professional lives exhibit some form of resistance. Skilled coaches go beneath the surface to help their coachees get past their own inner obstacles that prevent forward motion.

So much is written in educational research about change. Much of it focuses on external issues and challenges. However, to make true change, it is necessary to look deeply at both the *external* system, which includes performance measures, processes, resources, and other outer factors, and *internal* issues that block individuals, such as communication style, leadership capabilities, self-doubt, assumptions, beliefs, and negative self-talk. This chapter focuses on internal issues, the softer but necessary and often ignored side of change.

Think about a time in your life that you held back, that your inner voice told you "no." I remember sitting on a beach in Mexico thinking about going parasailing. I thought about it for days, watching dozens of people sail up and land laughing. I was on the edge. Maybe I'll try it. No, something held me back—fear. That was before coaching entered my life. I'd do it now in a heartbeat. What holds you or your colleagues back? What inner obstacles have to be released to allow courage to enter?

> *If you can find a path with no obstacles, it probably doesn't lead anywhere.*
>
> —Frank A. Clark
> (www.brainyquote.com)

I have found that people can be extremely clever about camouflaging the doubts, beliefs, and fears that keep them in the status quo. However, in a coaching relationship, defenses melt away, and people can look directly at those issues and notice how they impact them. In my experience as a coach, no matter what the external, organizational goals are, typically by about the third coaching session, we are addressing *internal* issues, such as limiting beliefs, negative thoughts, lack of courage, fear of failure, and embarrassment and related issues, such as time management, delegation issues, self-control, problem solving, and team building. Coaching addresses how each individual coachee will deal with internal challenges to achieve external results.

In organizational settings, these issues are rarely discussed and purposefully avoided. We don't want to admit our shortcomings. We think we're the only ones who have them. We keep our doubts to ourselves, like some kind of dark secret. The truth is, everyone is a work in progress, if we believe in continuous, personal improvement. With coaching, there is a safe, trusting, confidential relationship in which to reveal our deepest fears and doubts. When a coach is successful with a coachee, it is usually because the coachee has taken risks, stepped out of the comfort zone, broken through resistance, changed beliefs and thoughts, and took bold action. When this happens, coachees are energized and highly motivated to continue on their change journeys.

Skillfully coaching through resistance is gratifying for a coach. We want to help people change. It's why we want to coach others. However, it is no easy task for a coachee to push through obstacles, internal or external. Change is about going in a new direction, taking bold steps, doing what you thought was impossible. It's powerful. And for some, it can be scary or sad. Often, change is accompanied by letting go of what is not working, letting go of ways of behaving and long-held beliefs. Be aware that some coachees will experience fear and sadness as they embrace new ways of being. As a coach, you want to be aware of that and provide inspiration and possible comfort for them.

To be successful in coaching, a coach requires an understanding of what's going on inside the coachee's head. Together they explore limiting patterns of thinking, age-old beliefs, and bring them to the surface. Together they look for the breakthrough.

There can be dozens of reasons why people resist change. Here are some:

- They don't see a need to change.
- Their needs are being met.
- They're invested in what they have now.
- They don't know how to change.
- They don't like the in-between stage.
- The change comes from an external source and they haven't embraced it.

In the following pages are concepts and strategies that address inner blocks coaches will discover hidden within their coachees. They are like keys that will help coaches unlock the resistance code.

LIMITING BELIEFS

We have all adopted a set of beliefs that have been told to us by teachers, parents, or ourselves. Often, we hold onto beliefs that are not true for us, that hold us back from achieving the greatness within each of us. Think of limiting beliefs as the internal, mental chatter that goes on within your mind in silence and is rarely spoken. They are usually negative, self-imposed, old "tapes" from the past, thoughts you adopted at some time in your life that now curb your personal and professional growth. They might be thoughts about how you view others or what you think is possible for you to accomplish. These may have become your reality and part of your identity.

> *You can have anything you want if you are willing to give up the belief that you can't have it.*
>
> —William Purkey
> (*www.cygnoir net/quill/2003/11/06/*)

What we accomplish is directly related to what we think is possible. It's likely everyone has some limiting beliefs, yet we don't often discuss them. Limiting beliefs keep us trapped in the past and trapped in our own heads. Here follow some sample limiting beliefs:

- I have nothing really important to say.
- I'll never lose those last 10 pounds.
- I'm not a good writer.
- I'm shy.
- I'm not creative.
- I don't have what it takes.
- I can't sing.
- I'm not smart enough.
- I'm not lovable.
- I don't deserve that.
- I won't pass that math test.
- The budget won't pass. Why even try?
- I'm not good at networking.
- I'm uncomfortable speaking up.
- I'm not good with numbers.
- My staff won't support that project.

Limiting beliefs are like an inner critic, an inner voice that puts limits on what we think. Imagine what would happen if they weren't there. Imagine what would happen if those limiting beliefs were removed or better yet, transformed into positive thoughts. What would it be like for a coachee to think . . .

- I have a lot to contribute to this project (group, work, world).
- I can lose those last 10 pounds.
- I am becoming a better writer.
- I can create all the resources I need.
- I have good ideas.
- I am smart.
- I am lovable.
- I can do that.
- I can do anything.
- The budget will pass with flying colors.

> *Whether you think you can or think you can't, you are right.*
>
> —Henry Ford

A masterful coach helps a coachee eradicate limiting beliefs by reframing them, by turning negative thoughts into powerful, positive ones. When coachees see how limiting beliefs have actually restricted them in their work or personal lives, how they've caused stagnation, frustration, judgment and negative consequences, they soar. Transforming beliefs is central to coaching and the heart of change. Coaches are always listening deeply to every spoken word, and they challenge coachees when they hear a limiting belief. By helping a coachee identify and change limiting beliefs, a coach helps the coachee change from the inside out. (See Resource E: Examining Limiting Beliefs.)

COACHING TIPS:

- ❖ Ask participants to share their limiting beliefs. (They are likely to be relieved to find that other people have the same ones.)
- ❖ Have participants brainstorm limiting beliefs that they have heard from their colleagues.
- ❖ Have participants write a "turnaround statement." (For example, from "I'm not a good speaker" to "I am becoming a better speaker every day.")

Everyone has self-doubts at some point in their lives. What happens in organizations is that we rarely discuss them or don't have a trusted relationship with someone with whom we can discuss them. They're like our dark secrets we don't want anyone to know about. My coachees have shared many self-doubts: "I sound immature," "I don't sound professional," "I'm too old to get another job." People get stuck when they avoid examining those beliefs that keep them trapped. When they start to look closely at them, they see how their beliefs are holding them prisoner, and a whole new outlook begins to surface. New thoughts + new beliefs = new possibilities.

ASSUMPTIONS

How often have you noticed that the moment someone speaks, you instantly form an impression or an opinion? It's common to react that way. Assumptions are another personal and organizational growth killer. Assumptions are another form of negative inner thinking that keeps coachees and entire organizations stuck. We form assumptions when we've had certain experiences in the past and believe the results of similar experiences will be the same in the future. We think we already know the outcome and *act accordingly*. We then dwell in the land of negativity with such certainty that the result is already known, so why bother?

Unspoken assumptions can run rampant in organizations and squash any efforts to progress unless they are out in the open. Assumptions can destroy the future by placing limits on the innovative thinking necessary for transforming an organization. They can become the silent underlying threads of thought that, collectively, create a stagnant culture.

I can think of countless times when a staff member would resist joining a school improvement committee (*"We never get anything accomplished."*), or not apply for that new job (*"I won't get that one."*), or neglect an important conversation (*"I know what they'll say about that program."*). What happens is we make no effort, we stay frozen. When a new change initiative is attempted, we often don't try the new because we believe we can predict the result based on old experiences.

If we want to achieve new results in schools, we must take a deeper look at the assumptions people are holding onto. If you're in a building with a veteran staff, it is highly possible that people are holding onto memories, past history and personal issues that hold them back.

If a coachee's actions are the "same old, same old," naturally the result is likely to be the same. A coach helps them see that a new result is *sure* to happen with a different action or a fresh attitude.

For Example

I was enrolled in a beginner class at a professional acting school. We were each assigned a partner and asked to rehearse and perform a skit. I felt intimidated by my talented fellow-student and had a number of limiting beliefs wreaking havoc (*"I can't remember my lines," "I have no talent," "I sound like a jerk."*). I struggled with these nagging self-doubts for weeks. During a vacation, we were expected to rehearse twice before our next class and perform a short skit the following week. I called my partner—twice to schedule our rehearsals—and didn't receive a return call. I was convinced it was all about *me*. I invented assumptions—she knew I was a horrible actress, she had no desire to work with me, and she probably wanted a different partner. She didn't return my call because, *I assumed*, she hated the idea of working with me. She knew (so I thought) I had no talent whatsoever. I lost sleep and felt as though I must be a total waste as an acting partner. When class resumed, I *acted on* my assumption, intentionally arriving late, feeling upset and uncomfortable, and announcing to the teacher "I need a new partner." My partner whipped around and gave me a very surprised stare. After class, she simply said, "I didn't get two messages. I got one, was busy, and just thought we'd schedule a time when we saw each other." Imagine how I felt! It wasn't about me at all! If I had not let my limiting beliefs and assumptions determine what actions I took, the result would have been far more positive.

COACHING TIPS:

❖ Ask participants to think of a time they or a colleague acted on an assumption that turned out to be false. How might the outcome have been different if the assumption had not ruled the situation?

❖ Ask participants to role-play an experience they've had, but this time, change the outcome by eliminating the assumptions. What is the result now? How is it different?

FEAR

Few people on the planet are completely fearless. Most people harbor some level of fear about something. For some, it's speaking in public, for others it's a fear of failure or taking risks. Often, it's a fear of success. People can frequently give themselves fear-based messages that cause high levels of resistance.

> *Courage is not the absence of fear, but rather the judgment that something else is more important than fear.*
>
> —Ambrose Redmoon and Rich Fettke (2002)

Fear is different from limiting beliefs in that it is more intense and paralyzing. Imagine what would happen if suddenly your fears were dissipated, if you were free to be as big and bold in this world as you wish. When coachees step past their fear, they experience success and freedom. They experience confidence in manifesting anything they desire.

To surpass a fear usually requires the support of someone you trust and who totally understands you. The coaching relationship provides that safe space. An intuitive coach knows that action is always the result of coaching, and when dealing with deep fears, small actions are better than no action. Taking a small step can be frightening. With an empathetic coach, fears can be explored and a commitment made to moving forward.

In my experiences coaching school leaders, I've encountered people with fears of the following:

- Confrontation
- Speaking up
- Rejection
- Being successful
- Losing the known self
- Embarrassment
- Failure
- Networking
- Losing control
- Losing a job
- Disappointing others
- Disappointing oneself

Fear can be immobilizing. You know when it arises. You can feel it physically. It is at that moment, when the tendency is to back off, that you *must* go forward. It is in that moment that change happens. You take the step, move past the fear, ever so slightly, and you feel exhilaration! You discover it was not nearly as hard as you imagined. In fact, it probably wasn't hard at all.

> *Fear is an invisible barbed-wire fence.*
>
> —Anonymous

In my experience coaching and being coached, I have learned that it is *when you get out of your own comfort zone* and into what I call the *discomfort zone* that lasting, permanent change occurs.

For me, the moment came when I attempted the Quantum Leap activity during the filming of the *Life Makeover Project*. I like adventure but noticed that in my favorite activities, my feet were always on the ground. Hiking, bike riding, dancing, and skiing always appealed to me. Bungee jumping, parasailing, rock climbing, scuba diving . . . never. Safe adventures were my style—until I faced Quantum Leap, a 30-foot-high telephone pole adventure course activity with my coach, Cheryl Richardson, and six others. The goal was to climb to the top and stand, hands free, on a 10-inch disc. Terrified, I began my ascent. "One step at a time," is what I told myself. "Others can do it, why not me?" I had my coach and other supportive friends cheering me on. All was well until I got close to the top. Telephone poles are very wobbly at the top. There was nothing to hold on to. I was hunched over, paralyzed with fear, for what seemed like hours. I was 30 feet in the air and determined to do this seemingly impossible act. I didn't. I fell—and felt like a huge failure. Thirty minutes later, I made a second attempt, this time more determined than before. This time, I confess, I practiced first on a two-foot-high practice pole. Guess what: It was easy, just like climbing stairs. Still trembling from my fall, I began the climb again. As I approached the top, I focused, not on the difficulty of the task but on the *ease* of it, the incredibly accomplished feeling I would have standing on top of the pole, feeling free, seeing the world from a new perspective. There is nothing like the feeling of success that stems from accomplishing a scary, huge, challenging goal. I fear nothing now and know I could never return to living small-minded. I know that breaking out of your comfort zone is a *must* if you wish to create lasting change that occurs from the inside out.

In *Learning to Fly*, Sam Keen (1999), former editor of *Psychology Today*, talks about letting go of fear *in the moment*. At age 62, he became a flying trapeze artist. Although he sought this adventure and challenge, he acknowledges the accompanying fear that comes with such a feat. Standing on a tightrope high above the ground isn't the moment to dwell on what could happen. He suggests dealing with the fear *as you learn* the new task. But when you're *doing it,* you can't possibly dwell on it and have a successful outcome. You have to let go of the fear and just enjoy the experience of flying.

> When I neither force myself to be fearless nor run away from the danger, an area of freedom opens up within which I discover new options. I cease to be a victim of my fear and I break the hypnotic cycle of dread, the vicious feedback loop; the self-fulfilling prophecy of failure that shrinks my world. (Keen, 1999, p. 44)

That's great advice. Educator-coaches can support coachees *through* fear by encouraging them to process the fear during their coaching sessions. When they're taking action and leave the fear behind, they are free of the angst that holds them back. Fear can be a great catalyst for attaining powerful change.

Success Story

Corey was a central office administrator seeking a new position in another district. After many years in her current district, she realized that her fear of networking would get in the way of obtaining a position. She knew networking was a key element for her, and it was a huge stretch for her to take on the challenge of improving in that area. She literally felt paralyzed by the idea of approaching a stranger. We met at a national conference, where I was conducting coaching sessions. What a perfect place to begin.

After only one coaching session, she had a clear goal (to increase her comfort approaching strangers) and an action plan. She agreed to introduce herself to five new people in the next 24 hours. The thought terrified her, yet she was willing to get out of her comfort zone and take steps toward her goal. She successfully completed her actions, became acutely aware of how she felt as well as of her limiting thoughts and fears and began to shift them to a healthier belief.

Change happens in small daily actions.

JUDGMENTS

Most of us hold on to the natural tendency to maintain the status quo and stay in our routines. We feel a stronger pull toward the known than a push toward the unknown. Judging others or judging ideas keeps us in the present. It keeps us from being curious, and we remain opinionated and closed. Letting go of judgment is like opening a huge door for new opportunities, creative possibilities and a whole new array of options to enter.

Think how often and how quickly we judge others and new ideas. In an instant, we've formed an opinion and closed the door. We've taken a stand, often without consideration, and blocked a new possibility or another way of observing something. Coaches suspend judgment with their coachees, and in doing so, open up honest, trusting collaborations. Often what holds coachees back from growth is their anticipation of the opinions of others, of situations, or of programs and projects. When there's judgment, there's usually an emotional response going on; that is a ripe opportunity to explore it farther with a coachee.

Suspending judgment is no simple task. I find when I am training coaches, it's a huge challenge for them to let go of opinions. As they improve their ability to release their own viewpoints when coaching, they are more able to help coachees free themselves of disapproving opinions that stifle their growth.

INTERPRETATIONS

Another trouble spot that prevents change from occurring is in how we interpret situations and the world around us. Whenever we see or hear something, we create meaning for it by assigning a way of seeing it, and then we hold onto our view of it for dear life. Two people rarely see the same situation in the same way.

For one person, New York City is intense and crowded; to another, it's energetic and exciting. It's the same city, yet how they see it and interpret the experience of being there is completely different. We respond according to our interpretations.

For Example

I worked with someone who'd had her first shot at a central office position. She'd brought to the interview some nervousness and more than a little self-doubt. She was asked numerous, difficult questions. She *interpreted* those questions as doubting on the part of the interviewers. She was sure they were skeptical about her. She responded with timidity. Instead, she could have interpreted those questions as *interest,* and her responses would have been vastly different. She had numerous limiting beliefs and fears and let her *interpretation* of the interview distract her from being her best self.

In coaching, we look at how coachees interpret issues they're facing. We probe and explore and uncover if and how those perceptions may help or hinder them. Interpretation is related to observation. We view a situation filtered by our perspectives, opinions and judgments.

EXTERNAL OBSTACLES

Obstacles are those external things that *appear* to be in the way of reaching a goal. When coachees reveal obstacles, they are likely to believe there's no way around them, or they simply can't see a way to get past them. Often, coachees adopt a blaming role and give up. Coachees are reminded by their coaches that they have choices, every day, in every interaction, in how they think and what they do. Obstacles are to be anticipated and expected. Obstacles will always come up, and a wise coach will help a coachee anticipate them and develop strategies to deal with them. When coachees talk about an obstacle, a coach needs to guide them to explore their choices. Obstacles are not dead ends; they are openings for new actions.

Educators face many external obstacles. Among them may be the following:

- New federal regulations
- Decreased funding
- New board members
- High absenteeism
- Leadership turnover
- Lack of time
- Lack of professional development opportunities
- Lack of parental involvement
- High level of poverty in the community

During coaching, a coach will help a coachee brainstorm various ways to bypass the obstacles or reframe how the obstacle may, in fact, be an opportunity. Obstacles present opportunities for learning. If we plan and prepare for them, we can successfully overcome them.

> When flowing water meets with obstacles on its path, a blockage in its journey, it pauses. It increases in volume and strength, filling up in front of the obstacle and eventually spilling past it.
>
> —Anonymous

What does it take to surpass external obstacles? After all, they seem to be things out of our control. Sometimes a new state regulation is approaching, a grant wasn't renewed, a new board member is coming on board, and we feel like just giving up. We see the situation as impossible and blame the government, the president, the funder—anyone. Focusing on the external problem keeps us from creatively developing solutions to deal with it. But committing to the goal, making sure it's a high priority goal, and developing a team of support will help us or the organization negotiate those ever-present obstacles and achieve the goal we desire.

In my coaching workshops, we practice this process with a portable obstacle course. Blindfolded, we negotiate through a field of fears, self-doubts, lack of time, and lack of resources and other supports. We experience and learn what is needed to overcome external obstacles.

Keys to overcome obstacles:

- Be fiercely passionate about your goal.
- Anticipate obstacles; there will always be some.
- Develop strategies to overcome them during the planning phase.
- Build a support system; nothing big happens in isolation.
- Allow others to help you; be open to receiving assistance.

CHANGING INDIVIDUALS, CHANGING SYSTEMS

There have been scores of studies done about the challenge of change. Yet organizations have historically struggled with and been ineffective at creating lasting results, which is frustrating for the leadership and very costly to the organization. So what do we do? We can forever look at the hard issues: declining budgets, new federal and state regulations, challenging new standards and graduation requirements, for example. It's easy to adopt an attitude of "It's too much," or "We don't have enough resources."

As educators look at creating systems that support and achieve extraordinary results, we must look at the softer, people issues. We must look at the people within the organization and their attitudes toward change. We must look deeply at the silent system of resistance that can sabotage change efforts, if not addressed. How do individuals, teams, and building staff interact with each other? Are they supporting or resisting change? What strategies are leaders incorporating to confront and address them?

> Change doesn't happen from a leader announcing the plan. Change happens from deep inside a system, when a few people notice something they will no longer tolerate, or respond to a dream of what's possible. We don't have to start with power, only with passion.
>
> —Margaret Wheatley (2002)

Many factors affect large-scale change efforts in complex organizations, such as school systems. You can have a well-designed improvement plan created by a crackerjack planning team that will incorporate the best-researched programs known to improve schools. You can have the resources, the funding and the support of the board of education backing the plan. However, without the support of every *individual* to implement the plan, achieving very high levels of success will be a daydream. Individuals must support the changes as evidenced by their *actions on a daily basis*. Attitudes, habits, confusion, perceptions,

> *It doesn't take long for distrust, poor communication, resistance, cynicism, and hidden agendas to take root. Those become real obstacles to producing change and improved performance.*
>
> —Juechter, Fisher, and Alford (1998)

judgments, and a focus on the past are all factors that can rapidly thwart a change effort. Without attention paid to the minds and hearts of the people involved, intended change will likely be a scattered attempt and fail to achieve lasting results.

The coaching process addresses both minds and hearts. Coaches support individuals to make the needed shifts in attitude to clarify confusion, shift the focus to the future and align their personal attributes and strengths with the intended change. A coaching approach to changing people or accomplishing change for an organization is an individualized one. The coach considers where the coachee is *now* and moves forward. Together they traverse the bumpy road to successful change.

In the following pages are several practical models or strategies for dealing with the people side of change. I believe we need all the help we can get to obtain successful change; therefore, several are included, allowing readers to select any that resonate with them.

ABANDONING THE COMFORT ZONE

Most people have had personal experience confronting change. Whether it was a chosen change or came from an external source, you had a chance to *feel* the change. You may have felt anxiety or stress, nervousness or excitement. You may have felt out on a limb, alone or vulnerable.

I believe lasting change occurs when you take a step *out* of your comfort zone. Have you ever heard the saying, "Feel the fear and do it anyway?" In my experience, personally and as a coaching professional, I believe it is true. All of the coachees I have worked with have experienced varying levels of discomfort when trying on a new behavior. It's important for new coaches to be aware of this and assist coachees in *staying with it.*

I've identified three zones that I see people going through during a change process: the *comfort zone*, the *discomfort zone* and the *anything's possible zone* (see Figure 6.1). Coaches can help individuals take the first step out of their comfort zones into the discomfort zone and maintain progress until they reach the "anything's possible" zone.

The Comfort Zone

There's comfort in the known—the comfortable, numb, existing state. People know what to expect. They know their job, their responsibilities,

Figure 6.1   Discomfort Zone

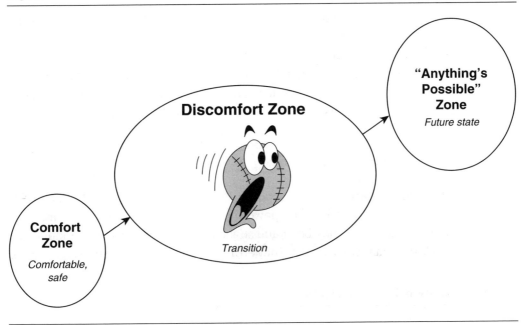

their skill level, and so on. They like being in the comfort zone. It feels normal.

In this zone, it is common to feel safe; things are predictable and status quo. Life hums along. Even if something isn't working or there is a high level of stress, it is less stressful than confronting or making a change.

Coaches encourage people out of the comfort zone because they know that is the path to successful change.

The Discomfort Zone

This is the transition space where people often get stuck. They may stagnate, move slowly, move backwards or not move at all. Resistance, doubt, and fear emerge. In this state, it is common to feel anxious, uncertain, lonely, doubtful, excited, or elated. Even high levels of happiness, joy, and accomplishment can cause discomfort.

> *Consider your discomfort and welcome it as an ache necessary for you to become more deeply attuned.*
>
> —Jacqueline Winspear (2005, p. 61)

Coaches keep people moving through the discomfort zone, day by day, step by step, obstacle by obstacle. They provide ongoing support so coachees don't fall back into the comfort zone.

The "Anything's Possible" Zone

This is the place where success is felt down to the bones. Accomplishments are recognized and celebrated. Challenging goals have been met, and people feel an enormous sense of achievement.

In this zone, it is common to feel optimistic, energized, the sky's the limit.

Coaches honor the coachees for arriving at their goal. They garner energy and enthusiasm as they set new, bigger, broader goals.

THE CYCLE OF CHANGE

The Cycle of Change was developed by Bruce Schneider (2001), PhD, founder of Institute for Professional Empowerment Coaching. He identified four stages of change a person may be in and suggested different ways for working with people depending on the stage they are currently dealing with (see Figure 6.2):

Figure 6.2   Cycle of Change

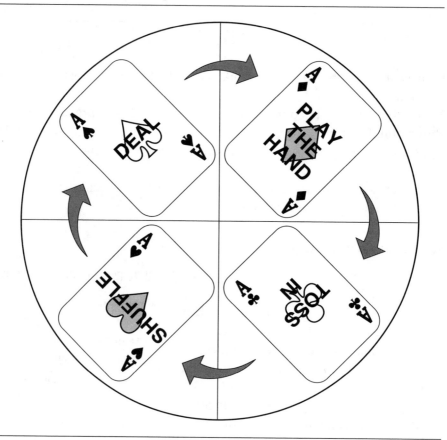

Source: Cycle of Change Contest of Bruce D. Schneider and IPEC Coaching.

The Shuffle Phase

The Shuffle phase is a period of detachment from what wasn't working. It's a time-out phase during which a person will reflect on a pending change, undertake some research and seek out a new way. In this stage, the person is in mourning and letting go of the past, creating closure on the old way of being or doing.

> The significant problems we face cannot be solved at the same level of thinking we were at when we created them.
>
> —Albert Einstein

It's an in-between place, a transition stage where people often feel both sadness and a low level of excitement as they anticipate the new. There's both loss and hope, especially toward the end of the cycle. Common feelings in this stage are fear of the unknown, emotional ups and downs, and anticipation about the future. At the end of the cycle emerges a plan, with new purpose, renewed energy and strength.

During this stage, the coach and coachee work together and devise plans for exploring and researching new possibilities, taking small to moderate levels of action.

For Example

Robert was a new assistant superintendent in a new district. He missed his old staff, people he worked with for many years. He missed seeing students on a daily basis. He was truly mourning what he lost. He had one foot in the past, another in the present. But he felt neither here nor there. Little by little, he began to create new relationships. He devised a plan to be in the presence of students on a more frequent basis and felt a renewed sense of excitement about the changes he hoped to make in the new district.

The Deal Phase

In this phase, the coachees are actively doing; they have a direction and are implementing an action plan. There's a high level of confidence, they're eager to explore and stretch themselves to new heights. They may take things one step at a time in the beginning of this stage and find themselves more committed as they progress.

> The death of a caterpillar is the birth of a butterfly.
>
> —Anonymous

It's easy and fun to coach someone in this phase. They're feeling excited, and energy is high. Feelings of failure or success or limiting beliefs might slip in during this phase as they surge forward.

For Example

After deliberating between two different positions and finally choosing one, Casey was charged. She used every available minute to learn about her new organization. She spent one day a week at her new district, even before beginning. She wanted to absorb everything. She fit everything into her day that had long been a struggle: walking, gardening, having lunch with colleagues. Her energy level was flying, and coaching her was a breeze. She also began to wonder how she'd learn enough, quickly enough, to dispel the self-doubt that lingered in her mind.

The Play-the-Hand Phase

This is a great time during a change phase. We're energized by the changes we've made and are seeing the fruit of our labors. We feel successful and have achieved a state of well being. We're doing it! It's happening! Goals and dreams are becoming reality. At times, we find setbacks, disappointments and new challenges we may not have anticipated. The excitement may lessen later on in this phase; it starts to feel like work.

You may feel overwhelmed and wonder, "Now what?" "How can I manage it all?" There's a mixture of feelings ranging from fear of failure to fulfillment. A coach knows and anticipates this stage. It's where there *could* be a decrease in progress. It *could* be easy to slip backwards, without the support of the coach. But the coach is right there by your side, holding you up, keeping you going, cheering you on. Together you look at what is working and correct what isn't. The coach reminds you that success *is* happening, it's in progress, and it is normal to feel uncertain in this phase.

For Example

Janice was experiencing some interpersonal struggles with her supervisor in the district office. She wanted to improve the relationship from one that felt strained to a collaborative and friendly one. She was in her first year, still felt like an outsider and made many assumptions about the relationship. She began a proactive plan for communicating and confronting her supervisor. Coming face to face with difficult conversations was draining. Although she felt excited at the thought of a solid, positive, professional relationship, she felt very shaky as she approached uncomfortable conversations. In our coaching sessions, we brainstormed various ways she could approach her next discussion. We role-played each one and they boosted her confidence in her ability to confront the supervisor.

The Toss-In Stage

People in this stage tend to feel victimized and stagnant. They're ready to throw in the towel. They can no longer remain where they are. Change is imminent. The end is near.

A coachee may be thinking "I can't deal with this any more" or "it's time to move on." They feel fearful of the unknown, depressed, or abandoned. Their energy level is low and they may withdraw. A wide range of emotions can surface, depending whether or not the pending change is chosen or has come from an external source.

Coaches know the signs, and know the coachees' thoughts and feelings are normal. They're in a grief stage, and taking small, baby steps is preferable. It is likely that coaching sessions will include much venting as the coachees absorb reality. Deep levels of listening and empathy are important on the part of the coach.

For Example

Eleanor, a subject area director, was in her last year before receiving tenure and had a new assistant superintendent. She was aware of the supervisor's dislike for the work Eleanor was doing. She experienced a very high level of stress for many months. She knew the end was coming. Her position would be eliminated, and she was extremely upset and angry. She strongly disagreed about the quality of her work. She felt she was being treated poorly and her elimination was not justified. In our coaching, she admitted to a probable mismatch between her tendency to be a risk-taking maverick and the conservative district she was in. I listened empathetically to her saga as we explored the deep causes that had led to this point. Although she was personally distressed and was grieving the loss, we very slowly began taking steps toward a better match for her and a new future.

When coaching, be aware of these stages and determine which one a coachee may be in. Discovering where the coachees are along their change pathways helps the coach know what they need in moving forward. Using the Cycle of Change helps the coach understand what the coachee is experiencing and design successful coaching experiences.

In spite of warnings, nothing much happens until the status quo becomes more painful than change.

—L. J. Peters (http://legendinc.com)

THREE STAGES OF TRANSITION

In his well-known book *Managing Transitions*, William Bridges (1991) talks about transition as a specific state people go through during any change. Transitions are different from changes and are often neglected in change management processes. According to Bridges, any change has three distinct phases: the ending, the neutral transition phase, and a new beginning.

Ending

Every new beginning is accompanied by a letting go of the old. Whatever used to be will become a thing of the past. There is loss that people experience and different people react differently, in their own time. There is a necessary period of grief in which people may feel varying levels of anger, sadness, anxiety, disorientation, and depression.

Neutral

The neutral zone is the in-between place. You're not here any more or there just yet. As Bridges (1991) says, "People are caught between the demands of conflicting systems and wind up like immobilized Hamlets trying to decide whether 'to be or not to be'." People may feel tense, frustrated and lack motivation. For effective change to occur, it's important to manage the neutral zone.

New Beginning

Beginnings can bring to the surface many feelings, from excitement to relief to fear. The beginning of the new change is a reality check. The old, known way is really over. It is no longer a fantasy or a threat.

Coaches help organizations maintain momentum, accept and manage the transition phase, and support people through transition, to arrive successfully and ready for the new beginning.

THE FOUR LAWS OF CHANGE

The Four Laws of Change (Stevenson, 2005) is another simple model passed down from the Shawnee nation a thousand years ago. The Four Laws of Change is used to enhance the effectiveness of big decisions and aligns well with a coaching approach to change.

Change Comes From Within

Change always comes from within the *individual*, from within the *group*, or within the *organization*. Ideally, the change will be like a pebble thrown into a lake where the change ripples from within all of these configurations.

Permanent Change Requires a Vision

Unless a clear and compelling picture is held of the change that needs to occur, the initial insight, energy or reason for changing can fade into the background, until triggered by the next difficult reminder.

A Great Learning Must Occur

This means that change is accompanied by a personal insight or a group awareness that is shared with the larger community. For an individual, it could be an insight that they are actually creating most of their problems by how they behave toward others. To make it a permanent change, the individual needs to share it with others, who in turn can support them in the change.

For an organization, it could be a shared awareness that each person within it is responsible for how the organization functions. What grounds the change is that the insight or shared awareness becomes the *responsibility of the group to sustain the changes*.

A Healing Forest Must Be Present

For any change to be permanent, it must have the support of the larger community. For an individual, it could mean that the insight or vision is shared with family and friends. For an organization, it could be that the change is shared with people inside and outside the group who can support the changes.

An example of these concepts can be seen in the 2002 movie *Antwone Fisher*. An angry soldier is struggling to break from his difficult past and change his belligerent behavior. Eventually, he comes to see how it is *he* who must change. There's a great moment of awareness when he realizes that he must change or his life will be ruined. He stands frozen in his psychiatrist's office and realizes he doesn't

> A basic underlying resistance to any change process is the analytical, critical, adversarial system of thinking we presently use.
>
> —Edward de Bono
> (www.debonogroup.com)

know *how* to change. "I don't know what to do. I don't know what to do," is all he can say. He is clueless how to *be* any way other than the one way he knows. He knows he must step out of his comfort zone into discomfort to arrive at a new state. He progresses through the various stages of change noted in the Cycle of Change, from shuffling around, knowing he must but not yet ready, to recognizing he can no longer conduct his life with so much rage, to dealing with it, being ready to change.

Looking at his situation through the Four Laws of Change, he is finally prepared to do the inner work and confronts himself instead of blaming others. He holds a vision for his future that propels him forward. He wants to be a better person. He travels to his childhood home and learns about his mother who discarded him and finds a new, supportive loving family he never knew he had. He found his healing forest in his new family and psychiatrist. He had all the elements to create lasting change and eventually became able to move forward with his life. He navigates the transitions by ending his negative behavior.

The foregoing four models are simple, fresh ways of looking at complex change. Change is a process, not an event. Helping people through the rough stages of change is precisely where and why coaching succeeds where other interventions have not. The coaching process provides a methodology for addressing change by zooming in to those areas where individuals, departments, teams, and entire organizations may be stuck. Educator-coaches can consider one or all of the change models described when working with coachees. Doing so will help them identify where a coachee may be when beginning and during the coaching process.

In the past, change efforts have focused on external strategies—more training, more funding, more staff—to accomplish them. Although leaders may have tried to address the people issues, without an internalized coaching process to directly and confidentially address the soft issuess—the attitudes and beliefs of the *people*—change efforts are likely to be unsuccessful. New programs, new systems and new policies will have limited impact unless the mindsets, attitudes and belief systems are uncovered and aligned with the change.

POSSIBILITY THINKING

In the 1970s, a young director met with a special effects expert in Hollywood. He had an idea for a new movie. He dreamed of creating a science fiction film showing realistic, fast-moving ships zooming through space. It would be a first. The special effects experts told him it couldn't be done . . . it was technologically impossible. They sent him away. The man did not give up. George Lucas founded his own special effects company to make the impossible possible. After two years of trial and error, the movie George saw in his mind was a reality. *Star Wars* was the most technologically innovative movie ever made—and the most profitable. Industrial Light and Magic has provided special effects for 8 of the 10 highest-grossing movies of all time and has won 12 Academy Awards.

It's probable that most of you reading this book grew up in homes with one or more land-based telephones. Then, it would have been incomprehensible to think that someday, everyone would have their own portable telephones. If anyone had suggested that we'd be able to speak to

> There isn't enough darkness in all the world to snuff out the light of one little candle.
>
> —Gautama Buddha

anyone anywhere without wires, what would you have said? Many would have laughed it off or deemed it ludicrous: "No way, can't happen, that's impossible."

There are thousands of other inspiring examples throughout history: explorers who discovered new worlds, scientists who challenged current thinking to create new cures, inventors who believed a new gadget

> It is impossible to begin to learn that which one thinks one already knows.
>
> —Epictetus

or gizmo would help others. It is essential to bring that kind of "yes" thinking to school systems. It's essential to do it, for our children and their future.

What conversations have occurred in school systems that focus on the impossible? In my work with school systems, I have cringed at the count-

less negative thoughts and comments I've heard. How would your school be different if *everyone* were a possibility thinker instead? We have no place for nay-sayers in school systems. Well-trained and skilled coaches in your district will help convert the impossible to the possible. Old, stale

> We are the only creatures on earth who can change our biology by what we think and feel.
>
> —Deepak Chopra

thought patterns cause stagnation in organizations and stifle their transformation. When we're able to transcend the limits of our thinking, fresh ideas emerge. To make them reality, individuals and organizational leaders need passion, determination, perseverance and action. To believe anything is possible, we have to surrender the belief that it's not. That becomes a choice. We can choose to believe in possibility or we can choose to stay inside our boxes.

When old beliefs are gone, there's an open space for new possibilities and new results to pour in. While thinking outside of the box is a first step,

> *The difference between can and cannot are only three letters. Three letters that determine your life's direction.*
>
> —*Remez Sasson*
> *(http://successconsciousness.com)*

acting outside of the box becomes a daring act of courage. Change begins with new thoughts and possibilities; acting on those possibilities is where transformation begins to happen in school systems.

Becoming a Possibility Thinker

If you weren't born or raised with the gift of being a possibility thinker, don't fret. You can change. Here's how:

- Be constantly curious.
- Be open-minded.
- Be interested.
- Be wildly creative.
- Be a contrarian.
- Be a courageous risk taker.
- Believe passionately in your vision and goal.
- Shift the focus from what's not possible to what is possible.
- Dream big and often.
- Ask "why not" instead of "why."

COACHING TIPS:

❖ Encourage coachees to simply notice their negative thoughts throughout the day. Become aware of how many and how often they appear. Jot them down.
❖ For each one, reframe the thought and create a "new possibility" thought.

For example, an old thought would be, "There isn't time for that new program." New thought: "This program is valuable and worth finding the time to implement it."

The concept of possibility thinking can be infectious. Positive energy flows from the possibility thinker to others around them. It spreads, expands, and inspires, and in my opinion, it is *the* reason why coaching has created profound paradigm shifts for individuals and organizations.

Let's go back to my vision: that all the adults working in schools and with children are possibility thinkers. How can this impact school improvement? Imagine the possibilities. Picture your school improvement team at a planning session, and everyone around the table believes that it *is* possible to achieve high levels of learning for *all* students, no matter the past history or current roadblocks. Everyone is brainstorming the short- and long-term strategies utterly convinced that success for all is possible. Everyone is focused on the successful outcome. The planning process and discussion is energized, positive and productive. It's a more creative process generating multiple possibilities.

Or envision faculty meetings in a coaching culture where there's a commonly held belief that anything is possible for the students within the school. You're a principal proposing that teachers increase their knowledge about using classroom data effectively. Rather than hearing groans from your staff, you hear enthusiasm and support. Doubt and skepticism are things of the past. With a room full of possibility thinkers, together you look at *how* versus *if*. The enthused energy of individuals, the group and the organization will create a successful outcome.

VISIONING A NEW FUTURE

Suppose one day you decide to buy a yellow convertible. All of a sudden, you start to notice them on the road. When you see an image of the reality you wish to create in the future, it's like sending out a message requesting it to happen and receiving the resources needed for it to appear.

Most educators are aware of vision statements, already have one and are familiar with the process for creating one. For school systems, it is a message to the community that describes their collective future. A strong, compelling vision should encompass the values and dreams of everyone involved in creating it. A well-developed vision that everyone's excited about creates optimism. Energetically, people are pumped up; they see it as possible. Ideally, they are so enthused they forget their fears or limiting thinking. Having a vision for an organization is essential to keep the dream alive. It stretches, inspires, and motivates. Living the vision is a necessity for accomplishing it.

> *The future never just happened. It was created.*
>
> —Will and Ariel Durant

Holding a detailed image of the future creates a picture in our minds that we can see and relate to. The human mind thinks in pictures. It doesn't know if the picture in the mind is real or a dream, a wish or a hope. In our conscious minds, the left side of the brain, we think about the future and determine what concrete steps it may take to achieve it. It's in the conscious mind that we can easily talk ourselves out of our goals. "It's too expensive, it's impossible, there's no time," are messages the conscious

> To succeed, we must have a desire so strong that it permeates our subconscious minds.
>
> —David Batchelor (n.d.)

mind can create as we consider the new. It stops the progress and can stop the project.

However, it's in our subconscious minds, involving the right side of the brain, where dreams and the ability to examine new possibilities on another level reside. Visioning is a powerful process because it's where we conduct possibility thinking. The right brain processes emotions. When we want to make a change, we *feel* a driving force about the change. Therefore, we want to maintain the visual image to keep us emotionally connected to the outcome.

So much is now known about the brain and how it functions. It's been discovered that we've been gathering images since we were born, making interpretations about them and storing them in the subconscious. The trick is that it's stored as reality, *whether it is or not.* Let's say you're considering a school improvement initiative. The school improvement team wants to implement collegial circles as a model of staff development. You don't think it's possible. You can't imagine finding the time or that it's worth your time. Your brain stores the image of it *not working, as if it happened and is real.* That's pretty powerful.

> Vision without action is a daydream. Action without vision is a nightmare.
>
> —Japanese proverb

On the other hand, using visioning techniques, you can imagine the new initiative as successful. Instead, you see teachers as collaborative and having sophisticated professional dialogue on a daily basis. The culture of the building has improved and teachers are making changes in their teaching practice based on their new learning. Seeing something as possible stamps an imprint on the brain. When we see it as possible, we tend to create it.

For Example

The great tightrope aerialist Karl Wallenda fell to his death in 1978 traversing a 75-foot high wire in San Juan, Puerto Rico. His wife, discussing her husband's fateful walk, recalled that, "All Karl thought about for three straight months prior to it was falling. It was the first time he'd ever thought about that, and it seemed to me that he put all his energies into not falling rather than walking the tightrope." Mrs. Wallenda added that her husband even went so far as to personally supervise the installation of the tightrope, making sure that the guy wires were secure, "something he had never even thought of doing before" (as quoted in Bennis, 1985).

COACHING TIPS:

❖ Focus only on what you want to create versus what you don't want.
❖ Use pictures and images of the future vision.
❖ Make the future picture very specific.
❖ Share the vision with others.

Visioning techniques are commonly used to achieve peak performance in the training of athletes. Let's look more deeply at the essential five components of mental training mentioned in Chapter 1, developed by Bobby McGee (2001). I met Bobby several times while training to run a 10K. He trains some of the best athletes in the country as well as the Navy Seals. He certainly addresses the physical realm in his training: laying out a schedule of physical tasks, providing feedback on stance—how a runner might lean more forward to gain a few seconds—and many other useful tips. However, when physical directions don't result in accomplishing the goal, the root cause is mental. Notice in the discussion to follow that the essential five address *only* the mental realm and are the major differentiators between accomplishing a goal and surpassing it: winning, achieving victory and extraordinary goals and peak performance. Isn't that what we also want from our school's leaders?

FIVE ESSENTIAL COMPONENTS OF ACHIEVING PEAK PERFORMANCE

- **Strategy**: Use positive affirmations based on realistic but high standards, written down, and repeated often and out loud. This is one of the more successful techniques used by winning athletes rivaled only by visualization as the most effective tool to access potential.

How can this thinking apply to education? A negative statement, such as "Oh no, this team meeting is going to be a tough one," can be reprogrammed to elicit a key coping strategy, set in motion by a well-rehearsed instruction you can say to yourself: "I am organized and prepared to deal with the challenges of today's meeting." Same situation, different self-talk, better result.

- **Focus**: Elite endurance athletes focus inward. They do not attempt to take their minds off their running or the race by thinking of something else. What actually happens is that by focusing on *not doing something, you are in fact accessing the very thing you are trying to avoid.* Tell the mind what *to* do, not what not to do. By not being in the present, you dwell on things you have no control over—the past or the future. By getting into the present, you can work on so many things.

How can this thinking apply to education? When your school system is faced with an enormous challenge that appears overwhelming, instead of fretting over the difficulty of the task, stay focused on the present, today, the very moment you are in. Avoid thinking about how difficult or seemingly impossible the task is. Give your all in the present. Instead of worrying about what will happen if your school doesn't achieve the desired state test scores, for example, focus on each day's tasks toward them.

- **Anxiety and relaxation**: Most elite sportsmen and women have a specific pre-event relaxation routine, which they repeat exactly before each competition. There is an optimum level of anxiety and relaxation for each of us; find yours and help your coachees to do the same. Talk to people who have a calming influence on you. Keep your mind in the present, and stay task oriented. Keep your mind on what you are doing rather than projecting to what might or might not happen. Stick to a formal, well-rehearsed warm-up routine. Reinterpret your feelings of anxiety as feelings of excitement.

How can this thinking apply to education? Anticipate the situations when you may feel especially stressed or anxious. Develop a set of strategies to create a sense of calm. Whether you are a school leader facing a difficult conversation or an instructional coach feeling upset about an interaction with a particular teacher, *prior* to confronting an anxiety-producing scenario, take a few minutes to de-stress.

- **Visualization:** Create your own movie with yourself as the hero. The more realistically you create the picture, the more accurate the outcome. Visualization is self-fulfilling. Create a clear picture of yourself as successful. This is the single most successful mental training drill you can do. All it involves is going to the movies in your mind's eye, picturing how you successfully compete in and succeed in an upcoming event. The following guidelines, which use the metaphor of running a race, will help you achieve successful visualization:

❖ Always imagine a positive, yet realistic outcome; in other words, aim high but within reason. Never fail in the movie you have created. Develop strategies for when you come unstuck or make a mistake but not during visualization. Stop the film and develop a strategy for when this *might* happen to you. Then commit to executing the strategy should things go wrong. After this, return to running the movie of visualizing the perfect race.

❖ Use *all* of your senses, not only vision. Feel the sensations of rubber meeting road, the smells (sunscreen) and tastes (salt water) and even hear (race announcer) all the race-associated sounds.

❖ Visualize your race as often as possible, completing sections of it at a time, if need be; a two-hour visualization session for a standard triathlon might prove prohibitive.

❖ Visualize at race pace, and physically time some of your visualization exercises. Imagine you're running the 7th kilometer in the 10-kilometer leg in vivid detail, and time the process. A perfect movie segment will bring you to the 8-kilometer marker in your target time.

❖ Be sure to visualize from your own perspective: See this all happening as if you are actually racing. This is more effective than looking down on yourself competing.

❖ Enjoy and believe in visualization. This greatly increases the chances of success and is a maxim that applies to all facets of life. We mastered visualization as kids, so get back there again.

How can this thinking apply to education? There is so much untapped power and potential for educators in the same visualization techniques athletes use to win gold medals. Think of the daily challenges you face. Think of just one, and try the techniques just described. Suppose you have a school board meeting tonight and you already know that several angry parents will be there to confront a specific issue. You dread the meeting. Using the foregoing techniques, you can prepare yourself by focusing on a successful outcome. See yourself leaving the meeting feeling confident, feeling successful in your ability to communicate key points. Imagine the conversation and rehearse it beforehand. By doing so, you set yourself up for success.

- **Dealing with discomfort**: The secret of dealing with discomfort is to *reinterpret what it means.* The discomfort of effort is an indication of performance. The more you can take on, the better you perform. The key to success lies in progressively taking on more and more discomfort, by continually reassessing what you are prepared to tolerate, until the end of the race coincides with the peak of sensation. By following this approach, you are assured of feeling satisfied that you gave your very best in each moment. A good interpretation is to consider that your discomfort as you race hard is the clearest indication that you are performing at a high level. Reinterpret uncomfortable situations as something to enjoy, something that is bringing fulfillment.

How can this thinking apply to education? These comments correspond well with the earlier concept of the discomfort zone. When we are there, we know we are at another level. Instead of feeling stressed by the discomfort of trying something new or going for a yet untried goal, recognize that you are out of your comfort zone, and it is a positive sign. Discomfort is a symptom of personal and professional growth. If we're not uncomfortable, we're not growing and changing. Acknowledge that discomfort as positive; without it, we are likely stagnating or not making changes large enough to make a big difference. Support people during their time in the discomfort zone, inspire them, cheer them on to victory.

Finally, put all 5 points together. Having the ability to create and utilize a powerful mental strategy will heighten your racing experience and turn you into a competitor who fully accesses his/her potential and training. Before races I discuss this strategy in detail with each of my athletes. I have known and worked with some of the world's greatest endurance athletes, and what sets them apart from the rest is not so much their physical attributes, but their utter refusal to quit, born of supreme mental toughness and confidence. This is a trainable attribute. (McGee, 2001, n.p.)

In a nutshell, what you focus your attention on is what you create. Therefore, when individuals, teams or entire staffs focus on what they *want,* they are actually neurologically strengthening the likelihood and possibility for achieving it. A poor outcome is precisely what you'll create by *thinking* about it. Individuals, school planning teams and entire organizations need to spend their time and energy on creating and communicating a shared future vision that stakeholders feel excited about accomplishing.

What does this have to do with coaching? Everything! Coaching is about bringing the impossible to life. Coaches assist coachees in bringing into reality that which they imagine. Using various visioning processes is a common and effective technique coaches use to create a crystal-clear picture of the future. Following up with action is what makes it reality.

THE LANGUAGE OF CHANGE

Take a walk down the hallways of your school or sit in the faculty room. Listen to the *language* being used. I don't mean grammar, diction or foreign languages. Listen for tone, for attitude, and for outlook. What are you hearing? What mindsets are behind the words? You can learn volumes about people by simply listening to the words they choose to use.

Our spoken words are powerful reflections of our inner thoughts. They can attract other people to us or repel them. They can be a catalyst for gathering forces toward a goal or helping to destroy one. Everything we think and speak is a reflection of who we are; what we value; and our intentions, attitudes and opinions. In an instant, we learn a great deal about each other and make decisions that influence the future. Our words can limit us when we choose words that hold us back and inhibit us from reaching our full potential.

> *Language is the biggest barrier to human progress because language is an encyclopedia of ignorance. Old perceptions are frozen into language and force us to look at the world in an old-fashioned way.*
>
> —Edward de Bono
> (www.developingteachers.com)

For Example

As mentioned in Chapter 2, Corey was a high-level administrator looking for a superintendency. For years, her self-talk was, "I'm not good at networking. I'm a great worker and know my stuff, but in social situations, I shrink." This level of thinking kept her from going out there; it kept her from meeting and interacting with people who could help her, support her, or become mentors for her. Many people shrink in social and work settings. I find, in my coaching practice, it's more common than you'd imagine. In this example, it is Corey's inner dialogue and the language she used with herself that kept her small and safe. She aligned herself with similar-thinking people, safe people. Going to a professional networking event was a quantum leap out of her comfort zone. To accomplish it, she *had* to change her inner dialogue, the language she used on a daily basis. Instead, she created new messages:

- I am sociable.
- I am capable of changing.
- I am enthused about meeting new people.
- Others enjoy knowing me.

> *The word is a force. It is the power you have to express and communicate, to think, and thereby to create the events in your life.*
>
> —*Don Miguel Ruiz (1997, p. 26)*

Our words are our most precious creative source of personal power. With them, we create *everything*. Our integrity and credibility are based on whether or not we follow through with our words, missions and promises. Organizational leaders are supported, or not, based on how congruous their actions are with their words. Do their words align with their actions? There is so much power and promise for growing and strengthening our school systems by paying careful, thoughtful attention to what we say and how we say it.

Have you ever noticed that when you feel down, you seek others who are also down? You look for someone who agrees with you, with whom you can corroborate your miseries and complain together. All that really does is keep you both stuck. After all, it's so much easier to ruminate over something than *do something* about it. You cannot move forward when you're in complaining mode.

Coaches work intentionally to help people shift their internal language patterns by avoiding words that keep them in stagnation, words like the following:

- I'll try
- If
- Maybe
- I might
- I hope
- I don't know
- But
- I'd like to

When we use words such as those listed, we have already created an out. If we say we will *try* to do something, we probably won't. Intentions drive our actions. When we use weak language, our intention is also weak, and the action is not likely to occur. By becoming more aware of our language and changing it to reflect stronger commitments, intended actions follow. Instead of weak words, the language of commitment sounds like these examples:

- I will
- I agree
- I promise

- I resolve to
- I commit to

As school systems seek out and search for methods of improving schools, listen closely to the voices heard within the school's walls. When positive possibility thinkers are present, the language of change is in the air. Conversations change

> By understanding and paying close attention to our speech patterns, we can move ourselves from mere desire for change into commitment and action.
>
> —William R. Miller (2005, p. 45)

From	To
I'm not interested in trying that.	Sure, let's try it.
There isn't time.	Let's find time.
I don't think that will work.	I wonder how that can work.

Successful coaches must be highly attuned to the language and words their coachees are using. They are clear signs and signals telling the coach what inner thoughts are either helping them or hindering them.

SUMMARY

Change has to start with the individual before organizational change can happen. When coaching is embraced, lasting change can occur, first within the person, then a team or school, and then the entire organization. And individual change happens from the inside out.

When there's a trusting relationship between a coach and coachee, there's an opening to explore one's inner beliefs and for new thoughts to enter. Once individuals confront the internal issues that have blocked them, huge breakthroughs can be anticipated. Old limiting thoughts, fears, assumptions, judgments, and interpretations have provided a service for keeping people stuck in one place and ideas from manifesting. They keep the status quo and inhibit change. For successful change in individuals and school systems to occur, people must be willing to redirect their fear, stay focused on what they *want*, be ready to adopt new thoughts and take a leap into the unknown.

Educator-coaches need to have a deep understanding of the causes of resistance, a sense of where a coachee is when they begin, and practical strategies to bypass them. Coaches become the facilitators of change. They change minds and attitudes and help people become possibility thinkers. When the halls of our school systems are lined with possibility thinkers, when all adults are functioning at their peak levels of performance, a quantum leap toward achieving high levels of performance can result.

Reflective Questions

- Think of a time when you, a staff member, or a team resisted a change. What was at the root of it?
- Notice limiting beliefs you may hear among staff, administrators, or board members. How can you begin to shift them toward a positive belief?
- Brainstorm a list of changes or programs that have come and gone in your district. Can you identify the breakdown?
- Coach yourself to create new possibilities. In what areas are you or your staff stuck? How can you encourage them to become possibility thinkers?

Powerful Coaching in Action

To exist is to change, to change is to mature, to mature is to go on creating oneself endlessly.

—Henri Bergson (www.creatingminds.org)

IN THIS CHAPTER

POWERful Coaching Framework™

Phases of the coaching relationship

Aligning goals and action

Creating a coaching plan

Using assessments

You probably think you've already implemented more than enough school improvement strategies and programs in your district. You've explored and implemented cooperative learning, data-driven planning processes, learning communities, problem-based learning, and other positive, helpful programs. Yet you may wonder, "Where are the results we hoped for? Why aren't we achieving the high levels of performance we want?"

Earlier in the book, I discussed coaching as an appropriate strategy both for those who need it for performance improvement purposes and also for any professional who is interested in and committed to growing and improving themselves to reach their full potential. As you consider coaching as a professional development opportunity to maximize the gains you hope to achieve, consider a broader plan for coaching than only for *some* teachers or *some* leaders.

In previous chapters I defined coaching as an individualized, customized professional development process. As such, it is useful for *every* educator within a system that is focused on continuous improvement.

THE POWERFUL COACHING FRAMEWORK™

All the background knowledge and textual information in the world won't provide educators with the practical methods, hands-on experience and tools for effective coaching. Yet forming a philosophy of people and change is necessary before jumping into the how-to phase.

You've arrived at a point where you can synthesize the learning of the previous chapters into practical, easy-to-use methods to implement coaching. As you begin to apply the model, keep at the forefront of your mind what has already been addressed earlier in the book:

- Professional coaching core competencies
- The coaching mindset
- The attributes of a great coach
- The whole-coachee concept
- Strategies to break through resistance

I created a simple model, the POWERful Coaching Framework,™ to help coaches touch on important issues during every coaching session. It's an organizing tool that sets in motion a process of continuous improvement. It is a tool for the *coach* to use to address important issues.

Coaching is successful when there are changes made in what a coachee does. Remember: Coaching is about action—doing something different to yield a desired change. This section will help coaches create change by providing a model and structure to follow during *every* coaching session, long or short. It will help coaches create accountability with their coachees, create agreements with them to take action toward their goals and explore obstacles that may be looming.

I have found success with my coaching participants by using a simple model I developed known as the POWERful Coaching Framework™. Using this model will assure a powerful and successful experience and point coachees toward their desired goals. Having a specific structure for conducting a session is highly valuable, especially for new coaches.

Why use a structured model?

- To gain confidence as a coach
- To ensure that the coachee leaves each session with committed action steps
- To consider available options
- To organize time
- To ensure effective use of time
- To ensure a focus on results
- To yield maximum results in any period of time

In my experience, coaching sessions typically range between 20 and 60 minutes. The POWERful Coaching Framework™ can be effective for any length session in that span and even for one as short as 10 minutes. In the early stages, new coaches could keep the Framework by their sides as a reminder to address each component. Eventually, it will become automatic.

What Is the POWERful Coaching Framework™?

It is a five-part, structured, easy-to-follow framework for conducting a coaching session of any length. It contains the key elements that should be addressed in all coaching sessions. By using this framework, the coach creates the conditions for success that the coachee needs:

- Clear and meaningful goals
- Action and momentum
- Specific tasks
- Assessment of coachee's mindset and perceptions
- Examining obstacles in advance
- Emotional support and inspiration
- A record of promised steps
- Follow up

Each coaching session should include all five parts of the POWERful Coaching Framework™. They can be addressed in order, although it's not necessary, with the exception of the last step: recording the actions.

POWERful Coaching Framework™

P: Purpose (What is the purpose for this session or the future?)

What does the coachee or the organization want to accomplish?

What does the coachee want to achieve by the end of this session?

What are the desired short- and long-term results?

O: Outlook and Obstacles (What perceptions are at play? What obstacles does the coachee perceive to be in the way?)

How does the coachee see the issue(s)?

What obstacles may be in the way of accomplishing them?

Examine limiting beliefs, doubts, fear, and thought patterns.

Help coachee recall past success. Build on success.

Create a new vision.

Help coachee see a successful outcome.

How aware is the coachee of the current reality?

Are inner and outer goals in alignment?

W: What (What can the coachee do? What choices are there?)

What possibilities exist? Help coachee see other possibilities.

Brainstorm actions when stuck.

Help coachee see the many options.

What actions will the coachee commit to take?

Choose actions.

E: Empathize, Empower, Encourage (Offer emotional support, boost their spirits.)

Inspire and champion new behaviors.

Help coachees visualize themselves as successful.

Manage time to achieve the goals.

Assess how much inspiration and cheerleading the coachee needs.

Provide empathy, if and when needed.

Acknowledge and validate the coachees' concerns.

R: Recap and Record (Review commitments, record assignments.)

Review the discussion and commitments.

Reinforce strategies to overcome obstacles.

Coach and coachee each record the promised actions to be taken.

Let's look at a sample:

Purpose

- Create and deliver a well-received graduation speech by June 30

Outlook and Obstacles

- The coachee perceives herself as inexperienced and naïve.
- The coachee believes that others view her as childlike.
- There are only three weeks to prepare for the speech.
- The coachee lacks confidence.
- The coachee never previously gave or wrote a speech.
- The coachee believes it will be scary.
- The coach views the coachee as capable.

What

- Brainstorm ways of learning to write a speech.
- Go to the library or bookstore and find or buy books on speech-writing.
- Search the Internet for already written graduation speeches.
- Devote two hours per week to practicing speech-writing skills.
- Find a trusted colleague to deliver draft speeches.
- Videotape self giving a speech.
- Brainstorm ways of finding out about and learning presentation skills.
- Investigate organizations that can provide help.

- Visit and join Toastmasters.
- Rehearse speeches.
- Recall numerous successful classroom presentations.
- List classroom presentations.

Empathize, Empower, Encourage

- Coach reminds coachee that she has been successful in classroom presentations.
- Coach communicates that she knows how it feels to have that level of anxiety.
- Coach reminds her that she has what it takes; she projects her voice well and has a confident presence.

Recap, Record

- Coach and coachee review the conversation and agree on actions for the current week:
  - Buy a book on writing speeches.
  - Write an outline.
  - Find a Toastmasters group near my home.
  - List three times I gave a successful classroom lecture.

In the next coaching session, actions will be reviewed and new ones identified. The process continues weekly until the result is met and the coachee feels successful. (See Resource F: Conducting a POWERful Coaching Session.)

This model can be used with anyone—superintendents, principals, colleagues, teachers, students—in any time frame. When coaches are competent in integrating the core coaching competencies and specific coaching techniques, have adopted a coaching mindset and possess an understanding of possible causes of resistance, and use this format for coaching sessions, they will discover how quickly and effectively change *can* happen. The coaching process becomes a continuous improvement loop creating successful outcomes on a daily basis.

PHASES OF A COACHING RELATIONSHIP

Nothing in life stays the same. Everything is always evolving, including the coaching relationship. It is normal for a coaching relationship to go through various stages. Like any relationship, it develops and changes over time. As a coach and coachee progress, the coach should be aware of the various phases of the coaching relationship. Doing so helps coaches prepare themselves to provide positive support for the coachees during each phase. While there is some overlap with the change models in Chapter 6, the phases focus on the relationship between the coach and coachee.

The Start-Moving Phase

This is the getting-started phase, when the coach and coachee are establishing and developing their personal relationship. They are establishing trust, and the coachee is learning about the coaching process—what to expect and what not to expect. They agree on their schedule of meeting times—when and for how long. The early weeks of a coaching relationship are about discovery, for both participants. The coach listens and learns about the coachee, listening for what matters most, for blocks, obstacles, fears and challenges. Everything that was identified in Chapter 3 is part of the start-moving phase. The competencies identified are those that the coach needs during this phase.

The length of the start-moving phase will vary, depending on coachees' readiness and attitude toward coaching. If they *chose* coaching, it's likely they are ready to go and will zip through this phase quickly. If coaching is chosen *for* them, the coach and coachee are more likely to spend more time in this phase, learning about each other and the process, developing trust and clarifying the roles and relationship.

It can be useful for the coach to administer assessments during this phase to learn about more the coachee and provide a baseline of information for the coachee to learn about him or herself. Data and feedback from assessments help formulate performance-based goals. (See Using Assessments later in this chapter.)

In this phase:

- The coachees may be wondering what to expect from coaching.
- The coach is learning about the coachee.
- The coachees are learning about themselves, exploring what is most important to them.
- The coach and coachee explore the current challenges.
- The coachees discover and identify their core values.
- The coachees feel either uncertain or enthused.
- The coach is getting the big picture, taking it all in.
- The interpersonal relationship is developing.
- The coach is learning about the organization's goals and challenges.

- The coachees become aware of their most important values.
- Coach and coachee agree on a meeting schedule and policies for changing session times.
- The coach is deeply listening to the coachee's language and thoughts.
- The coachees are becoming more aware of their own thoughts.
- The coach may be learning about the coachee's personal life.
- The coachee begins to see situations with a new lens.
- Assessments may be used to identify strengths and areas for development.
- The coachee might be thinking
  –"I'm not sure what will happen."
  –"What is this coaching all about?"
  –"I'm excited about coaching."

The Keep-Moving Phase

In the keep-moving phase, coachees are on a roll. They're moving forward, sometimes rapidly. They're feeling excited and sometimes overwhelmed and exhausted. They may be recognizing losses, what has to be let go of to allow the new to enter—old, stale thoughts, fears, favorite lesson plans, their old selves.

This is the goal-setting and action phase. Coachees are usually excited about the progress they're making. The coaches and coachees set specific goals and performance targets. With the support of their coaches, they're taking steps, even baby steps, toward their agreed-upon goals. Even if the two already know one another, when coaching, they'll get to know each other in brand new ways. The coachees will reveal far more about themselves than in a typical work-related relationship.

In this stage, there may be a temptation to stop or slow down. Coachees may want a rest or a break from coaching. Coaches should realize this is a normal feeling. It is at this point, in this stage, that a backwards slide can happen if coaching is not present. This is where the coaching role is effective in helping the coachees stay on track, maintain the pace, and continue the momentum. This is a critical time for coaches to encourage and inspire them, support them, remind them of their success (see The Cycle of Change section in Chapter 6).

In this phase,

- Specific goals are established and defined.
- Bold actions are taken.
- Obstacles are considered.
- Coachee needs support.
- Coachee might feel either exhilarated or exhausted.

- Action planning occurs on a regular basis. Weekly actions are identified during the coaching session.
- The coachee is into the routine.
- The coach and coachee agree on methods of measuring results.
- There's a high level of energy and momentum; progress is being made.
- The coach is supporting the coachee through obstacles.
- The coachees know they're held accountable for completing tasks.
- The coachees become aware of how they may stop themselves.
- There a solid foundation of trust between coach and coachee.
- The coachee is more willing to take chances, try new behaviors.
- It's not unusual for the coachee to feel exhausted. Change takes effort and can take an emotional toll.
- Coaches are likely to hear comments like,
  –"I'm making progress."
  –"I'm focused and in control."
  –"I'm pooped. I need a rest."
  –"Life isn't controlling me any more."

The Renewal Phase

In this phase, the coachees have experienced success and are aware of their inner obstacles, fears and self-doubts that have inhibited them from achieving outer success in the past. The coachees have begun to internalize new ways of thinking and see life from an entirely new perspective. Often, new goals are set, bigger goals, beyond those first considered.

Usually, coachees want to keep moving. Sometimes, there are environmental factors to be considered. When one person changes, unless he or she lives in a bubble, it's likely others may want to pull that person backward into the old ways. It can feel like a very strong pull. During this phase, the coach and coachee may focus on creating a supportive environment for the changes to stick. It is in this phase that most changes fail.

In this phase:

- Initial goals have been met.
- New goals emerge.
- The coachee feels confident.
- The coachee is open to new possibilities.
- The coachee has developed renewed feelings of unshakable confidence.
- The coachee is integrating a new outlook and new attitudes into daily interactions at work and home.

- The coachee seeks more.
- The coachees may feel pressure from others in their life.
- The coach helps the coachee attain new levels of achievement.
- The coachee might be thinking:
  - "I wonder how far I can go!"
  - "I'm unstoppable."
  - "I can do anything!"

ALIGNING GOALS AND ACTIONS FOR EXTRAORDINARY RESULTS: SETTING GOALS

Another important aspect of the coaching process is short- and long-term planning and goal setting. With the coachee or the organization, determine the *overall* purpose for coaching. What is the specific intention? What new future do you wish to create? What is the motivation that has led to a coaching approach? What does the organization hope to gain?

Identify the long-range goals as well as any short-term goals for both the organization and the coachee. Determine the professional goals as well as any personal goals with the coachee during the start-moving phase. Among them may be

- Acquiring new skills
- Improving performance
- Making a difficult decision
- Managing time or stress
- Improving teamwork
- Developing leadership capabilities
- Creating a coaching culture for the organization

Coaching is about creating extraordinary results. You don't need coaching to achieve good, good enough or mediocre. Just as in the athletic world, coaching in education is about achieving superhuman results. It's about every person reaching his or her absolutely highest potential, in order for school systems to reach the lofty goals they are striving for. When all educators are performing at his or her peak potential, with fully aligned personal and professional goals and values, the results they produce for their schools, districts, or universities will surpass their challenging goals,

Any well-developed school improvement plan has specific goals with aligned actions. A coaching plan destined to achieve outstanding results is an individualized, customized plan for each person, aligned with the district plan, improvement, and respecting the needs of the individual.

Values Clarification

Exploring what an organization and an individual values is a useful process to align behaviors and actions. Planning processes typically include a thorough discussion and identification of specific values that describe the guiding principles and behaviors of an organization.

Our personal values are those things we hold close to our hearts; without them, we wouldn't be who we are. They define our true selves. Discovering your personal values, and *living* them, are key to aligning your life with your work. Each of us has and chooses the set of values that we live by. Often they are unconscious and may evolve over time.

> Events shape values, as much as values shape events.
>
> —Charles Handy (as quoted in M. Albion, 2000, p. 98)

Have you ever struggled with a decision? Were you undecided between the convertible car and the gas-efficient one? If you have ever been stuck or torn between two choices, it is probable that you were wrestling with two important values, each choice representing a different one. Maybe you've had a choice to make between two new positions. One had the potential for a much higher salary. The other would require you to relocate. You're undecided because the practical side of you thinks the higher salary would be good for your family. The adventurer in you wants the chance to start over in a new community. Your two values of financial security and living an interesting life of adventure are in conflict. When you are clear about what you value most, it becomes easy to say yes or no to your choices.

Focusing on values helps coachees make decisions that are aligned with their purposes, strengths and interests. Organizations in strategic planning mode identify their common values to clarify and communicate those that the organization agrees to uphold. The coaching process helps individuals identify their personal core values that guide how they choose to live. Coaches will help coachees explore and identify the values that are theirs alone and incorporate them into their lives to achieve greater fulfillment. Being clear on your values increases commitment to goals and can strengthen successful hiring practices when your personal values are shared with an organization's values. If you value risk taking, how happy will you be in a conservative district? If your priority is open communication, how good a fit will you be in a district where open communication is a foreign concept and not valued by others?

Identifying Goals

When individuals seek a coach and plan to use their own resources to pay for coaching, there are clearly two people in the coaching relationship;

the coach and the coachee. Goal setting is a snap. However, when an organization opts for coaching, regardless of whether it is using external or internal coaches, there are technically three players: the coach, the coachee, and the organization that chooses to invest in coaching.

Earlier in the book, it was discussed that coaching is more successful when the coachee has a voice in choosing goals; that's easy when the coachee is paying for coaching. This concept is a tad more challenging when the organization is paying. Naturally, the organization will want the coaching goals to be the organization's priority goals. However, a top-down management style of telling others what or how to do something can result in defensiveness and action by compliance. Coaching seeks action by choice.

So how to accommodate both the district's goals and personally chosen goals? How do coaches proceed? How do they meet the individual needs of the coachees while supporting the organization's goals?

Let's remember that coaching is a supportive process for aligning the internal self with outer results. Coaches seek to bring out hidden abilities and help individuals live their lives on purpose, stemming from a clear picture of their strengths, values and a sense of their personal mission. Taking action toward a new goal can be challenging, scary and anxiety producing for anyone, even when it is by choice. When we choose, motivation is high. When we are given goals by an external source, that can cause us to go right into the discomfort zone mentioned in Chapter 6, and resistance is more likely to occur than cooperation.

When coaching for improving the performance of the organization, it is important for those who invest in coaching to understand that results and commitment to coaching will be greater when the coachee has some say in the goals that emerge from the coach-coachee relationship. Coaches can surely offer and discuss the organization's improvement goals, while allowing the coachees some freedom to choose how and when they are integrated into the coaching plan. An effective strategy can be to ensure a balance between the organization's goals and the coachee's goals. I find there are always benefits to the organization. For instance, a district goal is related to improving reading scores, and the coachee chooses to focus on classroom management. Or a district has a new focus on data analysis and a principal coachee chooses a goal for improving the relationship with an assistant principal.

During the goal-setting phase, the coach is listening and probing, seeking motivation and commitment. Usually, when people seek to achieve a big goal outside of their normal frame of reference, they want to *feel* differently than they do today. Coaches are wise to listen for the driving force and emotions and tap into how achieving the new goal will cause the coachees to feel something else: more confidence, more happiness, more connected, and so forth. It is that feeling that will keep them moving and motivated and help them accomplish the results that have evaded them without coaching.

COACHING TIPS:

❖ Assess the current situation with the coachee; identify what is working well and what is not.

❖ Set a specific number of goals for a set period of time. Two to four goals quarterly are usually manageable.

❖ Be open and frank about the organization's goals. Tell the coachee what they are and include them in the conversation.

❖ Review goals quarterly or as they are reached. Set new goals.

School systems will engage in and continue with coaching when the individuals receiving coaching are enthused and supportive of the process and when there is a resulting value to the organization. When we acknowledge and communicate the coaching process as one of continuous improvement versus one of corrective action, coachees will be far more amenable and open. There will be reduced defensiveness and resistance and increased productivity, enthusiasm and action.

ALIGNING GOALS AND ACTIONS FOR EXTRAORDINARY RESULTS: DEVELOPING A PROFESSIONAL COACHING PLAN

Creating a coaching plan typically takes place during the first few coaching sessions. The coaching plan should include clear objectives and goals for the coaching process. They can be

- Developmental goals
- Performance-related goals
- Skill development goals
- Inner personal development goals

Having an overall coaching plan creates a strategic direction for the coaching process. Just as in the development of a results-focused school improvement plan, a professional coaching plan sets and defines expectations and creates a picture of the future for the coachee.

Step 1: Exploring

During the first few coaching sessions, the coach's intention is to assess, probe, identify and clarify issues of concern for the coachees. The coach will ask numerous questions to help the coachees gain a clear perspective and determine their motivation for making changes in their professional performance or personal life. To assist in the goal-setting stage, here are some helpful questions:

- Where do you see yourself 3, 5, or 10 years from now?
- Why do you want to achieve that? What purpose will it serve?
- What do you want to create? Why?
- What impact do you want to have on your district, students, or colleagues?
- What is your personal mission?
- What values are you honoring?
- How does that align with your values?
- What do you hope to accomplish in our coaching relationship?
- What is your ultimate goal?
- Suppose you had no fear and unlimited resources. What would you do with your life? Or in your district?
- What does success look like for you?
- What does success look like for your classroom (building, district)?
- What would you want to be remembered for when you leave this district?
- What is your definition of the ideal teacher (or principal or superintendent, etc.)?
- What brings you the most joy?
- What changes do you need to make to achieve that?
- What would you do if you could do anything?
- Why is that important to you?
- Why might you be resistant to the district goal?

Notice that some of the questions help coachees think beyond today. Initial questions help coachees think bigger and more strategically about their work and their life. That way, setting coaching goals can stem from a longer-term view of themselves and their lives and work. (See Resource G for a tool to record goals.)

These can be challenging questions which may need some reflection time. Before jumping into action, it is helpful that the coachees be crystal clear about their purpose and their rationale. This is an important part of the coaching conversation in relation to goal setting. The questions get to the heart of the coachees. What is the driving motivation behind their goals? This is beneficial information for the coach. When the change process becomes challenging or difficult, the coach can use this information as a reminder and help keep the coachees on track.

Motivation is the internal compass that steers people toward a desired result. The results are seen externally. The more a coach learns about what motivates a coachee, the better the chance of a successful outcome.

Most people are motivated to perform well on the job. No one goes to work intending to do a poor job. Leaders want to develop high-performing teams. Teachers want to make a difference in the lives of students. Often, when the performance does not match the expectation of the organization, a number of factors may be influencing an individual or a team:

- Lack of meaningful feedback
- Unclear expectations
- Fear of failure
- Unclear payoff
- Mismatch between employee and position
- Lack of experience
- Limiting beliefs

A coach intervenes, helping to uncover either the motivation to do something or the resistance behind not doing it. Motivation increases when coachees become clear about their purpose, personal mission and values and align them with their work.

Step 2: Defining and Committing

Discuss the coachee's priorities and begin to identify specific goals. Remember that there will be more progress made when the coachees select goals that matter *to them*. It is perfectly okay to discuss the organizations' goals with the coachees, remembering that it is preferable the coachees choose those they wish to work on *at this time*. Balancing professional with personal goals is very common, as I've said. Doing so energizes the coachees and keeps them in forward motion with joy.

> Make the most of yourself, for that is all there is of you.
>
> —Ralph Waldo Emerson

Don't overwhelm the coachee with too many goals. Agree on a reasonable number—in my experience, *three* goals at a time works well. I suggest a 3-month time frame as a minimum, although 6-month to 12-month goals are fine. Often coachees feel overwhelmed by a longer window of time; keeping it short enables them to feel successful, while keeping the longer-term goal in mind. Three months is a reasonable time frame for new behaviors to become new habits. Coachees aren't overwhelmed by a longer time frame and perceive three months as realistic. I also suggest that any coaching relationship be no *less* than three months to enable time for new thoughts to become integrated and new habits to be established as routine.

Goals should be written in SMART goal format: specific, measurable, achievable, reasonable, and timed. Avoid creating goal statements that sound too broad or general. Specificity is necessary to create a very clear picture of the goal. For example, "90% of all students will achieve a score of 80 or better on the reading assessment by May 1." Without clarity, how will you know if you've arrived? Measurable goals are necessary to analyze progress toward them. To assist in defining and committing to goals, the following questions may be helpful:

- On a scale of 1 to 10, how important is it to achieve that goal?
- How ready are you now to do what it takes to achieve that?
- What will achieving that goal do for you?
- How will we know when you've achieved it?
- By when?
- What will it look like when you have achieved it?
- How will you feel when you accomplish that?
- How does that align with the district goals?

For Example

Goal 1: By June 30, I will write and deliver a successful graduation speech.

Goal 2: By June 30, all third-grade teachers will participate in a minimum five hours of staff development about data-driven decision making.

Goal 3: I will run a half-marathon before summer.

Coaches can use the Professional Coaching Plan: Quarterly Goals and Initial Actions form, found in Resource G, to record goals and establish initial actions (see Figure 7.1). Use a separate form for each goal once clear goals are established with the coachee. For an example, see Figure 7.2.

Step 3: Action Planning

Create actions. For each goal, identify actions to take that will ensure that the goal is met. The Professional Coaching Plan: Quarterly Goals and

Figure 7.1   Professional Coaching Plan: Quarterly Goals and Initial Actions

---

Professional Coaching Plan

"Never mistake motion for action." —Ernest Hemingway

Coachee Name: _____   **Date:** _____

Identify **three** goals; fill out one of these forms for each one. Goals should be SMART: Specific, Measurable, Achievable, Realistic, and Timed.

Goal:

Measure of Success:

Possible Obstacles:

Possible Solutions:

Initial Action Steps:	By When	Review Date	Completed

Notes:

Figure 7.2   Sample Professional Coaching Plan: Quarterly Goals and Initial Actions

---

Professional Coaching Plan

"Never mistake motion for action." —Ernest Hemingway

Coachee Name: _____   **Date:** _____

Identify three goals; fill out one of these forms for each one. Goals should be SMART: Specific, Measurable, Achievable, Realistic, and Timed.

Goal:

> *By June 30, I will write and deliver a successful graduation speech.*

Measure of Success:

> Students and staff will report feeling inspired, at least an 8 on a 0-10 scale.

Potential Obstacles:
Lack of confidence
Lack of experience

Possible Solutions:
Positive self-talk
Gain experience

Initial Action Steps:	By When	Review Date	Completed
Research well-written speeches	April 1		
Find and join a Toastmasters group	May 1		
Write draft of graduation speech	May 15		
Rehearse with feedback	May 22		

Notes:

Initial Actions tool (Figure 7.1) also outlines a schedule of actions and strategies on a quarterly basis. It breaks down big tasks into manageable actions with deadlines for accomplishing them. For busy educators, it is helpful to envision the overall action plan as a doable one.

The Weekly Coaching Action Planner (Figure 7.3 and Resource H) can be used at each coaching session on a weekly basis (or other schedule) for actions to be taken *before the next session*.

Brainstorm possible actions, allowing the coachees to choose the actions they will commit to act on. Call them assignments, commitments or promises. They should be treated that way by both parties. Discuss any obstacles or challenges that may arise and develop strategies for overcoming them. List the next set of actions at the bottom of the Weekly Coaching Action Planner. Both coach and coachee keep copies.

Accountability is a key aspect of the coaching relationship that keeps coachees in action and ensures the likelihood of them committing to taking the promised steps. The coach checks in with them each week, and this creates an ongoing, continuous cycle: goal → action → accountability → new actions.

Request that coachees e-mail or deliver the completed Weekly Coaching Action Planner to their coaches *prior to* the next session, enabling the coach time to review it. It has been my experience that coachees may resist completing it. While no one wants or needs busywork or additional paperwork, I *strongly* recommend that they take the few minutes to do so; it's an excellent way to create awareness that action is occurring, for noticing progress and gaining a sense of accomplishment. It's an ongoing record of actions taken, issues that have arisen, and hints of what the coachee may need from the coach. It becomes a cyclical tracking system helpful to both coach and coachee. In my practice, I request that the Weekly Coaching Action Planner log be e-mailed to me prior to the coaching session, giving me time to review it and prepare for the session.

The coach's role is far more than making a list of actions. This is where the coaches hold high expectations for the coachees and maintain a picture of them as successful. With a mindset that the coachees are capable of accomplishing anything, they urge them and nudge them to do a little more, to spend more time or more effort, while providing inspiration as appropriate. Resistance can arise quickly during action planning, as the coachee may not see time to do something or shrinks back due to inner fears. Action planning is a critical stage for stepping out of their comfort zones and making a bigger commitment than they ever would have on their own.

Figure 7.3   Sample Weekly Coaching Action Planner

Weekly Coaching Action Planner

Coachee Name: _____   Date: _____

Actions I completed since the last session: (coachee lists these and sends to coach prior to the session)

    Identified five graduation speeches, and read them

    Found a Toastmasters group nearby

    Identified data workshop leader

    Ran four days this week

What I didn't get to:

    Attend first Toastmasters group

    Write a speech

Why? What challenges arose?

    Didn't have time; conflict with PTA meeting

    Brain freeze during writing time

What supports or possibilities exist?

    No PTA meeting next week

During the next session, I need help with . . . :

    Courage to speak up at Toastmasters

    Boosting my confidence to write first speech

What I commit to do by the next session: (List actions below during coaching session)

    Attend Toastmasters Thursday at 7 p.m.

    Write a draft graduation speech by Friday 5 p.m.

    Tell myself I have what it takes; I can do this—three times a day, every day

    Contact workshop leader and schedule the data workshop by Wednesday

    Run four days, two mornings and two evenings, at least two miles each

---

For Example

The principal in an earlier example wanted to strengthen his relationship with the assistant principal. The assistant was providing far more touchy-feeling, interpersonal support to staff than actual concrete help as the principal's right hand. The principal was drowning in work and needed the assistant to step in and take on more responsibility. The principal's solution, initially, was to move the assistant out, to another position. To him, that seemed easier than confronting the problem, than working with the assistant to improve the situation. That was too uncomfortable for him. Left to his own resources, he would have avoided a conversation to move toward improvement. With coaching, we brainstormed and role-played until he was able to agree to actions to improve the situation.

Helpful questions during action planning are

- What possibilities exist?
- What choices do you have?
- What might prevent you from doing that?
- What are you willing to commit to this week?

Step 4: Interim Communication

When possible, invite informal communication between formal coaching sessions. Doing so ensures that the coachees feel supported while in the discomfort zone and gives them a chance for midpoint coaching, if needed. This helps deal with obstacles, time management issues or other challenging moments for the coachee and provides ongoing encouragement and inspiration. Additional benefits are increased trust and improved relationships. Communication can be in person, by telephone or by e-mail.

For Example

Continuing the foregoing example, I knew the principal was highly uncomfortable facing the discussion with his assistant. I offered support by inviting him to call me the night before and call me right after the discussion to discuss the outcome.

Step 5: Continuation

The next coaching session arrives. Unless a period of venting a stressful event is needed, the coach begins by reviewing the progress on actions promised in the previous session. Using the Weekly Coaching Action Planner as a guide, discuss any obstacles that arose and actions for the next week. Offer congratulations for every success. The process continues.

USING ASSESSMENTS IN COACHING

As you know, when I began coaching, one of my first coachees was an assistant principal in her first administrative position. Although she had great confidence in her abilities as a new leader, many times, she said "I'm not sure how people view me. I think they perceive me as childlike." She formed a perception about herself without any concrete information or data to confirm her thoughts.

This type of self-doubt is more common than people would guess. I have been quite surprised by similar comments from dozens of school leaders in my coaching work.

I cannot underestimate the importance of assessments to the coaching process. Among the benefits for using assessments with coachees are the following:

- To identify performance strengths
- To identify developmental opportunities
- To determine the effectiveness of the coaching process
- To validate hunches about performance
- To provide insight into skills necessary for a particular role
- To provide a foundation for future development
- To identify leadership strengths
- To evaluate the fit for a leader in a new district or team effectiveness
- To identify personality attributes
- To identify preferred work style
- To learn conflict style
- To determine emotional intelligence
- To identify behaviors that impede success

Identifying Strengths and Opportunities

When I began my coaching work, I spoke with a number of human resource professionals outside of the education field. In corporate America, it is common to administer various assessments during a hiring process or when promoting people to a higher position. They are used to determine a person's fit with a team as well as personality, leadership strengths and team functioning. They can uncover key development areas that may be inhibiting or sidetracking an individual or an organization from achieving desired results. School leaders, professional staff, and team members can benefit from knowing their specific strengths, styles, attributes, and areas for professional growth.

In coaching, assessments are effective tools that provide concrete data: feedback and information often missing from one's frame of refer-

ence. "How do I know how I'm doing?" is a common question coachees ask. They want to know, very specifically, how they are perceived and how they can improve. Assessments provide much-needed information, talking points, and a basis for setting important leadership goals.

> Leadership is a personal journey for each person.
>
> —Donna Riley, IBM (as quoted in Tischler, 2004, p. 112)

Self-Assessment

The coaching process normally begins with *self-assessment*. The coach and coachee explore professional goals, personal goals, and reasons for seeking coaching. They discuss what *is working* and what *is not* working. This type of self-assessment is based on the individual's perception of his or her professional and personal (if applicable) life. The coaches help the coachees examine their driving purposes and personal values. The coach may help them verify and validate their perceptions by asking questions and gathering data informally.

For Example

One assistant superintendent I worked with, who was in a new district, sent a brief survey to district principals asking for feedback about how she was doing. In doing so, she set a precedent for others to be open and vulnerable.

Sample Self-Assessment Questions

What is working well for you?

What is not working? Why?

In what specific areas would you like to improve?

How can you find out for sure?

How can you learn more?

Who can you ask?

What burning question do you have in relation to your career?

Self-assessments can be interviews, questionnaires, or observations. They can be personal reflections that help coachees increase awareness about how others perceive them, or they can request input from colleagues, supervisors and peers. Normally the coach and coachee develop questions based on the coaching issue being explored.

Without data and feedback about their perceptions and performance, coachees are often in the dark. As mentioned earlier, it's a wise move to conduct assessments at the beginning of the coaching relationship. Doing so provides useful, specific data about the coachee's competencies and opportunities for development that can serve as a baseline for identifying coaching interventions that will ultimately improve the coachee's performance.

> Be patient with yourself. Self-growth is tender; it's holy ground. There's no greater investment.
>
> —Stephen Covey
> (www.worldhealing.net)

Published Assessment Tools

There are dozens of appropriate, published assessments on the market ideal for use with coachees. Determine what needs to be assessed, then research appropriate, credible tools. Some common assessment tools are

- Myers-Briggs Type Indicator (MBTI)
- Fundamental Interpersonal Relations Orientation (FIRO-B)
- CPI 260 Coaching Report for Leaders
- CPI 260 Coachee Feedback Report
- Genos EI Emotional Intelligence
- Emotional Quotient Inventory
- Emotional Competence Inventory
- Leadership Practices Inventory
- Thomas-Kilmann Conflict Mode Instrument (TKI)
- DiSC (Dominance, Influence, Steadiness, Conscientiousness)

The coach determines appropriate assessment tools to use in the coaching process. Some are appropriate for leaders and top level executives; others can be used by teams and other staff members. Assessment data should be kept confidential between the coachee and the coach. Results of wider-scale assessments taken by large groups of people can be shared publicly while keeping personal information private. (See Resource I for the publishers and their addresses of the listed assessment tools.)

Midpoint Assessment

It is also wise to conduct a midpoint assessment several weeks or months after coaching has begun. The purposes of a midpoint assessment are to track progress, deal with any relationship or coach matching issues, and in general, check in to make sure that the coachee is feeling helped and the process is being meaningful.

A midpoint assessment *could* be conducted as a three-way meeting with the coach, coachee and supervisor. The purpose would be for the supervisor or the sponsor of the coaching to be part of the conversation *without* breaking any confidentiality agreements. The coachees may wish to divulge their private interactions with the coach, but only with the coachee's permission should that information be part of the conversation. Otherwise a three-way midpoint assessment agenda would be to discuss progress and attitudes toward continuing coaching.

Midpoint Informal Assessment Questions:

On a scale of 1 to 10, how effective is coaching in helping you achieve your goals?

What changes have you made since you began coaching?

What insights have you had since you began coaching?

Are your goals acceptable, or do they need revision?

What impact on the organization has coaching had thus far?

Exactly how has coaching contributed to your achievements so far?

On a scale of 1 to 10, how effective is the coach-coachee relationship?

Is the coaching relationship working well?

What, if anything, isn't working or needs improvement?

How effective is the coach-coachee match?

Final Assessment

Coaching can be ongoing as long as the coachee is benefiting from the relationship and improvements are being made that satisfy the coachee and the organization sponsoring coaching. An end point can be determined in advance or whenever goals have been reached, as determined by the sponsor. A final assessment can be conducted that would address the following:

- Goal attainment
- The quality of the relationship
- The coaching process
- Feedback for the coach
- A plan for follow-through with changes the coachee has made
- Possibility of new goals and continuation of coaching

SUMMARY

The main purpose for coaching in organizations is to improve performance and effectiveness so the purpose and mission can be fulfilled. School system leaders and school board members exploring coaching as a potential strategy for helping districts accomplish their challenging goals should expect extraordinary results from engaging in the process, especially when it permeates the system. A number of factors can enable that level of success: highly trained and skilled coaches, a deep understanding of various phases of a coach-coachee relationship, and numerous processes for ensuring that goals are meaningful and that coachees take regular action steps to achieve them. Coaching is productive and meaningful when there is action toward a goal that is important to the coachee, and the organization reaps results.

The POWERful Coaching Framework™ provides a model for addressing important issues in each coaching session. It helps establish the purpose for the session, address challenges and create a set of actions, all of which can be accomplished in any time frame.

Each individual professional coaching plan is based on a set of coachee-chosen goals that are aligned with the inner person and the desired outer results. The organization, school system, building, classroom, and students benefit by supporting the individual's personal and professional growth. An investment in coaching is an investment in the future of the organization by supporting the individuals who compose it. Aligning the organization's goals can be accomplished and successful when they are also aligned with the individual's goals. Allowing freedom of choice increases motivation and decreases resistance and resentment. Ultimately, the coaching relationship and process are successful when there is a high level of trust and freedom to grow in areas recognized by the coachee and supported by the organization.

Professional assessments must become a more regular aspect of professional growth and self-reflection. Educators need specific feedback about their leadership abilities, capacity for team building, problem solving, decision making, communication effectiveness, and other factors necessary for success. They need credible data and information about their strengths and areas for growth. Assessments are used in coaching to gather this information, which is then used as a springboard for goal setting. They are essential for developing personal and professional attributes that strengthen the ability of educators to perform at their peak and in turn, lead their schools to achieve superhuman results.

Reflective Questions

- Try the POWERful Coaching Framework™ model with a colleague. What is the result?
- What are the pros and cons of allowing coachees the freedom to choose their own goals during the coaching process?
- What has been your organization's experience with assessments for professional staff? How can you benefit by using them? Discuss the benefits of using leadership, teaming, emotional intelligence, and other assessments with your school leadership team.

Implementing Successful Coaching

Challenges are what make life interesting; overcoming them is what makes life meaningful.

—Joshua J. Marine (www.equalearth.org)

IN THIS CHAPTER

Creating conditions for success

Confidentiality

Communication

Policies and decision making

Selecting and training coaches

Leadership coaching

A coaching approach to continuous school improvement

During a lunch break at an education conference, I recall speaking with a school board member distressed over the district's dysfunctional coaching program. The program was more than two years old. Instructional coaches were trained and making classroom visits. From a bird's-eye view, it might look like it was working.

Yet rather than a successful coaching program, there was pervasive distrust. Teachers lacked the belief that the coaches were there to help them. Instead, they believed they were being supervised. Teachers were cautious, resisted coaches entering their classrooms, and the coaching model was less than productive. There were unclear boundaries, uncertain avenues of communication, lack of sufficient coaching skills, and little understanding of the coaching role. A culture of suspicion and doubt had developed; it was a broken system.

As with any new initiative, coaching is successful when it is well planned, well communicated, well supported, and when all the crucial elements are considered in advance. Moving toward a coaching approach holds enormous potential for improving an organization's culture, its ways of communication. The more that coaching is integrated, the more people who are receiving coaching or competently coaching one another, the greater the result can be.

As a rapidly emerging profession, coaching is certain to become a greater presence in schools. It will be successful when certain conditions are considered in advance and understood throughout the system. This chapter contains recommendations and issues to consider in the planning stage of a coaching program implementation. (See Resource J: Successful Coaching Implementation Checklist.)

CREATING CONDITIONS FOR SUCCESS

Since the majority of educators have not experienced the potential and power of a coaching process or a professional coaching relationship, it can be difficult to create a solid plan for the unknown. I have observed a number of key considerations that ensure the success of a coaching initiative. They are derived from my personal experiences and observations with coaching, school improvement planning and managing change initiatives. Review and discuss these following items:

1. Have key decision makers experience coaching. Most professional coaches are willing to offer a complimentary session. Doing so will affirm what coaching is and who may benefit.

2. Create awareness of coaching and how it differs from mentoring, consulting, training, and other roles. Be sure that district stakeholders can articulate the differences.

3. Make sure that key stakeholders support the rationale for coaching and agree to sponsor it. Sponsoring implies providing resources: time, skilled coaches and funding.

4. Adopt ICF Professional Coaching Core Competencies for educator-coaches. Ensure that either external or internal coaches have been trained in necessary skills and processes for successful coaching.

5. Create a confidentiality policy. Coaches uphold confidentiality with the coachees at all times.

6. Set realistic objectives, timeframes and outcomes for coaching.

7. Provide a cadre of coaches and the opportunity for coachees to have input in their choice of coach.

8. It is preferable that the coachee be willing to be coached. You can't force coaching on anyone and expect success. The coachee should be informed about the coaching relationship at the onset, and agree that it is a process he or she is willing to commit to.

9. Align coaching objectives with organizational, professional and personal goals.

10. Action is the motto. Coachees understand and agree to take weekly action toward their goals.

11. Provide ongoing training and support for internal coaches. What process will the district develop to coach the coach? What will coaches do when they feel stuck or when the coachee is stagnating? Who will support them and provide troubleshooting?

12. Make sure that coaches receive sufficient coach-specific skills training and practice. Thrity hours at a minimum; 60 or more is preferable.

13. Make sure that coaching training is provided by an ICF-credentialed coach or program. Coaches with this credential are trained and knowledgeable of the Core Coaching Competencies.

14. Provide a minimum of three months of coaching for any coaching engagement. Doing so allows new behaviors to become integrated and comfortable.

15. Agree on who is the coachee: In organizational coaching, when the organization foots the bill, it is the *sponsor*. The coachee is the person receiving coaching with whom the coach maintains confidentiality.

CONFIDENTIALITY

The most successful coaching relationship and program design will include confidentiality as an *essential* ingredient in the recipe for success. Coaching is highly effective in improving organizations for a number of reasons; confidentiality is one *major* one. It is a given, among professional coaches, that confidentiality is *always* maintained in a coaching relationship. The only exception is threat of suicide or other danger to the coachee or others (see Resource D, ICF Standards of Ethical Conduct). Confidentiality enables honesty and creates privacy for the coachee to experiment with new behaviors.

In the safety net of a coaching relationship, coachees undergo a process of self-revelation. They look deeply within themselves and explore their beliefs, innermost thoughts and fears. They uncover and reveal to their coaches what makes them tick, what stops them from doing something, and what motivates them to do something. Defensiveness melts away; the coachees can be themselves; they can freely discuss their professional performance or personal issues. A protective space develops in which the coachees can try on new behaviors and new thoughts and take new bold action. A high level of trust is formed *because of* the confidentiality that is promised.

> We can't stop the waves, but we can learn to surf.
>
> —Jonathon Kabat-Zinn
> (www.inspirationalspark.com)

Without confidentiality, the connection between the coach and coachee would be vastly different. Among the educators I've spoken with who have not developed confidentiality policies, programs are weak and teachers are defensive, viewing the coach in a supervisory role reporting behavior to the principal versus an ongoing supportive role in which the coachees can grow and develop themselves at their own pace.

I have had several lively conversations with educational leaders who prefer to know exactly what is going on in classrooms and are resistant to confidentiality between the coach and coachee. Confidentiality is of critical importance to the coaching process. I recommend it be nonnegotiable. Principals and supervisors can observe and witness changes the coachees make, and they are free to discuss issues with the coachees. The coachees can, if they wish, discuss their coaching progress with others. However, discussions between the coach and the principal or other sponsor remain private.

COMMUNICATION FLOW AND CONFIDENTIALITY

In organizations where the district sponsors the coaching, there's an obvious investment of time, staff, and resources. It is understandable why some people may have a concern about a confidentiality policy. However, it is in the best interest of the coachee and the credibility of the coaching program to uphold it. The ultimate goal is to achieve higher levels of performance, increased confidence among leaders and teachers, and acquisition of new skills for the good of the district. Here follow some recommended guidelines and strategies for three-way communication for complex systems adopting a coaching approach to change (see the table below and Figure 8.1).

Who	*Confidentiality*	*Notes*
Coach – Coachee	Confidentiality is kept, always.	These two discuss everything with each other: goals, actions, thoughts, resistance.
Coach – Sponsor	Coach maintains confidentiality regarding coachee's issues. Sponsor respects confidentiality.	These two discuss issues such as scheduling, whether or not the coachee is keeping appointments, general attitude toward coaching.
Coachee – Sponsor	Coachees keep confidentiality agreement unless they choose to share any goals, actions or obstacles. Sponsor respects confidentiality.	Coachee chooses if and what to share with the sponsor. These two discuss issues such as coach-coachee match, general attitude toward coaching.

As you can see in the diagram, communication can flow between all parties involved in the coaching relationship. It is in *what* is discussed where clarification and protection of privacy become a concern. Issues acceptable to discuss between the coach and sponsor include the coachee's willingness to be coached, whether regular action is being taken, and scheduling issues. The coachee's goals are kept in confidence as are conversations. While this may be controversial and disagreeable to some, it is necessary to maintain a high level of trust. The sponsors should be seeing progress externally. Perhaps they will witness the coachees trying new teaching techniques, or taking more risks, or taking on more of a leadership role. They should be seeing a demonstrable *result*. It is beneficial to all when the sponsor lets go of attachments to a specific outcome and trust the process. Change takes time, and coachees need time to perform new actions without judgment or reprimand.

Figure 8.1 Communication Flow

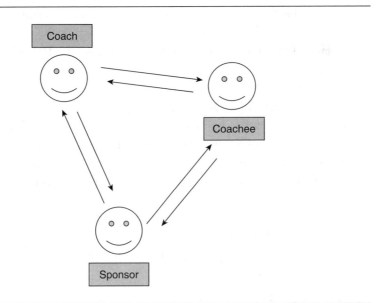

On the other hand, coachees are free to share anything they wish with the sponsor, at their discretion, *when* the time is right for them, and without pressure. They don't have to; they only do so if they choose to.

Often, periodically, or midway through a coaching agreement, it is common to hold a three-way meeting between the coach, the coachee, and the sponsor. The purpose of such a meeting is to acknowledge progress without breaking confidentiality and to assess sufficient willingness for continuation and continuous improvement.

POLICIES AND DECISION MAKING

Important decisions regarding successful coaching implementation should be discussed and considered early on in the planning process. Doing so will ensure smooth sailing in the future and prevent difficult issues from arising before it's too late to address them. Districts may need to establish formal policies regarding some issues:

- How will coaching be made available? Could coaching be available to any staff member who requests it? Will coaching be for developmental or performance purposes or both?
- Who is eligible to receive coaching? Which teachers or administrators? Is it for new or veteran staff? Which grade levels? Coaching

may be perceived as a punishment if it is only available to staff who need assistance. As a positive process for learning and growing, coaching is best viewed and conveyed as a perk.

- How will coaches and coachees be matched? Will the coachees have a choice of coaches?
- Establish a common definition of coaching. Create awareness throughout the organization.
- Will coaches also be mentors? If roles are combined, will the district ensure that coaches have sufficient coaching training?
- Establish a minimum amount of coaching training.
- Will the district or organization require credentials for external coaches?
- How will the district create partnerships or alliances with credentialed, professional coaches?
- Will assessments be available? For whom?

SELECTING AND TRAINING COACHES

Neither content knowledge nor experience in the coachee's role or situation are needed for successful coaching to take place. For instance, people think, erroneously, that only a principal can coach a principal . . . not so! Choosing a potential coach is more a matter of rapport, experience, connection and training. While some may feel a greater personal connection with a coach who has been in their role and knows what it's like to be in their shoes, from a coaching perspective, it is far more important that a coach be skilled and experienced as a *coach*.

In my practice, I have worked primarily with educators because I have a personal mission to support, serve and increase the effectiveness of school systems. When coaching, I rarely use my experience as an educator to guide a coachee. I use coaching skills, techniques, and processes. I have also coached business owners, salespeople, artists, and staff in nonprofit organizations and used the same array of skills.

Selecting Internal Coaches

Review the Coaching Mindset Self-Assessment found in Chapter 2 and in Resource A. Individuals who possess those attributes and are excited by fostering change in others are good candidates to become effective coaches. Educators make great coaches; they've already chosen a helping profession interested in helping students reach their full potential. You can use the Coaching Mindset Self-Assessment as an initial screening tool or as a discussion starter about behaviors and attitudes a coach needs. Consider individuals who are

- Active listeners
- Nonjudgmental
- Possibility thinkers
- Inspirational
- Personable
- Intuitive
- Sincere
- Trustworthy
- Risk takers
- Action oriented
- Focused on results
- Knowledgeable about or willing to learn coaching competencies
- Curious

Potential coaches should be aware that personal issues may emerge, and they should have a certain level of comfort dealing with them. They should be willing to extend coaching to include personal as well as professional performance goals.

The foregoing attributes are those to consider when the coach will be in a purely coaching role. It can be helpful in creating rapport, although not necessary, for a future coach to have experience or knowledge of the coachee's role or job. If a future coach is to function in a combination role, including consultancy and mentoring, a range of experiences and knowledge is necessary. Coaches best serve the coachees and the relationships when they communicate which helping hat they are wearing at a specific time. Moving between the roles of coach, consultant, and mentor requires specific communication with the coachee as to which role the coach is playing and the understanding by the coachee of what that means.

Selecting External Coaches

As mentioned earlier, I urge education institutions to rely on credentialed coaches trained in the ICF Professional Coaching Core Competencies. Look for coaches who are graduates of credentialed coach training schools. Training programs will range from 60 to 125 hours or more, including skill development and coaching practice. A second professional coach organization, the International Association of Coaches, founded in 2003, has over 7,000 members. It also offers a credentialing process based on its 15 coaching proficiencies.

Coaches with a professional credential adhere to a set of standards and ethics, as mentioned in Chapter 1. Dealing with certified coaches ensures competence and a greater return on an organization's investment in coaching.

External coaches are typically used with middle- and upper-level leaders. Interview several coaches to make sure there is a positive connection and a desired comfort level.

Training Coaches

If a district wishes to develop its own coach training program or revise a current one, a first step is to review the ICF Professional Coaching Core Competencies. Although some coaching-specific training is better than none, educators should be cautioned about too little training. Minimal coaching skills training is likely to result in frustration for the coaches and the coachees and little progress or results for the organization. A small amount of coach training is like learning to swim a little bit. Without all of the skills, techniques and sufficient amounts of practice, a person may drown. Coaches may make some progress with coachees, but when coaches face a difficult situation or reluctant, resistant coachees, it's likely that they won't have sufficient skills to effectively deal with them.

Consider the fact that to receive a professional coach credential requires a minimum of 125 hours of training. (Note: There is an "associate" coach credential that requires 60 hours.) Effective coaching is far more than asking reflective questions and listening. To help coachees make significant changes takes a range of knowledge, skill, and technique and a comfort level dealing with people on a very deep level.

Coach training should include skill development in the ICF Professional Coaching Core Competencies, role-playing and hands-on practice sessions guided by a credentialed coach. It is also helpful for coach trainees to identify one or more practice coachees with whom they can hone their skills and techniques during the learning process over the course of several weeks or months.

Most helpful would be a process for continuous training and problem solving. Professional coaches continue to learn and hone their skills through advanced training. Ideally, a credentialed coach would be available to the district or employed by the district to support coaches when they are at impasses with coachees. Providing a system of ongoing support is in the best interest of everyone involved in a coaching program.

LEADERSHIP COACHING FOR SCHOOL CHANGE

The practice of providing coaching for new and veteran leaders or to work with teams to create cultural change is in its infancy. School leaders need to be both recipients of leadership coaching to strengthen themselves as leaders *and* to learn to integrate a coaching leadership-management style into their interactions with others.

Once again, let me state that coaching has the power to transform individuals and entire organizations and to create a culture of continuous improvement for *everyone.* If we recognize that the culture of an organization is created by the beliefs, assumptions, and behaviors of the individuals within the

> *Self-development of the effective executive is central to the development of the organization.*
>
> —Peter Drucker (1967, p. 170)

organization, then by shifting those beliefs, assumptions, and behaviors on a large scale, the challenge of creating lasting organizational change is within reach.

In Chapter 1, a number of studies were mentioned that focused on the rising concern over the next generation of school leaders. Dwindling interest and lack of experience has resulted in fewer highly qualified applicants for leadership positions. High stakes stemming from challenging new standards has created fewer reasons for seeking leadership roles. In a high-pressured environment with the enormous challenges school district leaders face, meaningful support is a must. Executive and leadership coaching can provide personalized, customized professional growth and development that will strengthen leadership muscles and provide confidential support.

Executive and leadership coaching can be differentiated. Executive coaching is designated for the organization's leader: the superintendent, the dean, the executive director, or president. It is common for CEO's of large companies, hospitals, or other complex organizations to have access to executive coaches as they integrate into new positions, either for a specific period of time or on an ongoing or as-needed basis. Executive coaching provides confidential support to assist the leader in dealing with the challenges of leading people, teams, and departments; aligning talent; achieving high levels of performance; and initiating and sustaining improvement efforts to accomplish the organization's mission. An executive coach pro-

> *Change means movement; movement means friction.*
>
> —Saul Alinsky (en.thinkexist.com)

vides a confidential thinking partner for an organization's leader to brainstorm and strategize solutions, and to strengthen the leadership stance for the overall enhancement of the organization. Executive coaches are typically external to the organizations.

Leadership coaching provides a similar service to middle-level leaders; those who are responsible for the performance of individuals under their domain but are not individually responsible for the entire organization. Leadership coaching is beneficial for educators in new leadership roles or who have transitioned into new roles or new districts. Leadership coaches can be either external or internal to the organization.

Here is a sampling of issues that school leaders have requested coaching assistance with:

- Dealing with difficult personnel issues
- Confrontation; dealing with difficult conversations
- Managing school board relationships
- General decision making
- Deciding or determining readiness for becoming a superintendent or changing jobs
- Aligning staff and goals; getting leaders to agree on important issues
- Managing multiple priorities
- Delegating
- Managing time
- Managing stress
- Having a personal life
- Strengthening leadership attributes
- Building confidence
- Dealing with angry parents
- Dealing with resistant staff

Coaching for leaders is not an event. It's a system and a success partnership where the coach is invested in the success of the leader. Executive and leadership coaching can be conducted either in person or on the telephone. There are advantages to both.

On-Site Coaching

Advantages

- A coach can observe the coachee as new behaviors are adopted and integrated.
- A coach can observe interactions with other staff and provide immediate feedback.
- An external coach can meet with several coachees on the same day.
- A coach can work with a team, department or committee.
- An internal coach can be available to coach anyone.

Disadvantages

- External on-site coaching is not always convenient. As with many busy school leaders, last-minute meetings and issues can arise that may interfere with coaching sessions.
- It is more costly to engage in on-site coaching provided by an external coach.

Telephone Coaching

Advantages

- It's convenient; it can be conducted from home or office.
- It's efficient; 45- to 60-minute sessions are most common.
- It minimizes extraneous conversation; it's easier to stay focused.
- It's easy to arrange urgent sessions.
- It provides increased access to coaches.
- There are no geographic limits.
- It is cost-effective.
- There are no travel or associated costs.
- Privacy is possible.

Disadvantages

- Nonverbal communication is curtailed.
- Coachee's behavior changes and interactions with others cannot be observed.

A COACHING APPROACH TO CONTINUOUS SCHOOL SYSTEM IMPROVEMENT

I propose that the field of education is at the very beginning of a movement that has the potential to create true, deep, meaningful change in schools by using coaching. Thus far, there's the new role of school-based coach—a great start. However, as coaching expands, educators become more skilled and results become known, coaching can expand beyond the classroom to embrace and strengthen leaders and entire systems. It can become *the* strategy and method for communicating continuous improvement at all levels.

In the future, coaching in school systems is likely to look very different than it does today: Superintendents, principals, and other school system leaders have help in reaching for their organizations' goals they are striving to accomplish as well as their own professional goals. Leaders use a coaching approach in dealing with the people whose performance they are responsible for. Teachers are using coaching skills as effective ways to communicate with students and parents. Everyone is coaching each other. There is a support system for people when they're stuck, a "coaching the coach" program where a more experienced, trained coach is available when needed. Every building has a well-trained coach, and everyone within the organization is taking action on a daily basis toward the school or district's goals. That's continuous improvement in action.

As districts consider coaching as a professional development strategy to maximize the gains they hope to achieve, I urge that they consider a broader plan for coaching. In previous chapters, I described coaching as an individualized, customized professional development process. As such, is there an educator who could not benefit from such a process?

Let me say once more, as the use of coaching grows, as educators become more skilled as coaches and positive results become more known, coaching can expand and become a continuous improvement process available to anyone and everyone who wishes to improve themselves and their professional performance.

> *Anyone who stops learning is old.*
>
> —Henry Ford

Earlier I discussed coaching as an appropriate strategy both for those who need it for performance improvement purposes and also for all professionals who are interested and committed to growing and improving themselves to reach their full potential. (See Resource J: Successful Coaching Implementation Checklist.) Coaching can be offered as a perk, not a punishment. A coaching approach to continuous school improvement consists of

- Executive and leadership coaching available for superintendents, principals, and others in leadership positions—for both new and experienced leaders.
- Principals acting in more of a coaching role than a manager role, coaching staff and students to higher levels of achievement.
- Instructional coaches, highly trained in coaching skills and competence in helping teachers create classroom change.
- Department chairpersons using a coaching approach with teachers under their supervision.
- Teachers using coaching skills to boost and enhance student outcomes.
- School improvement teams coached individually and as a group, to optimize success.
- The reduction of teacher burnout, as teachers align their interests and talents with their work.
- The reduction in teacher turnover as teachers feel supported and energized.
- Every educator having a Professional Coaching Plan with specific goals and weekly actions to achieve them.
- Public and shared goals.

I see a world where schools fully embrace coaching as the means for creating continuously improving organizations with a "we can do anything" culture. I see a world where every district has a fully trained, professional coach available—better yet, in every school. I see leaders utilize coaching skills in their interactions with staff. School-based coaches know what it takes to be a great coach and are highly skilled. Teachers coach their students to higher levels of success. I see schools achieving the results they are seeking when all leaders, staff, and students are coaching and being coached.

SUMMARY

As a strategy for helping districts reach their challenging educational goals and for developing the leadership skills of current and future educators, the coaching process holds great potential. As coaching becomes widely used as a process and means of communicating and improving schools, it is essential that school system leaders create policies that will ensure successful implementation. A broader view of coaching is needed to create school systems where every educator knows and uses coaching skills as a means of continuous improvement for themselves and those they interact with. I urge that district leaders consider extending opportunities to be coached and to coach others beyond the classroom. There is no better time for school system leaders and others in leadership roles to have the availability and benefits of working with coaches to maximize their capability to lead complex school systems.

Setting important policies in advance will ensure that common understanding and key ingredients for success are in place at the onset. Decisions and policies are needed regarding how coaching will be offered, who coaches and who receives coaching, and how the training program will be designed and delivered. Will leaders be offered coaching? If so which leaders, when and how?

The use of external coaches is common for executives and leaders. Strengthening communication and confidence are natural outcomes for leaders, both qualities sorely needed by educational leaders.

The more training and guided practice coaches have, the more skilled and effective they will be in succeeding with individuals, teams, and entire systems. When districts choose to pursue coaching, seeking partnerships with credentialed coaches will ensure they have the skills, knowledge, and techniques to make lasting change . . . at last. Broadening their view of coaching, districts will be wise to consider expanding coaching beyond the classroom to create districtwide capacity for improving schools, one person at a time.

I have high hopes for coaching and the ability it possesses to transform school systems. It is time we recognized that each individual working to enhance the ability of students to perform at their peak must pay attention to themselves as well. When all educators who touch the lives of students are focused, aligned with their purpose and personal strengths and continually setting and achieving personal and professional goals for themselves, I have no doubt that schools and students everywhere will thrive as never before.

Reflective Questions

- What is the district plan for selecting and training coaches?
- What are the benefits of supporting a coaching process for school leadership?
- What policies need to be discussed and decided upon?

Conclusion

In the end, it is important to remember that we cannot become what we need to be by remaining what we are.

—Max DePree (1989)

The intention for this book was to clarify the mystery around coaching and highlight the necessary coaching skills, processes, and mindsets that successful coaches need. Moving toward a coaching approach to support the continuous improvement of leaders and educators of children is a wise investment of precious district resources. It is high time every school leader has access to skilled coaches to ensure that they perform at their peaks, to lead their schools and systems to greater functionality and increased results.

Creating lasting change in complex school systems has long been a challenge for school leaders and school board members. Many of us seek to create change in schools, and in the attempt, we invest in curriculum reform, technology and costly external solutions. Yet we also need to recognize and acknowledge that change only happens when people behave in new ways. Coaching addresses the internal aspect of creating successful change, one person at a time. Coaching must be part of professional growth programs for all adults in the system: school leaders, teacher leaders, and teachers. Everyone will benefit.

The competencies and skills identified in this book are a beginning, a baseline for developing a uniform body of learning for educator-coaches. It is by no means a complete package of skills and techniques. The Professional Coaching Core Competencies provide a standard for the coaching profession and are necessary and valuable for current and future leadership and school-based coaches. Training programs should include them in a format that enables sufficient practice. There are dozens of coaching-specific skills and even more techniques and tools that coaches use to lead coachees to breakthroughs, new awarenesses, and new insights that lead to new actions and permanent change.

In the purest form of coaching, a skilled coach need not be experienced in the role, the line of work, or the organization of the coachee. An experienced, professional coach can successfully coach anyone, in any field. Doing so empowers the coachee, strengthens confidence, and creates greater independence. The role of coach differs greatly from other common, helpful roles, such as mentor and consultant, both of which focus more on sharing specific expertise and experiences as a method for creating change. Coaches focus more on empowering the individuals to discover their own best solutions and pathways to change.

In reality, when educators become coaches or adopt a coaching approach, there is a greater tendency to combine roles. At times, a mentor or consultant approach may be appropriate. Coaches need to communicate the differences, be sufficiently trained and proficient as coaches, and combine roles when appropriate. The ultimate goal—transporting people from here to there via a coaching approach—creates lasting personal and organizational change and a meaningful strategy in boosting results.

My experience in coaching school leaders has only strengthened my commitment to this work. Here are some comments from practicing school leaders that highlight how coaching can enhance leadership practice:

- "Superintendents need [coaching] skill to work with parents, teachers, administrators, and board members."
- "Every district needs a trained coach to support them. Every superintendent needs training and awareness."
- "[Coaching is] very powerful if used throughout the organization."
- "The isolation experienced by experienced superintendents could be alleviated via sound coaching."
- "The coaching mode of support is needed for our principals."
- "I would recommend leadership coaching for current and aspiring administrators."
- "It helped me to see situations with a different pair of eyes. The coach "nudged" me to create possible solutions that I might not have seriously considered on my own. The coach provided the gentle support that kept me focused on attaining personal and professional goals."
- "Our sessions have had a tremendous impact on me—too much to name, but I want you to know that I like your style! You've given me a new way to look at time management; thank you for challenging me."

"Oh Yes We Can!" I've revised the Bolder Boulder motto mentioned in the beginning of the book to reflect that it is *we* who can make a difference in our school systems. Together, we can develop coaching as a significant strategy for growing each person in the education system for the sole result of strengthening schools to better serve the needs of our children. We can be coached, become coaches, and learn to coach our staff and students to peak performance.

School systems that embrace coaching can experience stronger, more confident leadership, more aligned systems, and a continuous improvement culture that involves all educators working toward significant goals, every day.

Resources

Resource A: Coaching Mindset Self-Assessment

Resource B: Coachee Readiness Checklist

Resource C: ICF Professional Coaching Core Competencies

Resource D: ICF Standards of Ethical Conduct

Resource E: Examining Limiting Beliefs

Resource F: Conducting a POWERful Coaching Session

Resource G: Professional Coaching Plan: Quarterly Goals and
Initial Actions

Resource H: Weekly Coaching Action Planner

Resource I: Useful Assessment Tools to Use in Coaching

Resource J: Successful Coaching Implementation Checklist

RESOURCE A

Coaching Mindset Self-Assessment

10	10	10	10	10	10	10	10	10	10	10	10	10	10
9	9	9	9	9	9	9	9	9	9	9	9	9	9
8	8	8	8	8	8	8	8	8	8	8	8	8	8
7	7	7	7	7	7	7	7	7	7	7	7	7	7
6	6	6	6	6	6	6	6	6	6	6	6	6	6
5	5	5	5	5	5	5	5	5	5	5	5	5	5
4	4	4	4	4	4	4	4	4	4	4	4	4	4
3	3	3	3	3	3	3	3	3	3	3	3	3	3
2	2	2	2	2	2	2	2	2	2	2	2	2	2
1	1	1	1	1	1	1	1	1	1	1	1	1	1
Active Listener	Non-judgmental	Possibility Thinker	Compas-sionate	Inspirational	Personable	Intuitive	Sincere	Trustworthy	Risk Taker	Action Oriented	Focused on Results	Knows Core Coaching Competencies	Curious

How to use the Coaching Mindset Self-Assessment Tool:

1. In each column, circle a number that indicates, from 1 to 10, how skilled you feel in your coaching now (with 1 meaning low and 10 meaning awesome).

2. Shade in the area with crayons or pencil from the bottom to the number you circled. Look at the completed "picture" of your skills as a coach.

3. Decide which three areas you wish to work on. There may be others; that's OK. Choose the three most important to you that you are willing to focus on for the next three months.

4. Repeat in three months.

Write three general goals here that you commit to work toward in the next three months to grow your coaching skills.

Goals	Actions
1. _____	_____
_____	_____
2. _____	_____
_____	_____
3. _____	_____
_____	_____

RESOURCE B

Coachee Readiness Checklist

The potential coachee

- ☐ Is excited to work with a coach
- ☐ Wants to grow in his or her professional life
- ☐ Is open to new ideas
- ☐ Is ready to take steps or risks
- ☐ Can visualize a preferred personal future as well as for the school, district, or university
- ☐ Has a positive attitude
- ☐ Wants to become more competent
- ☐ Is willing to think beyond the current mindset
- ☐ Is able to reach decisions through collaboration
- ☐ Is already successful and seeking more
- ☐ Wants to learn something new
- ☐ Wants to make a bigger difference in the district, university, organization, or have a larger impact on the world
- ☐ Has ideas and goals and is ready to move forward
- ☐ May need help focusing attention
- ☐ May need some inspiration
- ☐ May need someone to rein him or her in

RESOURCE C

International Coach Federation Professional Coaching Core Competencies

A. SETTING THE FOUNDATION

1. **Meeting Ethical Guidelines and Professional Standards**—Understanding of coaching ethics and standards and ability to apply them appropriately in all coaching situations

   a. Understands and exhibits in own behaviors the ICF Standards of Conduct (see list),

   b. Understands and follows all ICF Ethical Guidelines (see list),

   c. Clearly communicates the distinctions between coaching, consulting, psychotherapy and other support professions,

   d. Refers coachee to another support professional as needed, knowing when this is needed and the available resources.

2. **Establishing the Coaching Agreement**—Ability to understand what is required in the specific coaching interaction and to come to agreement with the prospective and new coachee about the coaching process and relationship

   a. Understands and effectively discusses with the coachee the guidelines and specific parameters of the coaching relationship (e.g., logistics, fees, scheduling, inclusion of others if appropriate),

   b. Reaches agreement about what is appropriate in the relationship and what is not, what is and is not being offered, and about the coachee's and coach's responsibilities,

   c. Determines whether there is an effective match between his or her coaching method and the needs of the prospective coachee.

B. CO-CREATING THE RELATIONSHIP

1. **Establishing Trust and Intimacy With the Coachee**—Ability to create a safe, supportive environment that produces ongoing mutual respect and trust

   a. Shows genuine concern for the coachee's welfare and future,

   b. Continuously demonstrates personal integrity, honesty, and sincerity,

   c. Establishes clear agreements and keeps promises,

   d. Demonstrates respect for coachee's perceptions, learning style, personal being,

   e. Provides ongoing support for and champions new behaviors and actions, including those involving risk taking and fear of failure,

   f. Asks permission to coach coachee in sensitive, new areas.

2. **Coaching Presence**—Ability to be fully conscious and create spontaneous relationship with the coachee, employing a style that is open, flexible, and confident

   a. Is present and flexible during the coaching process, dancing in the moment,

   b. Accesses own intuition and trusts one's inner knowing—"goes with the gut,"

   c. Is open to not knowing and takes risks,

   d. Sees many ways to work with the coachee, and chooses in the moment what is most effective,

   e. Uses humor effectively to create lightness and energy,

   f. Confidently shifts perspectives and experiments with new possibilities for own action,

   g. Demonstrates confidence in working with strong emotions, and can self-manage and not be overpowered or enmeshed by coachee's emotions.

C. COMMUNICATING EFFECTIVELY

3. **Active Listening**—Ability to focus completely on what the coachee is saying and is not saying, to understand the meaning of what is said in the context of the coachee's desires, and to support coachee self-expression

   a. Attends to the coachee and the coachee's agenda, and not to the coach's agenda for the coachee,

   b. Hears the coachee's concerns, goals, values, and beliefs about what is and is not possible,

   c. Distinguishes between the words, the tone of voice, and the body language,

   d. Summarizes, paraphrases, reiterates, and mirrors back what coachee has said to ensure clarity and understanding,

   e. Encourages, accepts, explores, and reinforces the coachee's expression of feelings, perceptions, concerns, beliefs, suggestions, etc.,

   f. Integrates and builds on coachee's ideas and suggestions,

   g. "Bottom-lines" or understands the essence of the coachee's communication and helps the coachee get there rather than engaging in long descriptive stories,

   h. Allows the coachee to vent or "clear" the situation without judgment or attachment in order to move on to next steps.

4. **Powerful Questioning**—Ability to ask questions that reveal the information needed for maximum benefit to the coaching relationship and the coachee

   a. Asks questions that reflect active listening and an understanding of the coachee's perspective,

   b. Asks questions that evoke discovery, insight, commitment, or action (e.g., those that challenge the coachee's assumptions),

   c. Asks open-ended questions that create greater clarity, possibility, or new learning

   d. Asks questions that move the coachee toward what he or she desires, not questions that ask for the coachee to justify or look backwards.

5. **Direct Communication**—Ability to communicate effectively during coaching sessions, and to use language that has the greatest positive impact on the coachee

   a. Is clear, articulate, and direct in sharing and providing feedback,

   b. Reframes and articulates to help the coachee understand from another perspective what he or she wants or is uncertain about,

   c. Clearly states coaching objectives, meeting agenda, purpose of techniques or exercises,

   d. Uses language appropriate and respectful to the coachee (e.g., nonsexist, nonracist, nontechnical, nonjargon),

   e. Uses metaphor and analogy to help to illustrate a point or paint a verbal picture.

D. FACILITATING LEARNING AND RESULTS

6. **Creating Awareness**—Ability to integrate and accurately evaluate multiple sources of information, and to make interpretations that help the coachee to gain awareness and thereby achieve agreed-upon results

   a. Goes beyond what is said in assessing coachee's concerns, not getting hooked by the coachee's description,

   b. Invokes inquiry for greater understanding, awareness, and clarity,

   c. Identifies for the coachee his or her underlying concerns, typical and fixed ways of perceiving him- or herself and the world, differences between the facts and the interpretation, disparities between thoughts, feelings, and action,

   d. Helps coachees to discover for themselves the new thoughts, beliefs, perceptions, emotions, moods, etc. that strengthen their ability to take action and achieve what is important to them,

   e. Communicates broader perspectives to coachees and inspires commitment to shift their viewpoints and find new possibilities for action,

   f. Helps coachees to see the different, interrelated factors that affect them and their behaviors (e.g., thoughts, emotions, body, background),

   g. Expresses insights to coachees in ways that are useful and meaningful for the coachee,

   h. Identifies major strengths vs. major areas for learning and growth, and what is most important to address during coaching,

i. Asks the coachee to distinguish between trivial and significant issues, situational vs. recurring behaviors, when detecting a separation between what is being stated and what is being done.

7. **Designing Actions**—Ability to create with the coachee opportunities for ongoing learning, during coaching and in work/life situations, and for taking new actions that will most effectively lead to agreed-upon coaching results

    a. Brainstorms and assists the coachee to define actions that will enable the coachee to demonstrate, practice, and deepen new learning,

    b. Helps the coachee to focus on and systematically explore specific concerns and opportunities that are central to agreed-upon coaching goals,

    c. Engages the coachee to explore alternative ideas and solutions, to evaluate options, and to make related decisions,

    d. Promotes active experimentation and self-discovery, where the coachee applies what has been discussed and learned during sessions immediately afterwards in his or her work or life setting,

    e. Celebrates coachee successes and capabilities for future growth,

    f. Challenges coachee's assumptions and perspectives to provoke new ideas and find new possibilities for action,

    g. Advocates or brings forward points of view that are aligned with coachee-goals and, without attachment, engages the coachee to consider them,

    h. Helps the coachee "Do It Now" during the coaching session, providing immediate support,

    i. Encourages stretches and challenges but also a comfortable pace of learning.

8. **Planning and Goal Setting**—Ability to develop and maintain an effective coaching plan with the coachee

    a. Consolidates collected information and establishes a coaching plan and development goals with the coachee that address concerns and major areas for learning and development,

    b. Creates a plan with results that are attainable, measurable, specific, and have target dates,

    c. Makes plan adjustments as warranted by the coaching process and by changes in the situation,

    d. Helps the coachee identify and access different resources for learning (e.g., books, other professionals),

    e. Identifies and targets early successes that are important to the coachee.

9. **Managing Progress and Accountability**—Ability to hold attention on what is important for the coachee, and to leave responsibility with the coachee to take action

    a. Clearly requests of the coachee actions that will move the coachee toward their stated goals,

    b. Demonstrates follow through by asking the coachee about those actions that the coachee committed to during the previous session(s),

    c. Acknowledges the coachee for what they have done, not done, learned, or become aware of since the previous coaching session(s),

    d. Effectively prepares, organizes, and reviews with coachee information obtained during sessions,

    e. Keeps the coachee on track between sessions by holding attention on the coaching plan and outcomes, agreed-upon courses of action, and topics for future session(s),

    f. Focuses on the coaching plan but is also open to adjusting behaviors and actions based on the coaching process and shifts in direction during sessions,

    g. Is able to move back and forth between the big picture of where the coachee is heading, setting a context for what is being discussed and where the coachee wishes to go,

    h. Promotes coachee's self-discipline and holds the coachee accountable for what they say they are going to do, for the results of an intended action, or for a specific plan with related time frames,

    i. Develops the coachee's ability to make decisions, address key concerns, and develop himself or herself (to get feedback, to determine priorities and set the pace of learning, to reflect on and learn from experiences),

    j. Positively confronts the coachee with the fact that he or she did not take agreed-upon actions.

RESOURCE D

International Coach Federation
Standards of Ethical Conduct

Professional Conduct at Large

As a coach:

1) I will conduct myself in a manner that reflects positively upon the coaching profession and I will refrain from engaging in conduct or making statements that may negatively impact the public's understanding or acceptance of coaching as a profession.

2) I will not knowingly make any public statements that are untrue or misleading, or make false claims in any written documents relating to the coaching profession.

3) I will respect different approaches to coaching. I will honor the efforts and contributions of others and not misrepresent them as my own.

4) I will be aware of any issues that may potentially lead to the misuse of my influence by recognizing the nature of coaching and the way in which it may affect the lives of others.

5) I will at all times strive to recognize personal issues that may impair, conflict, or interfere with my coaching performance or my professional relationships. Whenever the facts and circumstances necessitate, I will promptly seek professional assistance and determine the action to be taken, including whether it is appropriate to suspend or terminate my coaching relationship(s).

6) As a trainer or supervisor of current and potential coaches, I will conduct myself in accordance with the ICF Standards of Ethical Conduct in all training and supervisory situations.

7) I will conduct and report research with competence, honesty, and within recognized scientific standards. My research will be carried out with the necessary approval or consent from those involved, and with an approach that will reasonably protect participants from any potential harm. All research efforts will be performed in a manner that complies with the laws of the country in which the research is conducted.

Source: Reprinted with permission by the International Coach Federation. All rights reserved.

8) I will accurately create, maintain, store, and dispose of any records of work done in relation to the practice of coaching in a way that promotes confidentiality and complies with any applicable laws.

9) I will use ICF member contact information only in the manner and to the extent authorized by the ICF.

Professional Conduct With Coachees

10) I will be responsible for setting clear, appropriate, and culturally sensitive boundaries that govern any physical contact that I may have with my coachees.

11) I will not become sexually involved with any of my coachees.

12) I will construct clear agreements with my coachees, and will honor all agreements made in the context of professional coaching relationships.

13) I will ensure that, prior to or at the initial session, my coaching coachee understands the nature of coaching, the bounds of confidentiality, financial arrangements, and other terms of the coaching agreement.

14) I will accurately identify my qualifications, expertise, and experience as a coach.

15) I will not intentionally mislead or make false claims about what my coachee will receive from the coaching process or from me as their coach.

16) I will not give my coachees information or advice I know or believe to be misleading.

17) I will not knowingly exploit any aspect of the coach-coachee relationship for my personal, professional, or monetary advantage or benefit.

18) I will respect the coachee's right to terminate coaching at any point during the process. I will be alert to indications that the coachee is no longer benefiting from our coaching relationship.

19) If I believe the coachee would be better served by another coach, or by another resource, I will encourage the coachee to make a change.

20) I will suggest that my coachees seek the services of other professionals when deemed appropriate or necessary.

21) I will take all reasonable steps to notify the appropriate authorities in the event a coachee discloses an intention to endanger self or others.

Confidentiality/Privacy

22) I will respect the confidentiality of my coachee's information, except as otherwise authorized by my coachee, or as required by law.

23) I will obtain agreement from my coachees before releasing their names as coachees or references, or any other coachee identifying information.

24) I will obtain agreement from the person being coached before releasing information to another person compensating me.

Conflicts of Interest

25) I will seek to avoid conflicts between my interests and the interests of my coachees.

26) Whenever any actual conflict of interest or the potential for a conflict of interest arises, I will openly disclose it and fully discuss with my coachee how to deal with it in whatever way best serves my coachee.

27) I will disclose to my coachee all anticipated compensation from third parties that I may receive for referrals of that coachee.

28) I will only barter for services, goods, or other nonmonetary remuneration when it will not impair the coaching relationship.

Source: Reprinted with permission by the International Coach Federation. All rights reserved.

RESOURCE E

Examining Limiting Beliefs

No pessimist ever discovered the secret of the stars, or sailed to an uncharted land, or opened a new doorway for the human spirit.

—Helen Keller

Our inner thoughts are the secret to success. Begin to examine your thoughts by jotting down any limiting beliefs that may be part of your current thinking. You can change category headings to meet your needs.

Students	Curriculum	State/ Federal Regulations	Budget and Funding	Staff	My Leadership or Teaching Ability	Self-Confidence	Parents

Next step: Write each limiting belief on one of the lines provided. Next to it, write a turnaround statement that reflects the opposite thinking. Post them around you and repeat them frequently. Write the turnaround statement in the present tense, as if it is already happening.

For example:

I am a terrible writer.   *I am acquiring the skills to improve my writing.*

Limiting Belief   Turnaround Statement

_____   _____

_____   _____

_____   _____

RESOURCE F

THE POWERful Coaching Framework™

Conducting a POWERful Coaching Session

Each coaching session includes all five sections of the model.

Each session ends with a specific set of actions the coachee agrees to take prior to the next session.

P = Purpose

What does the coachee and the organization want to accomplish?

What does the coachee want to achieve by the end of this session (month, year)?

Agree on the topic and specific objectives for discussion.

O = Outlook & Obstacles

How does the coachee see the issues?

Assess the current reality.

Listen for self-limiting thoughts and beliefs.

What obstacles may be in the way of accomplishing them?

From what perspective does the coachee see the issues?

Help the coachee recall past success.

Create a new vision of possibility. Help the coachee see other ways.

Help the coachee see himself or herself as successful.

W = What to Do?

What possibilities exist?

What actions can be taken toward the goal?

Brainstorm—together.

Choose actions.

Help coachee see many paths toward the goals.

E = Empower, Encourage

Help coachee manage time to achieve the goals.

Provide inspiration as needed.

Build on past success.

How much cheerleading does the coachee need?

Provide empathy, if and when needed.

Let the coachee know you get it—you understand where he or she is coming from.

R = Recap & Record

Review your discussion and commitments.

Reinforce strategies to overcome obstacles.

You and the coachee each record the promised action steps.

RESOURCE G

Professional Coaching Plan:
Quarterly Goals and Initial Actions

Never mistake motion for action.

—Ernest Hemingway

Coachee Name: _____ **Date:** _____

Identify **three** goals; fill out one of these forms for each one. Goals should be SMART: Specific, Measurable, Achievable, Realistic, and Timed.

Goal:

Measure of Success:

Possible Obstacles:

_____

_____

_____

_____

_____

Possible Solutions:

_____

_____

_____

_____

_____

Initial Action Steps:	By When	Review Date	Completed

Notes:

RESOURCE H

Weekly Coaching Action Planner

Coachee Name: _____ **Date:** _____

Actions I completed since the last session: (coachee lists these and sends to coach prior to the session)

What I didn't get to:

Why? What challenges arose?

What supports or possibilities exist?

During the next session, I need help with . . . :

What I commit to do by the next session: (List actions below **during** coaching session)

RESOURCE I

Useful Assessment Tools to Use in Coaching

There are numerous assessment tools helpful in identifying specific personality traits, competencies, and behaviors that may be either helping or hindering personal or professional success. I have found the following to be appropriate during the coaching process.

✓ **Bar-On Emotional Quotient Inventory (EQI)**
MHS, Inc.
P.O. Box 950
North Tonawanda, New York 14120-0950
800-456-3003
www.mhs.com

✓ **CPI 260 Coaching Report for Leaders**
CPP, Inc., 1055 Joaquin Road, 2nd Floor
Mountain View, California 94043
800-624-1765
www.cpp.com

✓ **CPI 260 Coachee Feedback Report**
CPP, Inc., 1055 Joaquin Road, 2nd Floor
Mountain View, California 94043
800-624-1765
www.cpp.com

✓ **DiSC**
Inscape Publishing
6465 Wayzata Boulevard, Suite 800
Minneapolis, Minnesota 55426
888-575-8800
www.inscapepublishing.com

✓ **Emotional Competence Inventory (ECI)**
Hay Group, Inc.
116 Huntington Avenue
Boston, Massachusetts 02116
800-729-8072
www.hayresourcesdirect.haygroup.com

✓ **Fundamental Interpersonal Relations Orientation (FIRO-B)**
CPP, Inc., 1055 Joaquin Road, 2nd Floor
Mountain View, California 94043
800-624-1765
www.cpp.com

✓ **Genos Emotional Intelligence Assessment**
Institute for Professional Empowerment Coaching
Valley Park West, 2519 Highway 35, Bldg I–103
Manasquan, New Jersey 08736
866-72COACH
www.iPECcoaching.com

✓ **Leadership Practices Inventory (LPI)**
John Wiley & Sons, Inc.
432 Elizabeth Avenue
Somerset, New Jersey 08873
800-225-5945
www.wiley.com

✓ **Myers-Briggs Type Indicator (MBTI)**
CPP, Inc., 1055 Joaquin Road, 2nd Floor
Mountain View, California 94043
800-624-1765
www.cpp.com

✓ **Thomas-Kilmann Conflict Mode Instrument (TKI)**
CPP, Inc., 1055 Joaquin Road, 2nd Floor
Mountain View, California 94043
800-624-1765
www.cpp.com

RESOURCE J

Successful Coaching Implementation Checklist

☐ I (or school board, staff, coachees) know and understand the difference between coaching, mentoring, consulting, and other related roles.

☐ Our district has adopted a confidentiality policy.

☐ School-based and internal coaches are knowledgeable about and can demonstrate skill in the Professional Coaching Core Competencies.

☐ All internal coaches have had a minimum of 30 hours of coaching-specific training.

☐ There is ongoing training for coaches.

☐ There is a choice of coaches available.

☐ There are processes for problem solving and for coaching the coaches.

☐ Coaching is not forced on anyone.

☐ Coaching is available to anyone who requests it.

☐ There is access to or an alliance with certified, credentialed coaches.

☐ All school leaders have access to coaching when needed or requested.

☐ Coaches know and use the POWERful Coaching Framework™.

☐ Our district has discussed and agreed on an appropriate communication policy.

References

Agno, J. G. (2003). Copy cat or born leader. In *CEO refresher.* Ann Arbor, MI: Refresher Publications.

Albion, M. (2000). *Making a life; Making a living.* New York: Warner.

Austen, N., & Peters, T. (1985). *A passion for excellence.* New York: Warner.

Baker, J. H., & Baker, G. A. (2001, November). The power of knowledge communities. *WeLead Online.* Retrieved March 30, 2006, from www.leadingtoday.org

Batchelor, D. (n.d.). *A passion for success.* Retrieved April 10, 2006, from www.ksinclair.com/Article421.htm

Bennis, W. (1985). *Leaders: The strategies for taking charge.* New York: Harper & Row.

Berglas, S. (2002, June). The very real dangers of executive coaching. *Harvard Business Review,* 86-92.

Borisoff, D., & Purdy, M. (1996). *Listening in everyday life: A personal and professional approach,* (2nd ed.). New York: University Press in America.

Bridges, W. (1991). *Managing transitions: Making the most of change.* Reading, MA: Addison-Wesley.

Brothers, C. (2005). *Language and the pursuit of happiness.* Naples, FL: New Possibilities.

Cambridge Dictionary. (2006). Retrieved March 27, 2006, from www.dictionary.cambridge.org

Chappelow, C., & Leslie, J. B. (2000). *Keeping your career on track.* Greensboro, NC: CCL Press.

Cherniss, C. (2000, April). *Emotional intelligence: What it is and why it matters.* Paper presented at the Annual Meeting of the Society for Industrial and Organizational Psychology, New Orleans, LA.

Collins, D. (1997). *Achieving your vision of professional development.* Washington, DC: SERVE, Office of Educational Research and Improvement, US Department of Education.

Colorado Association of School Executives. (2003). *The view from inside: A candid look at today's school superintendent.* Englewood, CO: Author.

CompassPoint Nonprofit Services. (2003). *Executive coaching project.* San Francisco: Author.

DePree, M. (1989). *Leadership is an art.* New York: Dell.

Deutschman, A. (2005). *Change or die.* New York: Fast Company, Gruner & Jahr.

Drucker, P. (1967). *The Effective executive.* New York: Harper & Row.

Edge First. (2000, October 26). Retrieved March 29, 2006, from www.baldrigeplus.com/Edge_First_11.html

Eggers, J. H., & Clark, D. (2000, September-October). Executive coaching that wins. *Ivey Business Journal*, 4.

Executive coaching—with returns a CFO could love. (2001, February). *Fortune*, 19.

Executive couching. (2002, August 3). *The Economist*, 51.

Fournies, F. F. (2000). *Coaching for improved work performance.* New York: McGraw-Hill.

Fullan, M., & Stiegelbauer, S. (1991). *The new meaning of educational change.* New York: Teachers College Press.

Gibran, K. (1995). *The prophet.* New York: Knopf. (Original work published in 1923)

Goleman, D. (1998). *Working with emotional intelligence.* New York: Bantam.

Goleman, D., & Cherniss, C. (1998). *Guidelines for best practice.* Newark, NJ: Rutgers University, Consortium for Research on Emotional Intelligence in Organizations Guidelines.

Gratton, J. (2006, February 20). *The beatings will continue until morale improves.* Core Character. Retrieved April 11, 2006, from www.corecharacter.com

Hargrove, R. (2000). *Masterful coaching fieldbook.* San Francisco: Jossey-Bass/Pfeiffer.

Hesselbein, F., Goldsmith, M., & Beckhard, R. (1997). *The Drucker Foundation: The leader of the future.* San Francisco: Jossey-Bass.

Home Depot: Something to prove. (2002, June 27). *Fortune.* Retrieved March 28, 2006, from www.mutualofamerica.com/articles/

International Coach Federation. (n.d.). Retrieved March 13, 2006, from www.coachfederation.org

International Coach Federation and Linkage, Inc. (2000). *1999 survey on coaching in corporate America.* Retrieved March 13, 2006, from www.coachfederation.org

Joyce, B., & Showers, B. (1995). *Student achievement through staff development.* White Plains, NY: Longman.

Juechter, W., Fisher, C., & Alford, R. (1998, May). Five conditions for high performance cultures. *Training & Development Magazine*, 69-80.

Keen, S. (1999). *Learning to fly.* New York: Broadway.

Killion, J. (2002, Spring). Soaring with their own life coach. *Journal of Staff Development*, 19-22.

Killion, J., & Harrison, C. (2005, September) The 9 roles of a school based coach. *Teachers Teaching Teachers, 1*(1). Retrieved March 15, 2006 from www.nsdc.org/library

Lebow, R. (1990, May). Making heroes of workers. *Washington CEO Magazine*, 36-39.

Lombardo, M., & Eichlinger, R. W. (1989). *Preventing derailment; What to do before it's too late.* Greensboro, NC: Center for Creative Leadership.

Lunden, J. (2001). *Wake up calls.* New York: McGraw-Hill.

Manchester Inc. (2001). *Maximizing the impact of executive coaching, 6*(1). Retrieved March 24, 2006, from www.cpcusociety.org

Management Tid Bytes. (2004, September). Seattle: Washington University.

Maxwell, J. (2003). *Thinking for a change.* Boston: Warner.

McGee, B. (2001). *Optimize triathlon performance through mental training: Don't waste training by being a head case.* Retrieved March 24, 2006, from www.psychedonline.org/Articles/Vol5Iss2

Michael, K. (2000, April 7). Coaches can help guide careeer, life. *Triangle Business Journal*, 2. Retrieved March 31, 2006, from www.bizjournals.com/triangle/

Miller, W. R. (2005, February). Resolutions that work. *Spirituality & Health*, 45.

New York State Board of Regents' Blue Ribbon Panel on School Leadership. (2000). *School Leadership for the 21st Century: Statement of New York State's Blue Ribbon Panel on School Leadership.* Albany, NY: Author.

Oakley, E., & Krug, D. (1991). *Enlightened leadership.* New York: Fireside.

Rackham, N. (1979). The coaching controversy. *Training and Development Journal, 33*(11), 12-16.

Redfield, J. (1993). *The Celestine prophecy.* New York: Warner.

Redmoon, A., & Fettke, R. (2002). *Extreme success.* New York: Fireside.

Ruiz, D. M. (1997). *The four agreements.* San Raphael, CA: Amber-Allen.

Schneider, B. (2001). *The cycle of change.* Manasquan, NJ: Institute for Professional Empowerment Coaching.

Seiler, A. (2003). *Coaching to the human soul.* Victoria, Australia: Blackburn.

Sparks, D. (2002, Spring). Soaring with their own life coach. *Journal of Staff Development*, 19-22.

Stevenson, H. (2005). *The four laws of change.* Retrieved March 15, 2006, from www.clevelandconsultinggroup.com

Tichy, N. M., & Cohen, E. B. (1997). *The leadership engine: How winning companies build leaders at every level.* New York: HarperCollins.

Tischler, L. (2004, November). IBM's management makeover. *Fast Company,* (88), 112.

Volp, F. (2004). The fifth triennial study of school superintendents in New York State. In *Snapshot V,* p. 7. Albany, NY: New York State Council of School Superintendents.

Wheatley, M. (2002). *Turning to one another.* San Francisco: Berret-Koehler.

Whitmore, J. (2004). *Coaching for performance.* London: Nicholas Brealey.

Whitworth, L., Kimsey-House, H., & Sandahl, P. (1998). *Co-active coaching.* Mountain View, CA: Davies-Black.

Williams, P. (2004). Coaching vs. psychotherapy: The great debate. *Choice Magazine, 2*(1), 38-39.

Winspear, J. (2005). *Pardonable lies.* New York: Holt.

Index

The Corwin Press logo—a raven striding across an open book—represents the union of courage and learning. Corwin Press is committed to improving education for all learners by publishing books and other professional development resources for those serving the field of PreK–12 education. By providing practical, hands-on materials, Corwin Press continues to carry out the promise of its motto: **"Helping Educators Do Their Work Better."**